From the Imjin to The Hook

D1345307

From the Imjin to The Hook

A National Service Gunner in the Korean War

Jim Jacobs

Pen & Sword
MILITARY

First published in Great Britain in 2013 by
Pen & Sword Military
an imprint of
Pen & Sword Books Ltd
47 Church Street
Barnsley
South Yorkshire
S70 2AS

Copyright © Jim Jacobs 2013

ISBN 978 1 78159 343 1

The right of Jim Jacobs to be identified as the Author of this Work
has been asserted by him in accordance with the Copyright, Designs
and Patents Act 1988.

A CIP catalogue record for this book is available from the British
Library

All rights reserved. No part of this book may be reproduced or
transmitted in any form or by any means, electronic or mechanical
including photocopying, recording or by any information storage and
retrieval system, without permission from the Publisher in writing.

Typeset in Ehrhardt by
Mac Style, Driffield, East Yorkshire
Printed and bound in the UK by CPI Group (UK) Ltd, Croydon,
CRO 4YY

Pen & Sword Books Ltd incorporates the Imprints of Pen & Sword
Aviation, Pen & Sword Maritime, Pen & Sword Military, Wharncliffe
Local History, Pen and Sword Select, Pen & Sword Military Classics,
Leo Cooper, The Praetorian Press, Remember When, Seaforth
Publishing and Frontline Publishing.

For a complete list of Pen & Sword titles please contact
PEN & SWORD BOOKS LIMITED
47 Church Street, Barnsley, South Yorkshire, S70 2AS, England
E-mail: enquiries@pen-and-sword.co.uk
Website: www.pen-and-sword.co.uk

Contents

NEATH PORT TALBOT
LIBRARIES
CL 951.90424
DATE 7.13   £12.79
LOC SAN
NO 2000 615344

Acknowledgements

If Major C.F. Lane, Battery Commander, 170 (Imjin) Battery Royal Artillery, had not invited me to attend at the Officers' Mess, Woolwich Barracks, London, in October 1988 for the unveiling by General Sir Anthony Farrar-Hockley of a painting depicting 170 Independent Mortar Battery in action in Korea in April 1951, these memoirs would never have been started. Twenty-four years later, they have finally been completed.

I acknowledge the help I received from Major Lane, and also the following people, who held the positions shown in 1988: Charles Wilson of Mirror Group PLC, Lisa Wright of P&O Steam Navigation Company, Ian Mackley of the New Zealand Korean War Veterans, and Jane Carmichael, Keeper of Photographs at the Imperial War Museum, London, for whom I worked as a volunteer on the Korean War Collection in 1993, and the archivist at *Gunner* magazine in 1996. For those who have moved on in life, I thank you for your generous assistance, and apologize for taking so long. Photographs have been gathered from the above sources, who kindly waived copyright fees.

Over the years I have listened to the advice of fellow members of the British Korean Veterans Association, some of whom have written their own memoirs. Sadly, too many have had their last post sounded over the intervening years. Their passing has fired me with the will to write something meaningful before it is altogether too late.

I thank Brigadier (Retd) Henry Wilson, late Royal Green Jackets, Publishing Manager at Pen & Sword Books Ltd, for his insistence that I had an almost unique story that should be told … and read. Without his excellent advice and encouragement this record of my military career, mostly served in the defence of another country, would not have been published. And, of course, I thank my editor, Linne Matthews, for taking me through every step along the way, and my wife Sheila, for her support and reassurance that I would, one day, have my story published.

Preface

In times gone by, when a nation lusted after territory occupied by another, the king would mount his charger and lead his army into battle. Today, when territorial greed has reared its ugly head, or another dictator must be eliminated, wars are started by those who mostly remain remote from the danger: politicians sitting around conference tables in comfortable surroundings, who make decisions on how others will fight an armed conflict for them – others who will shed blood for them, and who will die for them

Immediately prior to 25 June 1950 there would have been many such meetings north of the 38th parallel, before the army of the Democratic People's Republic of Korea (DPRK) launched its overwhelming attack on the ill-prepared citizens living to the south of that artificial border. That army, the Inmin Gun, started a three-year war that was first reported as a 'police action'.

During those three years, 81,000 personnel of the British Armed Forces were involved in the preservation of independence for the country under attack in what would become known as the Korean War, the first war in which western nations were pitted against the remorseless spread of communism throughout Asia, the only war fought under the banner of the United Nations. Today, veterans of that distant conflict refer to it as the 'Forgotten War', consigned as it was to virtual oblivion by politicians and people alike.

The British people had only recently experienced six years of warfare; they wanted no more. Our politicians were more concerned that the conflict would draw too many of our service personnel to Northeast Asia, when they perceived the real threat was closer to home, in Europe, with the Soviets.

So in extreme contrasts of temperature, 56,000 British soldiers played their part in vicious ground fighting during Siberian winters and oppressive summer heat and torrential rain. Approximately 25,000 men of the Royal Navy and Royal Marines patrolled the seas off the Korean coast, with a Royal Marines Commando operating on land, and a small number from the Royal Air Force maintaining air supremacy while attached mostly to United States Air Force squadrons. For weeks on end, front-line troops existed in self-dug holes in the ground and squalid trenches, the like of which had not been experienced since the First World War. They were shelled and mortared daily, and assaulted by massed, fanatical enemy infantry.

In 1950, the British Army, reduced to 420,000 following mass demobilization after the Second World War, consisted of four categories of soldiers. There were the regulars who had taken the King's shilling – many of them experienced veterans of war. Then there were the reservists who had been recalled to the colours for a fixed period to serve in the Korean War. Others were known as 'K' volunteers, men who had left the service but had volunteered for service in Korea for a maximum of eighteen months. And there were also the conscripted youths, the National Servicemen, hastily trained in the ways of the military, and without whom Britain would have been unable to satisfy its many commitments across the world. By 1953, 70 per cent of the Army consisted of conscripts, swelling the number of soldiers to 443,000.

These personal recollections of my experiences of war in Korea are dedicated to all of my former comrades, regular, reservist, K volunteer and conscript alike, who served sovereign, country and the politicians to the very best of their ability; those who came home – and those who did not. We left too many behind in the superbly maintained United Nations Cemetery at Pusan, and also those who died in prisoner of war camps in the north. There were others whose remains were never recovered, who lie forever in that far-off land, including in excess of 300 National Servicemen whose families were never thanked by the government for their sacrifice.

An expression used on occasion today is that our soldiers in Afghanistan might be in 'the wrong place at the wrong time'. Were we in the wrong place at the wrong time? I don't think so. I believe we were in the right place at the right time, the result of which is only too evident today in the Republic of Korea. In the British Korean Veterans Association we have seen ample proof that we fought the right war. The people of Korea have never forgotten the troops of all the United Nations member countries who saved their country from communism, although we completely wrecked their cities, towns and villages in doing so. They have forgiven us.

The war in Korea has had no shortage of books written about it. There have been the war stories of journalists who were first on the scene, covering the early months of fighting as correspondents for the world's newspapers. My belief is that by mid-1951 they were few on the ground; Korea had gone stale. Few readers retained an interest unless a family member was actively involved. Headlines could be produced at less expense by weekly reports from 'our Far East correspondent', who was most likely holed up anywhere from the Strand Hotel, Rangoon, to the Peninsula hotel in Hong Kong. Those who still preferred to be closer to the action might be in the Marounuchi, Tokyo, from where they could scrounge space at short notice on a US Air Force flight to Seoul if anything of particular interest happened. Of course, they would be expected to send copy to head office of more interest than their inflated expense accounts.

Records of the exploits of individual fighting units have been written by regimental officers who had served in Korea, so that recruits might always be reminded of the part played by their illustrious predecessors, a part they might be involved in at some future time. Other senior officers have included a chapter or so on their experiences as a young officer thirty-odd years previously. Military and political historians have debated in minute detail the causes of the war, and the effect it had on the Korean people, both in the north, and in the south. Several of my colleagues, ordinary squaddies, have written their personal experiences of the war. To date, however, no full-length record exists of the major battles in the Korean War as observed by one of the lowest of the low in the Royal Regiment of Artillery, a gunner, the Royal Artillery version of a private soldier. I was a National Service conscript on whom that exalted rank was bestowed.

The typical boy called to serve generally thought little about military matters, and of politics he cared even less. We were unsophisticated young men who would emerge from our period of conscription rather more worldly wise. Many would see the world beyond the confines of their home town for the first time, unsettling them when returning to civilian life once more. Those who had been despatched, or who had volunteered to fight aggression and who had returned unscathed, could consider themselves blessed with good fortune.

So, these are the reminiscences of an eighteen-year-old who, following twenty-five weeks of intense military indoctrination, went to war. My writing is not intended as a military history of the Korean War, only a reflection of the very small part I played in it – just the story of a youth who experienced war close up. Some passages are written in light-hearted vein, others are much more serious, sourced from factual chronicles. My contemporaries might glimpse something of themselves they had forgotten as I attempt to combine the humorous – the boredom that was sometimes the lot of conscripts – with the ridiculous, the fear, and the horror: the sheer bloody awfulness that is war. It has been said that the Korean War will be the last one that will have been fought out in conventional trenches and bunkers, occasionally with combatants just yards apart, as in Belgium and France in the First World War.

I assure the reader that I have nothing gloriously heroic of which to boast. To my many friends and colleagues who find that I have not comprehensively included their own unit's commendable achievements in Korea, I offer my sincere apology. I make no pretence that my writing has any great literary merit. It is just an attempt by an old soldier to educate all who might otherwise never have heard of two major battles fought by the British Army in the middle of the twentieth century.

To recall life, and death, exactly as it was after so many years had passed did not come easily at first, but once started it was surprising to see how much detail could be dredged up from the inner recesses of the memory. Not that any of it was truly forgotten. The fuse was there all the time, waiting to be lit.

Jim Jacobs
Fareham, 2013

Glossary

AACS	Australian Army Canteen Service
A&SH	Argyll and Sutherland Highlanders
Baffs	British Armed Forces Special Vouchers
BC	battery commander
BCOF	British Commonwealth Occupation Force
BCR	battle casualty replacement
Bdr	bombardier
BEDS	Base Ejection Discarding Sabot
BHQ	battalion headquarters or battery headquarters
BK	battery captain
BKVA	British Korean Veterans Association
BOD	base ordnance depot
BQMS	battery quartermaster sergeant
Brig	brigadier
BSM	battery sergeant major
BW	Black Watch
Capt	captain
CATC	Commonwealth Artillery Training Centre
CAV	United States Cavalry Division
CBE	Commander of the British Empire
CIGS	Chief of the Imperial General Staff
COBU	Combined Operations Bombardment Unit
COD	Command Ordnance Depot
Col	colonel
Comwel Div	Commonwealth Division
Coy	company
CP	command post
CPO	command post officer
CRA	Commander Royal Artillery
DCM	Distinguished Conduct Medal
DF	defensive fire
Div	division

DMZ	demilitarized zone
DPRK	Democratic People's Republic of Korea
DSO	Distinguished Service Order
DWR	Duke of Wellington's Regiment
EUSAK	Eighth United States Army in Korea
FAB	field artillery battalion
FC	fire control
FMA	forward maintenance area
FOO	forward observation officer
FSMO	full service marching order
FUP	forming-up place
Gnr	gunner
GOC	General Officer Commanding
GPO	gun position officer
HAA	Heavy Anti-Aircraft Regiment
HE	high explosive
HF	harassing fire
HQRA	Headquarters Royal Artillery
HVM	high velocity missile
JRBD	Japan Reinforcement Base Depot
JRHU	Japan Reinforcement Holding Unit
KMAG	Korean Military Advisory Group
KOSB	King's Own Scottish Borderers
KRIH	King's Royal Irish Hussars
KSLI	King's Shropshire Light Infantry
K-type	volunteer for Korea
Lieut	lieutenant
L/Bdr	lance bombardier
Lt Col	Lieutenant Colonel
Lt Gen	Lieutenant General
LSH	Lord Strathcona's Horse
Maj	major
Maj Gen	Major General
MASH	Mobile Army Surgical Hospital
MATS	Unites States Military Air Transport Service
MC	Military Cross
MM	Military Medal
MMG	medium machine gun
MO	medical officer
MSgt	master sergeant
MSR	main supply route
NTR	nothing to report

OBE	Order of the British Empire
OP	observation post
ORBAT	order of battle
PFC	private, first class
PPCLI	Princess Patricia's Canadian Light Infantry
PSO	personnel selection officer
PTSD	post-traumatic stress disorder
R22eR	Royal 22eme Regiment
RAF	Royal Air Force
RAMC	Royal Army Medical Corps
RAR	Royal Australian Regiment
RASC	Royal Army Service Corps
RCHA	Royal Canadian Horse Artillery
RCR	Royal Canadian Regiment
RCT	regimental combat team
REME	Royal Electrical & Mechanical Engineers
RHE	repatriation to home establishment
RHQ	regimental headquarters
RIDG	Royal Inniskilling Dragoon Guards
RNF	Royal Northumberland Fusiliers
RNZA	Royal New Zealand Artillery
RNZASC	Royal New Zealand Army Service Corps
ROK	Republic of Korea
RTO	rail transport office
RTR	Royal Tank Regiment
RUR	Royal Ulster Rifles
Sgt	sergeant
SMLE	short magazine Lee Enfield
S/Sgt	staff sergeant
Tac HQ	tactical headquarters
TARA	Technical Assistant Royal Artillery
TC	tactical control
T/Capt	temporary captain
TRRA	Training Regiment Royal Artillery
TSM	troop sergeant major
UNKWAA	United Nations Korean War Allies Association
USAF	United States Air Force
VC	Victoria Cross
WO	warrant officer
WP	white phosphorous
WVS	Women's Voluntary Service

Chapter One

Another War 'Out East'

It promised to be a pleasant autumn day on 21 May 1982 as I stepped onto my balcony to watch the sun rise blood red above the Pacific Ocean. Autumn, that is to say, in Australia; spring in England. At that time of year the sun appeared dead centre between La Perouse and Kurnell, the twin headlands that marked the entrance to Botany Bay. The kookaburras had laughed at the dawn and moved on. Now it was the turn of the currawongs and parrots to screech and fight in the red gums that lined both sides of Trafalgar Street, Brighton-le-Sands, one of Sydney's pleasant beachside suburbs.

I had already watched the early television news and was aware that Britain was at war. Argentina had invaded the Falklands Islands – Las Malvinas, as Argentina calls those desolate islands in the South Atlantic. Another dictator, using a largely conscript army, had renewed his country's invalid claim to the islands.

Arriving at work, my boss, a New Zealander, commented, 'So, your Marines and Paras have gone in, then. They'll sort the bastards out, quick-smart.' I agreed that indeed they would.

Initially the Argentine invasion had not impacted to any great extent on the Australian public, although those with a direct interest would have been well aware that Britain had assembled a combined task force to secure the islands for the British, English-speaking inhabitants. The Royal Navy and a fleet of chartered civilian ships had transported the military component from the south coast ports of Portsmouth and Southampton, cities that were both well known to us. In New South Wales more people were concerned over reports that countless millions of mice were rampaging through the vast wheatlands out west and up into Queensland, devouring every living green shoot in their path. Watching their unstoppable advance on television, I was reminded of fanatical infantry attacks I had witnessed first-hand more than thirty years earlier.

Few Australians – indeed, few in Britain at the outset – had much idea where the Falklands were, unable to pinpoint them on a map. Now, after a voyage of three weeks or so, Britain's response to the generals and politicians in Buenos Aires was assembling on those sparsely populated islands. On that very day, as my boss and I spoke about what might happen, the young men of the Royal Navy, Royal Marines and the Parachute Regiment, the Scots and Welsh Guards, and the Gurkha Rifles, along with many support units, were preparing to take the fight to the invaders.

Over the following weeks, in excess of 250 of those young men would lose their lives in combat on land, at sea and in the air. Later, the evening television news confirmed that there had been early casualties. The cream of Britain's young men were laying down their lives so that others might be free. I was transported back in time to 1950, to another distant country that few people could find on a map. Even Winston Churchill had been heard to comment that he had never heard of that country until he was in his seventy-fourth year. That country was Korea, where war had commenced.

Koryo, the Kingdom of the White-clad People, the Hermit Kingdom, Land of the Morning Calm, Choson, Chosen – the country that we know today as Korea has, over the millennia, been known by all the foregoing names as well as others. During that time it has been said to have enjoyed '5,000 years of turbulent calm'.

Korea is a small peninsula bounded in the north by China, Manchuria and Russia, its land mass being roughly the same size as the United Kingdom. The first thing anyone arriving in Korea will notice is that they are never out of sight of the hills and mountains, forming as they do something approaching 80 per cent of the surface area. The tallest mountains are predominately in the north and east, with the heavy summer rainfall running off in a westerly direction, where there are many wide tidal estuaries of large slow-running rivers that become raging torrents in the wet season.

The Korean people are largely descended from nomadic tribes that originated in Central Asia. Archaeological discoveries indicate that the Korean peninsula was first settled in the Stone Age by tribes migrating from the north-west, and also by people of Mongolian origin. Today, the greatest proportion of the population display the facial characteristics brought about by the intermingling of the two distinct racial types. Chinese dynastic influences, the introduction of Buddhism and a Mongol occupation force all combined to form the Korean individual. The Mongols withdrew towards the end of the fourteenth century, their army being needed at home in mainland China to repel attacks from Ming Dynasty warlords. By the late sixteenth century, Japan had started to seek land beyond her own restricted confines, making two invasion attempts, both of which were successfully repulsed. In the early seventeenth century the Manchus invaded and occupied the peninsula, and by the middle of that century Korea began a policy of isolationism, until opening a limited number of ports to trade with the Japanese in the late nineteenth century.

Peace and trade treaties were concluded with the United States in 1882, followed shortly afterwards by similar treaties with other western nations, including Britain and Russia. By that time, however, Japan was casting a war-like eye over her mainland neighbour. These empirical aspirations culminated in the annexation of Korea by Japan in 1910. The nation, known at the time as Choson, was renamed as the Japanese colony of Chosen. During thirty-five years of Japanese colonization, several 'home rule' factions were formed in attempts to rid the land of the oppressor. A government in exile, headed by Dr Syngman Rhee, was formed offshore, waiting for the day when they might return safely to Korea to install their own brand of bureaucracy and to continue the subjugation of the people in yet another form. When Japan declared war on the United States in 1941, large numbers of young Korean men were forcibly conscripted into the Imperial Japanese Army, where they were treated as inferiors, mostly put into the lowest, meanest positions. By that time all Koreans had been compelled to take Japanese names, the Korean language press was banned, books of learning destroyed, and education continued only in the Japanese language.

Following the end of the Second World War the Korean people might have expected that they would at least gain independence from overseas influence and become masters of their own destiny. It was not to be. The Soviet Union, which had entered the war against Japan only in the final month of fighting, occupied the north of the country, while the army of the United States formed an occupation force in the south. After much prevarication regarding where the dividing line should be between north and south, it was arbitrarily decided that the 38th line of latitude would satisfy the requirement. The people would have this unnatural division forced upon them. From that time, both Koreas, north and south of what became known as the 38th parallel, would develop along very different lines. Groups of people who had originally taken to the mountains to fight guerrilla actions against the Japanese discovered new tyrannical oppressors, against whom it would be necessary to continue the fight. The north became a totalitarian socialist state, to be known as the Democratic People's Republic of Korea, with its capital in Pyongyang. The land to the south of the 38th parallel became Taehan Min-guk, referred to in the west as the Republic of Korea, or South Korea, with Seoul as its capital. Korea was now split in two, although the inhabitants remained one people with a common language and culture. In the north the Soviets equipped and trained a large army, as did the United States in the south, but on a much smaller scale. The north was equipped with heavy artillery and armoured units, chiefly of leftover Second World War Soviet T34 tanks and self-propelled guns.

The south was not, having mainly a defence oriented infantry force. In 1948 the Soviet Union withdrew her last troops to beyond North Korea's northern border, and the following year the last American ground forces left South Korea, leaving a Military Advisory Group (KMAG) behind.

Washington, and in particular General MacArthur in his Tokyo HQ, were satisfied that the army they had trained in the south would provide the essential buffer between the communist world that stretched from the 38th parallel in the east, all the way westwards to the border between East and West Germany, without interruption. The status quo was maintained by the provision of a military government in Japan, where three infantry divisions of the US Army and a Marine division were the occupying force, with a smaller British Commonwealth force holding the fort in southern Honshu and on the island of Shikoku. But disturbances in South Korea continued to disrupt daily life, the warring factions now opposed politically rather than militarily. In the south many people were displeased with the government of Syngman Rhee now that he had returned from overseas, but their political voices were ruthlessly silenced. The militant activists remained in hiding in the mountains, continuing the fight for freedom – until 25 June 1950, when for all the Korean people, in the cities, in the towns and villages, and in the mountains, three years of living hell began on both sides of the border. And that is where I begin my story.

These are the personal reminiscences of a young man who, like countless millions before him in the twentieth century, was pressed into the service of his country. A boy sent to do a man's job – although nobody forced me to go to war. I could have continued with a boring military job without ever going overseas, but I was one of the crazy minority: I was a volunteer. The war in which I participated is not remembered for glorious departures of the regiments, with bands playing and crowds cheering and weeping, with handkerchiefs waving. Nor is it remembered for joyful, tearful homecomings for the victorious troops. My war is the one the politicians had no guts for at the outset and quickly forgot as the troops returned home on troopships that mostly slipped into port on cold dawns completely without fanfare. In Whitehall the Cabinet hoped fervently that British participation would not cause a serious escalation into a third world war, with communism the common enemy, beyond the borders of a small Asian country that few had heard of.

Reluctantly, as a senior member of the United Nations Security Council, Britain had little choice in the matter of being involved in military participation. In 1950 Britain was still a supposed world power, albeit one that had been bolstered with massive financial and material loans provided by our United States ally. Financing six crippling years of war had all but bankrupted Britain. A third conflagration was all we needed.

For the British people life in 1950 was not a comfortable existence. We lived in a land of perpetual shortages and austerity, with the continuation of wartime food rationing. However, the government had to be seen to be doing something to assist a country that looked as though it was going to be overrun by communism. There was no real choice but to become involved.

I say that I became involved in a war, although in reality a state of war was never declared between the original combatants, nor has it ever ended. Following three years, one month and two days of killing, no peace agreement was ever forthcoming. A state of armed siege still exists between the two halves of the country that had for thousands of years been one. But it certainly was a war. A horrible, bloody war.

The early months of 1950 were good to me as I made the most of my leisure time. At eighteen years young I was only too well aware that in a few short weeks my life would be turned around dramatically. I had no real concept of how the enforced period of military conscription that awaited us all on reaching that age would affect me. No more would I be able to do as I wanted, when I wanted. During the forthcoming eighteen months I would be allowed no mind of my own. I would be told what to do, without any reason as to why I should do it without question. I accepted all of this without challenge. I was destined to travel far and see sights that I had never expected to see. And I would lose good friends that I had known only briefly. New emotions would be experienced, among them sadness and fear. And I would be changed forever by circumstances that were quite beyond my control.

During the fifty-odd years that have followed I have seen many more sights and visited many other countries across the globe, yet Korea remains the country that has had the most profound effect on me. It is the country where I and countless hundreds of thousands of young men from many lands played a part in securing freedom from tyranny for others – citizens whose country was devastated, but who were fired with the will to survive in the direst circumstances. That country was a long way from home. Before the days of mass air travel, it was a *very* long way from home.

My military career was not of my choosing for the first two years. At the beginning I was not exactly thrilled with all the stamping around on drill squares that gave men on the 'permanent staff' something to do in indoctrinating raw recruits.

In 1950, on reaching eighteen, three whole years before I would be eligible to vote in a general election, I had no say in being pressed into uniform. A letter arrived from a government department inviting me to mix with other fit young men. There was a selection process to weed out undesirables. After all, the British Armed Forces did not want any old riff-raff serving in the ranks. Having survived basic training, I committed the most cardinal of all sins in the military: I applied to be considered for service overseas. The lads told me I was crazy. There was an unwritten rule that nobody of sane mind ever volunteered for anything in the forces. But I volunteered regardless of the consequences. Hoping for a nice warm posting to the burning sands of Egypt, I tendered my body to get away, to anywhere. The wheels were set in motion. I was shipped off to where I was well aware that a violent armed struggle was in progress. Five years after the end of the Second World War, there was a new war, 'out East'.

Chapter Two

Called to Arms

In 1948 the National Service Act had been passed in Parliament, effective on 1 January 1949. Discounting the occasional mobilization of reservists, this would be the first time when Britain was not officially involved in a declared war that young men would be forcibly conscripted into the Armed Forces. From January 1949 men called to serve would be obliged to complete one year with the colours, followed by six years of reserve service. During the latter period they were liable for recall into uniform at short notice.

The forecast strength of the Army under this plan was supposed to be 305,000. However, due to escalating commitment overseas, by March 1951 the number would increase to 420,000, and to 443,000 by 1953. By 1950, further demands on the military would also mean that the period of conscripted service would increase to eighteen months, and then to two years. Reserve service was reduced to three years and six months. The prime minister at the time, Clement Attlee, who had strongly opposed rearmament prior to the outbreak of the Second World War, was also against National Service. His argument against outlaying vast sums from revenue on a conscript army meant much reduced funds would be available for the newly emerging Welfare State, in particular, the National Health Service.

Although the government had tried hard to convince the armed forces chiefs that an increase in the conscription period from twelve to eighteen months was an unnecessary luxury, the Chiefs of Staff were having none of it. They were unanimous in agreeing that eighteen months was the minimum acceptable period in which a man could practise the skills he had acquired in training when called upon to do so. With escalating overseas commitment, particularly in the Far East, the Chiefs argued, twelve months would eliminate most men from the reckoning, at a time when conscripts accounted for at least 60 per cent of the Army. Five or six months' minimum training, embarkation leave, kitting for overseas, medicals, plus a month at sea – both outward and homeward bound – would leave little more than four months for a man to serve with a unit in the Far East, while eighteen months would provide a trained soldier in Malaya, for example, for ten months, although still straining the replacement system to the limit. No commanding officer was thrilled to see a continual stream of competent, experienced men replaced with raw, untried youths straight off the latest troopship. As far as they were concerned, the longer the experienced men could be retained, the better.

Communist 'bandit hunting' in the Malayan jungle was keeping a number of infantry battalions at full stretch, most with a complement of 60 to 70 per cent conscripts. The rout of the Nationalist Army of Chiang Kai-shek in China by the communists, and the possibility that Mao Tse-tung might decide to continue his inexorable advance across the Shum-chun River into the Crown Colony of Hong Kong, was tying up an enhanced infantry division along the land and river border.

In 1950, Britain maintained garrisons or smaller establishments in Aden, Austria, Cyprus, Eritrea, Egypt, Germany, Gibraltar, Hong Kong, Jamaica, Japan, Jordan, Kenya, Libya, Malaya, Malta, Singapore, Somaliland, Sudan and the disputed Trieste territory. Other overseas postings were possible in smaller formations. Alterations to the structure of the Army in 1949 had reduced the Corps of Infantry to seventy-seven regiments. With the exception of the ten battalions in the Brigade of Guards, all retained a single battalion. In addition, four regiments of the Gurkha Rifles, each with two battalions, were in the Order of Battle (ORBAT), although they were not counted in British Army strength. The Royal Artillery fielded sixty-nine regiments: field, anti-tank, medium, heavy, coastal, and both heavy and light anti-aircraft units. There were in addition several specialized independent batteries. The Army's peak strength in 1952 was 440,000, more than half of whom were conscripts. The hope of most was that their period of military service would be on a home posting, within the United Kingdom, from where they would be able to take advantage of one weekend (forty-eight-hour) leave pass once a month to enable them to go home to all the comfort from which they had been removed. For the majority, as might have been expected, life would not be that simple. Large numbers were sent to West Germany to defend the border with Soviet Russia in the form of the East German Army. There would be no weekend passes from there.

Shortly after my eighteenth birthday, my attendance was requested at the local office of the Ministry of Labour and National Service on a specified date to register for National Service. On arrival I was asked to complete the standard registration form. There were many questions. Which service did I prefer? I entered Army. Which branch? How many branches were there, I wondered, as I gazed idly through the window across Osborn Road, where a smart red and blue painted sign caught my eye. I knew it to be the base of a local Royal Artillery unit, where I would no doubt have to serve three and a half years in the Territorial Army. I entered Royal Artillery. And that was all that was required to ensure that my service was as far away from bombs, bullets and shells as possible. A mate who was on embarkation leave to join his infantry battalion in Malaya, and another who had just finished his time in the Parachute Regiment, told me I would be quite safe and sound in the 'Nine-Mile Snipers', miles from any combat action.

Although I had enjoyed two years in the Sea Cadet Corps, I had already decided not to follow my father, who had served twenty-seven years in the Royal Navy. I would not have enjoyed a life on the briny, or, more likely, in a concrete battleship in Portsmouth, Plymouth or Chatham. Within a few weeks I received an official looking buff envelope inviting my attendance at Devonshire Hall, Portsmouth, for a full medical examination. The brigade of stethoscope wielders found little wrong with me, disregarding my short-sightedness, hammer toes, and the few pounds overweight I was for my height, about which one of them wrote 'will improve with training'. Unable to execute a passable limp, or a squint, I guessed that my body was just the right sort that was urgently needed in some Godforsaken part of Britain, West Germany or the outposts of Empire. I tried to fake the sight test by enquiring on which wall was the illuminated sign of large and small letters that I was asked to read from, but they had seen it all before. My Country had need of me.

Following another brief spell of waiting to hear the worst, it was not long before another buff envelope dropped through the letterbox. I believe it contained a postal order for four shillings – one day's pay – and a rail warrant, but the most important piece of paper instructed me to report to 67 TRRA, Wingate Lines, Park Hall Camp, Oswestry, Salop, where I would become 22358492 Gunner Jacobs J.W.

On the appointed day I stood cold and alone on the platform at Fareham station waiting for the first of three trains that would transport me to Salop (I had looked this word up in Fareham Library to find that it was the abbreviation for Shropshire). I had never been that far away from home in my young life. I supposed that the four-shilling postal order was to ensure I did not starve on the journey. If I had lost it I imagined that I would be expected to raid a station buffet for food, my first initiation test.

By the time I reached my destination the train was bursting at the seams with young lads, all heading for various training establishments. We who were destined for Park Hall Camp were loaded onto trucks and driven the short distance from the station. There I found a timber-hutted camp arranged around a menacing looking drill square. TRRA, I now discovered, was short for Training Regiment Royal Artillery.

After being told (ordered) to dump anything we had brought with us on a bed in the nearest timber hut, then to fall in outside in approximately three ranks, we were pounced upon by a man with two stripes on each sleeve, which we knew indicated he was a corporal. His opening words were, 'Listen up, you will note that I am *not* a corporal. In the Royal Regiment of Artillery a man wearing two stripes on his sleeve is a bombardier. Corporals are found only in the lower branches of the Army, the Royal Marines and the Royal Air Force.' Well, that straightened us out. Further, he announced that together with a man with one stripe who had been standing to the side, who we now knew was a lance bombardier, he would knock us into something vaguely resembling soldiers over the following two weeks. Then another man with three stripes approached. He told us he was our squad sergeant and his name was Sergeant McCampbell, which he spelt B–A–S–T–A–R–D, and that it would not be to our best advantage if we crossed him. Our next two weeks, it seemed, would be full of fun.

Next up was a young, pink-faced slip of a lad wearing a peaked cap and carrying a slim cane under his left arm who had been hovering in the background. The sergeant introduced him, name now forgotten, as the officer in charge of our intake.

'Now listen up,' said the officer in a cultured voice. 'How many of you chaps have played rugby?'

'The officer means rugby union, not rugby league,' interjected Sergeant McCampbell.

That was the first time I had heard of two different kinds of rugby. Four of the tallest lads put their hands up. 'Fall out and go with the officer,' they were told. Knowing full well about never volunteering, I thought they would most likely be put to task to paint white lines across an adjacent cow pasture, so that two teams of officers could attempt to kill each other while trying to carry an oval ball instead of kicking a spherical one.

Before our two weeks were up I discovered that as rugby union was only played in the better schools, this approach had been a provisional experiment to weed out potential National Service officers. They would be taken to places unknown, to qualify on passing out as second lieutenants – those who were supposed to be first 'over the top' in action, with a very brief life expectancy. Perhaps they ought not to have put their hands up – or should have stuck to football at school.

So, while the might of the Royal Artillery's crack training team had knocked the delights of very basic training into us, like how to press a uniform, get our arms and legs together when on the march, to salute, hold a rifle, perform basic arms drill, manage simple physical tasks to order, enjoy country runs in battle order, not to turn left when the order 'Right turn' has been given and how not to kill our instructor on the rifle range, we were informed that if we did not perform well on passing out parade at the end of the two weeks, we would be back-squadded. That meant having to go over it all again with the next fortnightly intake. It was more than a man could stand. We persevered, and passed out.

Before leaving Oswestry we were interviewed by the personnel selection officer (PSO), whose job it was to place us into various categories according to our intelligent responses to his questions. He asked what I had learned in the Sea Cadets, and if I was conversant with Morse code, to which I replied in the positive. 'Right,' he said, 'you will be trained as a regimental signaller,' without telling me that Morse code had just been removed from the training programme in the Royal Artillery. Maybe I would be expected to stand on the tallest hills and send messages with semaphore flags, as in the Royal Navy and Sea Cadets. The PSO continued by saying I would be posted to 38 TRRA, Kinmel Park Camp, Rhyl, North Wales. Some of the lads thought that after our passing out parade our basic training was finished. They had a lot to learn. It had hardly started. Taken back to the station with a group who were also to be trained as regimental signallers, our movement order was to change trains, I believe, at Chester, and connect with the North Wales line.

We all looked forward to Rhyl with confidence. That confidence was quickly dispelled. Kinmel Park Camp was several miles out of Rhyl, near the village of Boddelwyddan. First sight of the camp did not inspire me. It was exactly like Park Hall Camp, but built on a hill. Above us at the top of the hill was 31 TRRA, where other trades were taught. Also in camp was the Boys Battery, where underage youths were dumped by parents to learn the art of soldiering. They were trained on the bugle and cavalry trumpet or, for those with less puff, on the military side-drum. On reaching the appropriate age they would join service regiments.

To be trained as a regimental signaller sounded impressive, but in reality it meant dragging heavy pieces of wireless equipment called 22 sets to the tops of minor mountains, and spending days making coherent comments of a military nature into our microphones, using the 'Able, Baker, Charlie, Dog' phonetic alphabet of the era. Clambering up and down most of the hills in the vicinity, along with being tortured daily by the PT instructors in the gymnasium and on cross-country runs, probably made us fitter than any of us had ever been in our lives. And if that sounds bad, the food was worse. We were taught to read and understand military maps and how to find grid references. We became reasonably proficient on the rifle range and were trained on the Sten and the Bren (the latter of which was a neat piece of kit, but heavy to carry). By the time we passed out at Rhyl we had been in the Army ten weeks; looking down on the newly arriving drafts who had only six or eight weeks' service under their belts, we felt like old soldiers.

While we had been learning the art of the soldier, three events of international importance occurred. West Germany had been admitted to the Council of Europe, Yugoslavia had severed relations with Albania, and war had broken out in a place called Korea. Most people knew where West Germany was and, with a little prompting, a few could have found Albania in our old school atlases. But even the grammar school kids would be hard pressed to locate Korea. The papers and the BBC said that North Korea had invaded South Korea. Neither meant a thing to the average citizen of the United Kingdom. If we had been told that North and South Antarctica were at each other's throats, it would have been meaningful, but Korea, like Salop, was an unknown quantity.

On one afternoon each week we had classes under the horn-rimmed gaze of a conscripted school teacher, a sergeant of the Royal Army Education Corps, which was a nice relaxing afternoon. He displayed a map that pinpointed Korea, with Manchuria, China and Russia on the northern boundary, and the sea all around a rugged coastline with many offshore islands.

As the days passed it appeared that a full-scale war was in progress on the far side of the world, with the southern capital falling to communist forces from the north within days. The papers told us that American troops stationed in Japan might be committed to the fray. We said with great confidence that the Yanks would soon sort out that bunch of commies in no time at all. It rapidly became evident, however, that the unheard of army of North Korea was not going to be a pushover. Daily reports flowed thick and fast, together with hastily redrawn maps showing a shortening and withdrawing front line. A request had been submitted to the Security Council of the United Nations that member countries should send aid to South Korea, military or medical. In the absence of the Soviet Union delegate, who was boycotting the assembly due to the ongoing battle to have the China seat in the UN go to Communist China, not to the US-favoured Nationalist China of Chiang Kai-shek based on Formosa, the motion was carried. Within days the press were predicting that it would not be long before Tommy Atkins was told to pack his kitbag and head to the conflict, although first reports indicated that only a token force could be spared due to Britain's continuing commitment to police most of explored planet Earth.

Apart from dragging wireless equipment around much of North Wales, in our spare time we also had infantry training. There were fieldcraft exercises night and day in the pine forest adjacent to the camp; joyful nights in pouring rain being scared witless as a deer broke cover at the last second; drill on the parade square, with or without rifle; Sten and Bren practice on the firing range; and learning how to land with a satisfying squelch in the water jump on the assault course. We had great fun.

Once more we were threatened with back-squadding if we did not attain an acceptable level, or we could be transferred to a gunnery course or, worse still, to the Pioneer Corps. Eagerly we scanned the notice board to find our next posting. One notice caught everyone's eye: a request for volunteers to spend a week at the Cold Research Centre, Porton Down, Wiltshire. Successive governments have covered up the fact that many young men were invited to take part in this practice, denying that there had ever been any such establishment, passing it off by saying it must be a figment of the imagination. They ought to try telling that to a comrade of mine who lost his sight for a couple of days while there. There have always been rumours that nerve gas was tested at Porton Down, all of which continues to be denied by Whitehall.

The notice board informed me that I was being posted to 62 Heavy Anti-aircraft Regiment (62 HAA), at New Barracks, Burton Road, Lincoln. My new unit was based on a Second World War gun site that had been part of the protective screen around several RAF and USAF bomber bases, as well as Hull and Immingham docks. Once more I was housed in the ubiquitous timber hut, next to Sobraon Barracks, home of the Royal Lincolnshire Regiment, who at that time were busy swatting flies in the Suez Canal Zone. We soon discovered that they would allow us to use their assault course while they were away, provided that we did not damage it.

At Lincoln I was taught all the finer points of wireless communications applicable to a HAA regiment. It was pretty dreary stuff. Most of my daily life was spent in an underground operations room from where I could see neither the guns nor the aircraft that we practised shooting down based on my instructions. The general idea was that a formation of 'enemy' aircraft would be way out over the North Sea, where in time coastal radar would pick them up. I stood behind a huge sheet of clear perspex marked in grid squares, on which I had to draw a line and write backwards so that an officer on the other side, presumably the command post officer (CPO), could see where the approaching aircraft had reached. When they passed over the coast, where our own radar intercepted them, the officer would call out 'TC track'. On hearing that in my headphones, I had to instruct TC, the Tactical Control radar unit, to track. Then when they came within range of our guns, Fire Control took over, so I had to respond to the 'FC track' shouted out by the CPO, all the time writing backwards across the perspex sheet. At that point an early form of computer predicted height and speed of the moving aircraft, and the precise point where the shell would have to explode to shoot it down, and this information was transferred electronically to the guns. There could well have been more to it than that, but if so, it is long forgotten.

I thought there surely must be more to soldiering than that, but it was the best that 62 HAA Regiment could provide. I was doomed to spend my entire eighteen months shouting 'TC' and 'FC track'. And then, of course, the government increased the National Service period to two years. That did it. I had to get out: out to anywhere that would have me.

Around that time some important international events were again hitting the headlines. There was serious rioting in Belgium against King Leopold, who later abdicated in favour of his son, Prince Baodouin. In Hungary all religious orders had been dissolved and, in the UK, Hugh Gaitskell became Chancellor of the Exchequer – all riveting stuff. In the Malayan jungle British, Malay, African, Fijian and Gurkha soldiers were going through a successful period, killing many of the terrorists who wanted Malaya to become a communist state when the British left after the country gained independence. But the most important announcement by far that summer put everything else into the minor league. The Ministry of Defence announced that National Servicemen could volunteer to have their heads blown off in Korea. Wishful thinking, most men thought.

By the time I had finished my training, a hastily assembled and much under-strength 27 Infantry Brigade had been despatched from Hong Kong to Korea. They sailed with minimum equipment on the basis that good old Uncle Sam, or General MacArthur, would provide all field artillery, armour and necessary military stores, transport, etc. The infantry battalions selected from 27 Brigade were the Middlesex Regiment and the Argyll and Sutherland Highlanders. One troop of Royal Artillery 17-pounder anti-tank guns would accompany them. In the meantime, General MacArthur, Supreme Commander with his HQ in Tokyo, asked for more British troops. Waiting for the call, 29 Independent Infantry Brigade Group, the ever ready 'fire brigade', fully equipped and self-supporting with artillery and armour, was being readied at Colchester, Essex, although short of manpower. As our training was completed we could volunteer to join them. Unimpressed with their pleading, most of the lads in 62 HAA were pleased that, like flogging, the press gangs had been abolished in the previous century. But I had begun to give serious thought to Egypt.

One evening I spoke to a lad of the Royal Lincolns who had just returned from Suez. I asked him what it was like out there. 'Great,' he said, telling me only the rose-tinted spectacles version, leaving out the bit about having to fish dead donkeys from their drinking water supply most days.

There were three batteries in 62 HAA: 44, 214 and 218. I was in 214 Battery, and I felt certain they could manage without me. One morning, bold as brass, I marched into 214 Battery Office to enquire about vacancies out there for a keen young conscript with crossed flags on his sleeve. The Chief Clerk, a staff sergeant, told me no list was maintained of applicants for Middle East postings, but he made a note of my name, safe in the knowledge that I was a fool. Never volunteer, etc. … I thought I would let him mull it over for a couple of weeks.

For a change of scenery, 214 Battery was involved in a series of escape and evasion exercises with trainee pilots from RAF Cranwell. Simulating the pilots having parachuted into enemy territory, our job was to capture and interrogate them, without being too rough on them. It broke the monotony of the underground control room. On returning to barracks early one morning, on morning parade my name was called out and I was told to report to Regimental Headquarters (RHQ) as soon as the parade was dismissed. Now, RHQ was known to me only as the domain of Regimental Sergeant Major 'Tiger' Mitchell, who had a fearsome reputation. Wondering how on earth I might have fallen foul of him I entered RHQ with a heavy heart. A clerk directed me to the great man's office and I knocked on the door. A gruff voice called out: 'Come.' I went. I was standing in the Tiger's den.

Looking me up and down to see what miserable specimen of conscripted humanity was standing on his hallowed carpet, he enquired, quite pleasantly, I thought, 'Volunteer for the Middle East, isn't it?' I agreed that indeed it was. 'Can't help you there' he continued, 'but if you are interested in the Far East …?' letting his voice trail away. Well I knew nothing much about the Far East, except that it was further away than the Middle East, and wars were being fought in Malaya and Korea. I declined his kind offer, wondering if I was the first man ever to turn him down in all his years of service. 'Think it over, lad,' he continued, 'I have spent some good times soldiering in the Far East.' Nothing ventured, nothing gained, I thought.

'Where precisely would I be stationed, Sir?' I enquired.

Realizing that I was interested, he knew that he had me. 'Oh, Singapore or Hong Kong, I would think.' He continued with a smile, 'Of course, the regiment is looking for fifty volunteers for Korea!'

I thought, yes, I bet it is. But then I remembered the papers had reported that General MacArthur had handed out a press statement that concluded by saying the war with North Korea was won, and he would have 'all his boys' home by Christmas. Thinking it over for about two seconds, I thought that if the war was over, by the time I arrived out there I would be sent straight back, and the ocean voyage would do me no harm. I said, 'Put me on the list, Sir,' to which he replied, 'Be outside this office at 0830 hrs tomorrow morning with all your kit and in FSMO (full service marching order).'

Why the rush if the war is over, I wondered. Still, having volunteered I would be pleased to say goodbye to the underground control room, and to Lincoln (the barracks, not the city). It was with great interest that I looked forward to what fate had in store for me. As for Tiger, who seemed such a nice man, I thought he was more like a pussy cat. I could not imagine how he had acquired such a bad reputation among the men.

The next morning, staggering under FSMO and kitbag, fifty of us lucky lads, who were looking forward to the ocean cruise, were getting 'fell in'. Tiger gave up some of his valuable personal time to inspect us, to see if we were suitably fit to mingle with civilians on the train to London and to ensure we came up to his exacting standards. Dismissing us, he actually wished us well in our military careers. We boarded the trucks that would take us down the steep hill to Lincoln Station. Thankfully, we did not have to form up in threes and march down there. Tumbling out in a chaos of packs, kitbags and dislodged Blanco, we boarded the train for Grantham, where we changed onto the King's Cross flyer. At King's Cross we fought a valiant action, damaging a few civilians with our packs on the London Underground, and headed for Waterloo and the train for Woolwich, Depot of the Royal Artillery for something approaching 200 years, and transit point for gunners to and from overseas postings.

I was not at all impressed with the standard of accommodation. It looked as though it had stood there for the whole 200 years. We climbed an iron staircase on the outside of a long red brick barrack block. Some of the 'old sweats', who had by now joined our merry band, told us the ground floor was formerly the stables for the horses that until the 1930s had pulled the guns into action. It looked to me as though the horses had been moved out just that morning, that we would be issued with a nosebag and given orders to muck out before breakfast.

Our next order was to check our heavy kit into stores and march over to Field Wing Office, where our embarkation leave passes, food ration coupons and rail warrants to our home towns would be prepared. Then we were advised to make ourselves scarce for the rest of the day. Anyone found loitering in the barrack block, or in the NAAFI, would be found a job to do, like sweeping the barrack square, be put on fire picquet or even rostered for main gate guard. A lad with whom I had palled up and I decided to view the delights of Woolwich town to find some edible food that was within our mean price range and an improvement on army grub. As he was a Londoner, from Bow, his suggestion for a gourmet meal was to find a pie and mash shop, an experience that was obviously missing from my sheltered upbringing. And there was one right next to the railway station. The meal, a revelation to me, was cheap and cheerful. I was finding out how other people lived beyond the confines of Fareham.

The next morning, 22 December 1950, we lined up for our travel warrant, leave pass and a ten-day food ration card. Embarkation leave was in lieu of Christmas leave, or so it seemed. Then there followed a lecture on the dreadful fate awaiting any man who decided not to bother returning for his ocean cruise. I gained the impression that punishment could consist of ninety days in the 'glasshouse', the military correction establishment, followed by a voyage on the next troopship leaving for the most desolate posting possible. Somewhere like Tristan da Cunha, Ascension Island or Christmas Island, where A-bomb testing was in progress. I do not remember if firing squads were mentioned; probably not.

I spent a comfortable Christmas at home with my parents, had a brown ale or three at the Bugle and saw a movie with my mates, in which about ninety seconds of the newsreel was devoted to the war in Korea. It struck me that it was still continuing and there was mention that the Chinese Army had driven the UN forces back. I imagined that General MacArthur was annoyed. I listened to the King's speech on the radio on Christmas Day, saw the New Year in at the Bugle, and that was my leave over. Next step, foreign parts, as my father always called anywhere south of Portsmouth.

Back at Woolwich, our kit was withdrawn from stores for a complete kit check and new kit issued that was more suited to warmer climates. With webbing that did not need Blanco it pleased us no end, and with no brasses in sight, there was no polishing to do. Standard issue webbing in the UK was called 39 pattern, whereas our new webbing was 44 pattern, both figures indicating the year of first issue. We were given jungle green trousers and jackets – no shorts for where we were headed – and a strange new water bottle with aluminium mug attached. We appeared to have been well kitted out for overseas.

Next we underwent a very thorough medical examination by doctors of the Royal Army Medical Corps, so that our records could show we were complete in all respects on leaving for foreign parts. Various inoculations of all the latest scientific discoveries were pumped into our upper arms, and then it was the turn of the dentists to investigate the insides of our mouths. We had sight tests to determine that we would be able to see the enemy we were going to kill.

Boredom then set in for many, but I was put onto the most coveted fatigue duty in the whole of Woolwich Barracks, in the kitchen of the Officers' Mess, where life was made more pleasurable by close contact with the girls of the Women's Royal Army Corps who worked as mess waiters. The lads who were put on barrack square sweeping in pouring rain would have given their eye teeth for the opportunity. Another benefit was that the kitchen was just about the warmest place in Woolwich – and that included the town.

Came the big day; our day of departure. Our draft was off, headed now for the largely unknown. We knew that the Chinese forces had made a mockery of General MacArthur and his 'home by Christmas' boast, and the war was continuing, not necessarily to the advantage of the United Nations. Arriving at Waterloo Station, we first had to run the gauntlet of about a battalion of Royal Military Police, the Red Caps, and eventually board our troop train for Southampton, where our ocean greyhound awaited.

My last view of London was of the feverish activity preparing the Festival of Britain site along the South Bank of the Thames. By now the cynical old soldiers in our draft opined that, like most other places they had served in, Korea would not be worth the trip. After a couple of hours the train pulled alongside our transport to the Far East. HMT *Empire Fowey* looked huge – a white painted hull with broad Royal Navy blue stripe along the entire length, one buff funnel, and hopefully enough lifeboats to save us all if anything disastrous happened. Another battalion of Red Caps made sure no man made a sudden dive into the murky water and struck out for the far shore to avoid going to wherever he was being sent.

At the head of the gangway we were issued with a card that indicated in which part of the ship we would travel. It looked as though, as our Korea-bound draft would be the last to disembark, we had been placed just above the keel. We had been ordered to remove our boots and wear gym shoes for the voyage, apart from when on shore leave, as the owners of the vessel did not want their nice decks ruined by our hobnails. On the troop decks we found three-tier bunks that looked comfortable. There was quite a scrap for the top bunks because, as the old sweats had reminded us, when we hit the Bay of Biscay, seasickness would strike and Newton's law would prevail. Bottom bunks could become quite messy at short notice, they said, or no notice at all if men were desperate. Surviving all that the ocean could throw up, if you'll pardon the pun, on the fourth day we slowed as Gibraltar hove to on the port side. This was not a scheduled stop; a sick man was put ashore. We steamed on through the Mediterranean for Port Said, Egypt, where I had intended to spend my overseas service, until my discussion with the fatherly Tiger Mitchell.

I noticed that civilians had boarded – families, I supposed, headed for all ports to Hong Kong. Other drafts of men, including a few gunners, were bound for Singapore and Hong Kong. But first we had our indoctrination to the fascinating Orient. Port Said, our first landfall, appeared over the bow on about our eighth day at sea. We could smell it from a mile out, as our pilot boarded to guide us into the Suez Canal. The old soldiers had exaggerated the distance you could detect it to 10 miles when you are downwind. We packed every square inch of ship's rail to get our first smell of a foreign port. Wearing UK battledress, as it was winter here as well, we docked alongside a large pontoon of sorts from where we would be allowed to step ashore. Welcome to the mysterious East. A sandy beach stretched away into the distance and there was a large statue of M. de Lesseps, the Frenchman who had developed the canal.

Ashore the locals would be stretching and scratching, and gearing up for another day of relieving another shipload of innocent Tommies of their hard-earned wealth. On the other side of the ship we were being attacked by an armada of rowing boats bearing native traders with their shoddy wares – known universally as bumboat men, we had been reliably informed by those who had been there before. Some fools were buying rubbish from them, such as photograph albums that fell apart as the covering cellophane was removed. To them, we were all 'Johnny'. It was, 'You buy this, Johnny,' or, 'You buy that, Johnny, for you, special price.'

As we landed, we were attacked in earnest by sellers of flyswats, which seemed essential in Egypt, postcards, clean and dirty, cigarette cases, Turkish (Egyptian) delight, and all the usual tourist tat. I made certain I kept my few pounds well buttoned up. After a couple of hours ashore I had 'done' Port Said and agreed with the old soldiers that this was one place that was definitely not worth the trip.

If a man tried to get a refund on some piece of junk he had bought, he would be met with a tirade of a rapidly spoken mix of English and Arabic, all of which no doubt meant 'Up yours, Johnny' and indicated he was onto a loser. I elbowed my way onto the ship's rail as we departed, where I noticed some of the bumboat men had thin lines attached; it looked as though they were in for some high-speed surfing while pleading to have the lines removed. When this was refused there followed a blast of Arabic, which was probably an invocation of the wrath of Allah upon us, our children and our children's children. I feel certain they were not wishing us a pleasant voyage through the canal.

Continuing south, bound for Port Suez and the Red Sea, it was not long before we came upon British Army camps on the left bank, on our starboard. Perhaps it was a weekend as there were plenty of squaddies jeering at us as we passed by, yelling the time-honoured 'Get your knees brown' that was expected of them. We replied in our own style, something along the lines of the comments made by the bumboat men.

By the next day our convoy had cleared the southern end of the canal. We were in the Red Sea, and it was becoming decidedly warm. In fact, it very quickly became extremely hot, and it was not long before any exposed skin took on a pale pinkish hue, and then turned bright red and uncomfortable. I think that was when the crew raised canvas awnings over the few parts of open deck that were available to troop deck personnel. I imagined the ship's doctor might already have exhausted his entire supply of soothing cream to ease the burning for those who had overindulged in the tropical sun.

Aden was our next port of call, where the old soldiers reckoned it had not rained since 1936. We would have to avoid camel droppings once we were ashore and we would be well advised not to stare at the women, unless we might enjoy having our ribcages ventilated by the curved knives that the tribal men from the north carried tucked into their waistbands. We entered the harbour, which is, in fact, in a crater left by a gigantic volcanic eruption eons previously. As we slowly edged against two large floating buoys to which our bow and stern were secured we could see ships of many nationalities anchored out in the bay. Later we were ferried ashore in water-taxi type boats that were covered against the heat of the day. We were landed at a wharf where under a large archway were carved the names of British and Indian regiments that had served there in the past.

Once ashore, I could easily believe that Aden had not seen rain since 1936. It was hot. We probably felt the intense heat more as we had come from the chill of a northern European winter. Along with two mates I went, managing to dodge the droppings of the camels that pulled large water barrels to supply homes (probably most of them) that were not on a mains supply. We had a look at the shops along the main street called The Crescent, where I discovered that this was not the 'proper' Aden. This was just Steamer Point, and the real Aden town was some distance away. Walking with care past the tribal men and their knives, it was not long before we decided to head back to the shelter of our ship, which by now had become red hot. There was no air conditioning in troopships in those days and I knew that sleeping down below would be very uncomfortable. If someone had told me they had seen eggs frying on the pavements, I would probably have believed them. Sailing on the tide, we headed out into the Arabian Sea for Colombo, Ceylon.

Once ashore in Colombo, we were pounced on by the locals, who wanted us to buy all sorts of local produce – coconuts, pineapples, boxes of cigars called Burma Cheroots, carved wooden elephants in all sizes, and large tins of Lipton's tea that would have been appreciated if we'd sent them home as tea was still rationed. There were some decent buildings in the city, but the side streets did not look very inviting. Dodging touts who wanted to take us on a tour of their city and relieve us of a few rupees (we had changed our money into before going ashore), we decided to find somewhere to eat that looked reasonable. Many of the restaurants did not look too clean, so we decided on a Chinese establishment called The Nanking. Not being familiar with the pedigree of the pig that had gone into the sweet and sour pork, what part of the crustaceans the prawn balls had been extracted from, or what chops had been cooked in the chop suey, we stuck to good solid British fare and ordered fish and chips. We hoped that the waiters would not realize we were on our way to kill some of their fellow countrymen.

Back out on the streets we were immediately accosted by the touts again and we caught up with some lads who had bought elephants – the carved souvenirs, not the live animals. They told me the seller had said they were genuine ebony and the tusks were ivory. They looked to me as though they had been carved from ordinary soft wood, blackened with shoe polish, and, while the tusks had probably come from some long deceased animal, I thought it was more likely to have been cow than elephant. Other lads had started to smoke the Burma Cheroots, having no thought for what long-term damage they might be doing to their respiratory systems.

When we had seen enough we headed back to the ship, but not before one persistent local, on hearing that we would send postcards home from the post office, insisted on taking us there for a small fee. We could see the building about 50 yards ahead, but he suggested a few rupees for his service anyway. I suggested a fat lip, which sent him on his way. Back on board, we were off again, this time for Singapore, the crossroads of Asia.

Casually watching the flying fish and dolphins one day, I realized the ship was slowing, and then it stopped. A small boat nearby had run out of food or water, probably both, so supplies were delivered to them before we went on our way again. I looked forward to Singapore with relish to see if it lived up to my expectations, as related by Tiger back at Lincoln. But it was not to be. There would be no shore leave due to someone on the ship having contracted smallpox from places unknown, and as a consequence we were placed into quarantine by the health authorities on arrival in port. I guessed the culprit must have been one of the civilian crew, as all troops would have been vaccinated before leaving home. The only people allowed to leave the ship were troops and families to be stationed there, who would have been immediately quarantined on disembarkation. All I could hope for now was that there would be nothing to stop us going ashore in Hong Kong, another four or five days ahead. So, it was back to watching the dolphins, although they were not so prolific now as we were leaving the tropics astern.

As home service battledress was worn in Hong Kong during the cooler months we had to dig it out from the bottom of our kitbags and then try to find the shortest queue to grab an iron to press it to an acceptable standard. Before we entered harbour I was astonished at the number of small fishing boats and larger junks with the traditional slatted brown sails that we had to pass through. Our pilot expertly guided us into a wharf on what we had been told was the Kowloon side of the harbour. We were being allowed seven hours' shore leave, and we intended to make the most of it.

From the time we stepped ashore it was easy to see why Tiger had enthused over Hong Kong. On leaving the ship we took a short walk along Canton Road and then a right turning, which led us to the Star ferry, where hundreds of commuters were heading to be transported to a hard day's work at the office. We joined the ferry, sitting on the upper deck in first class for a very small charge, and passed by and through an amazing selection of ships and boats. Ships anchored in the bay were discharging cargoes from around the globe alongside several warships from various friendly navies, including two aircraft carriers – one American, the other French – and as oriental an assortment of junks and other boats of all sizes that could be seen nowhere else in the world.

Leaving the ferry on the Hong Kong side, with the aid of small maps we had been handed we headed first for the Cheerio Club for service personnel, where several who had left the ship ahead of us were already tasting steaks that looked about the size of two weeks' meat ration for a family of four back home. We stopped for a cold drink and then headed towards the China Fleet Club, a popular watering hole for the Royal Navy. As we felt we might not be welcome among the sailor boys, we moved on to the Soldiers and Sailors Home Club, more commonly referred to as the 'S&S'. As it was about midday, we decided to stop for a meal. I had never seen a menu with such a selection; it must have kept the chefs very busy in the kitchen. Managing to find a table, I ordered the first prawn curry of my life. There would be many more in the forthcoming years. The other lads reported that their meals were also excellent. We moved back towards the city centre, admiring the goods in the shops, dodging the shopkeepers who invited us in to inspect their wares, but buying nothing.

After a trip up to the Peak on the cable car and admiring the fabulous view across the harbour, we headed back to the Star ferry to see what Kowloon had to offer. We called briefly in at the YMCA, passed the huge Peninsula hotel without entering, as we did not wish to disturb the officers who would by then be taking their afternoon tea, and turned left into Nathan Road, which was another shopping paradise: luxury goods … jewellery … watches … cameras – they had it all. And to think that it was only five years since the Japanese occupiers had been sent packing. It was noticeable that most shops selling high value goods had a Sikh watchman with a shotgun seated at the entrance, daring would-be robbers to take him on. I assumed that the shotguns were loaded.

Passing along without entering the premises of the 'twenty-four-hour tailors', we turned right until we reached Chatham Road, where stood the Kowloon NAAFI, which was busy with service personnel and families. We met up with some of the lads off the ship, exchanging stories of our experiences ashore. We all agreed that Hong Kong would be a fine place in which to serve. Had I done the wrong thing by volunteering for Korea? Could a posting to Hong Kong have come up if I had waited a little longer? But it was my urgent need to get out of that damn control room at Lincoln that had forced my hand. I had to be content with Korea.

While we had enjoyed our shore leave a small party of officers had boarded our ship to provide us with updates on the war, and to interview us with a view to what lay ahead. In lectures they informed us that the entry of China into the war had driven the UN forces back from far into North Korea all the way beyond Seoul, where they had been halted. It seemed that China had found it difficult to maintain such a long supply line that was heavily dependent on mules and human effort. Their own troops and conscripted civilian labour was their main means of supply, whereas the Americans had a vastly superior logistics chain that was transporting vast quantities of men and material across the Pacific.

We were informed that the Canadian government had sent an infantry battalion that had joined with the original 27 Brigade, which also included 3 Royal Australian Regiment, and had been renamed as 27 Commonwealth Brigade. Christmas had come and gone, and in Washington and in General MacArthur's HQ in Tokyo, humble pie had been sliced generously but eaten without relish as the unbelievable had happened. The Americans, who had never lost a war, had been savagely mauled by a ragged peasant Asian army, styled the People's Volunteer Army. And now both sides faced each other, well back into South Korea.

Confident that the Yanks would still sort out the mess, some lads thought it likely we would only be needed for peacekeeping duty by the time we arrived at Pusan in another four days or so, without another shot being fired. Final training sessions for the infantry lads were rushed through. We lined up for final pay parade, where some of our hard-earned was spent on flat tins of fifty Players or Gold Flake at two shillings and threepence.

Noting that our route lay through the Formosa Strait, where the coast of China could plainly be seen on the port side, in case they tried to sink us,

I wondered if the Royal Navy had shadowed us from Hong Kong. It was decidedly cooler now, cold, in fact, and we had left the dolphins behind in their warmer waters. Our draft was called to a room in a part of the ship we had not previously been permitted to enter. An officer seated at a desk called us forward one at a time. He interviewed us and filled us in on the unit we would join in Korea. When it was my turn he told me that, whereas many of the lads would be leaving the ship in Pusan, I was in a group who had a different draft number stencilled on our kitbags. We would be continuing on to Kure, Japan. I had noticed the two different draft numbers when we left Woolwich, but had thought nothing of it.

We steamed on for whatever fate lay ahead for us. Perhaps I would get to stay in Japan. And pigs might fly.

Chapter Three

Arrival at My War

It was very cold as we turned into Pusan harbour, where many ships from different nations lay at anchor waiting to discharge war materials. We lined the ship's rail, straining our ears for any warlike sounds, although we were aware that battles were being fought at least 150 miles to the north. As we edged into the dock, a large US Navy hospital ship, USS *Haven*, was alongside the berth to which we were guided by the pilot, and a continuous stream of ambulances was bringing stretcher cases to be taken on board. What we saw was a timely reminder that the war was very much still in progress.

We were propelled into a wharf by a tug. On the quayside were Korean men in western clothing and ladies dressed in native attire carrying flowers. A few American Army and Navy personnel were leaning against warehouses; their jaws chewing rhythmically as they watched this latest bunch of Limeys arriving. The first man to leg it down the gangway was a senior officer, presumably the officer i/c troops, who was immediately mobbed by the ladies with their bouquets for having safely brought another shipload of top-quality cannon fodder all the way from Old England. The stream of ambulances continued to discharge their human cargoes, for transport to hospitals in Japan, we guessed.

There was a Korean Navy band playing on the dock, but we wondered where the one we had seen on the newsreels was, the one we thought played all troopships in at Pusan. Then, from the other end of the dock, led by the biggest drum major you would ever set eyes upon, there it was: the 56th US Army Band in all its glory. As they marched along towards us we could hear them playing *If I Knew You Were Coming I'd Have Baked a Cake*, a song that was very popular at home. I wondered if chapped lips might be a problem in the very cold air. But they played right through their repertoire, including another popular piece, the arrangement of *St Louis Blues March*, which later featured in the film *The Glen Miller Story*. They were great. What a way to be greeted to a war. Only the Americans could do it that way.

We said our goodbyes to those who were leaving the ship, wondering if we would ever see them again. I had already been told there were two reasons why the Korea/Japan draft was now off to Japan. Firstly, we were BCRs (battle casualty replacements). Secondly, some of us, yours truly included, had not reached our nineteenth birthday. It appeared that a group of mothers had petitioned Parliament to stop 'little Johnny' from going to war at eighteen. It had been decided by the politicians that to be killed in action at eighteen years and 364 days was not on, but one day older was no problem.

Later in the day we cast off the mooring ropes and headed for the Japanese coast through the picturesque Inland Sea to arrive the following day at Kure. We had been informed that Kure had been the operational base for the British Commonwealth Occupation Force (BCOF) after the end of the Second World War, with troops from Britain, Australia, New Zealand and India. By 1949, only 34 Australian Infantry Brigade remained, and by 1950, just a single infantry battalion. Now that the final infantry battalion had joined the Commonwealth Brigade in Korea there were only a few base units remaining. The British Military Hospital was also in Kure.

We were trucked out of town to Japan Reinforcement Holding Unit (JRHU), a camp that was good by British standards and had obviously formerly been used by the Australians. We changed our money, such as we had remaining, into British Armed Forces currency, Baffs, for short. When we bought anything from the canteen, operated by the Australian Army Canteen Service (AACS) – like the NAAFI, but better – we received Australian coins in change. Hoping to get out and into town as soon as possible to see something of this fascinating country, our draft members were sadly disillusioned. As BCRs we were confined to camp at short notice, or no notice at all. This was dependent upon casualty rates, which had been quite high in January while we had been at sea. As I had only a short time to pass before I would be nineteen, I was not in JRHU very long, but it still came as a surprise when I was called forward to pack up, head for the docks and get myself into action.

Taken back to the docks by drivers of the Royal New Zealand Army Service Corps (RNZASC), I looked for a troopship. There were none to be seen. The only ship I could see was some sort of tramp steamer with a tall black funnel called the *Po Yang*, registered in Hong Kong. And that was my transport to Pusan. It was a good thing Pusan was not much more that one day away, as the accommodation was basic, to say the least. As we arrived at Pusan, there was the US Army band again, playing us in. Ordered to disembark, we formed up in three ranks, were turned to the right and marched away smartly along the dock, much to the amusement of the watching Americans. Reaching the end of the wharf, our hobnailed boots crashed to a satisfactory parade ground style halt that caused a disturbance among the drivers of a line of US Army trucks who had been resting their eyelids. As they grabbed their sidearms, they realized it was just a bunch of Limeys showing off. They relaxed and asked, 'Are you guys for the war?' On receiving the affirmative from our officers, who had obviously made a mental note that they had not been saluted, we were told by the drivers, who were a cheerful bunch, 'OK guys, jump up,' and we were off to Pusan Station for our train to the north.

As we arrived it appeared that there was a serious riot in progress, with people milling around as though they had nowhere to go – which was exactly the situation. They had found space on the only transport available that would take them south to safety. I had seen the columns of refugees on the newsreels and had sympathy for their predicament, but where they would go now that there was nowhere further south to escape from the war I could not imagine. They were desperate people, living in desperate times.

As we had marched along the dock I noticed we had to pass under a large sign that told the arriving UN forces that through that gateway passed the best fighting men in the world – the United States Army. I wondered what would have happened if the United States Marines had been forced to pass under the sign. No doubt they would have ripped it down, set it on fire and erected their own sign reading something along the lines of: WHEN YOU ARE THE BEST IT IS HARD TO BE HUMBLE. *SEMPER FI*! (*Semper fidelis*, meaning 'always faithful', is the motto of the United States Marine Corps.)

As the smell of Pusan intensified with the rising sun, we boarded our train for the north. I had been informed that I was posted to the mortar battery. I knew that whatever the future held in store for me, it would be a whole lot better than that underground bunker at Lincoln. The train was in the charge of the US Army, with a crew on board under the command of a large NCO, who I guessed was a master sergeant, recognizable by the stripes over much of his sleeves. His opening words indicated that if we did not clear the centre aisle – inviting to us to 'get the lead out' and 'shake ass' – we could become another bunch of casualties to be shipped across to military hospitals in Japan. I climbed onto one of the two-tiered rough timber bunks that had obviously been used to carry south all those stretchers we had seen being loaded onto USS *Haven*. Wounded to the south, replacements to the north; that was the system. Struggling onto a lower bunk, dragging my belongings with me, at least I had a grubby window to see out of.

As I lay there wondering what to do next, our American master sergeant requested attention. In a strong southern monotone drawl he opened with, 'When we start moving, you are to lie on your bunks at all times, except when it is chow time or you need the latrine.' He continued, 'If we are attacked by guerrillas, get your asses off the train and lie down at the trackside.' I had not considered guerrillas, or having to leap from a speeding train. Of course, at that stage I had thought that the train would be capable of achieving rather more than the 6 miles an hour we were just about managing on the downhill stretches, with a following wind.

After a couple of hours the train crew moved down the centre aisle tossing three small olive green cans on each bunk – one hot, two cold. It was chow time so we were allowed to sit on the lower bunks with our feet on the floor. I picked up my hot can and read in black stencilled letters 'Ham & Lima Beans'. One of the cold cans was marked 'Apricots, halved', and the other was a composite pack. Opening the latter one first I was surprised to find twenty cigarettes, salt crackers, sweet crackers, a jelly disc, a chocolate disc, powdered milk, coffee and sugar, plus the *pièce de résistance*, a small roll of toilet paper. There was no end to Uncle Sam's ingenuity. Small folding can openers had also been provided, which we were advised to attach to our dog tag cords so as not to lose them.

Attacking my ham and lima beans with a plastic spoon, I discovered it was a pink mess with bits of green stuff embedded in it. I guessed that the pink bits had originally come from some part of a pig, and the green lumps were not unlike shelled broad beans. After eating this rather bland meal, I asked one of the lads what he thought of the ham and lima beans, to which he replied, 'What's a lima bean?' I told him they were the green bits he had just eaten. He said he had had no green bits in his can, and thought he had eaten hamburgers in gravy. It dawned on me that the idea was to swap around until we found a meal to our liking. There were many options, including chicken stew, ground meat patties in onion gravy, spaghetti and meatballs, frankfurters and beans, and so on. During our slow journey to the north we had two more meals of that variety thrown at us; we were told they were US Army combat rations, or C rations, called C6s and C7s.

At each stop – and there were many – we would be besieged by ragged urchins holding up string bags of apples for sale. But before any transactions could be completed our friendly master sergeant roared into action, telling us not to eat the fruit as hygiene standards were not up to much in the places where the apples had been packed. In the good old US of A people had become accustomed to deep-frozen, hermetically sealed just about everything. Such measures had not yet caught on in Britain, where fruit and vegetables were piled high on pavements outside greengrocers' shops, freely available to any passing dog, fish still came fresh from the sea, not from a freezer cabinet, and in butchers' shops, sausages hung in glorious coils above blood-encrusted chopping blocks – the hygiene factor being covered by the multi-corpsed flypapers hanging above. We threw our chocolate discs to the kids, then immediately regretted it, as the big kids beat up the little kids and grabbed their chocolate. It was a bloodbath. The first of many I would see.

Coffee was served at regular intervals. One of the lads, an Ulster Rifleman who was returning to his battalion after recovering in hospital in Japan from a wounding in a major battle in January, enquired if tea would be a problem. He was replied to in a very colourful version of the English language that indicated the American colonists had developed our language along very different lines since they had the audacity to tip our tea into Boston Harbor in 1773. We stuck with coffee.

Continuing our journey slowly but gradually, moving north, we eventually reached the railhead. Disembarking with two lads I had known from Rhyl, we said our goodbyes to the others and put ourselves and our kit on a truck bearing the red and blue square that denoted Royal Artillery. I was confused by the white '45' painted on the square, thinking I was on the wrong truck and heading for 45 Field Regiment. The driver put me at ease, telling me that the tac sign of the field regiment was 42, and that 45 was correct for 170 Mortar Battery. But anyway, I was still taken to 116 Battery of 45 Field, as B Troop 170, to which I had been posted, was temporarily attached to them. I was told that 116 Battery had been supporting 1 ROK Division, and they had been pleased with any artillery they could get, as they normally operated without any. So, I was a member of B Troop 170 Independent Mortar Battery, which was the troop designated to support the Royal Ulster Rifles.

On reaching a gun position 'somewhere on the western front', as the war correspondents put it, I dumped my kit on a piece of dry earth in a small tent and then headed to where a cook was heating water for a brew. He provided a meal of sorts – leftover stew with hardtack biscuits – but it made a change from C rations, and the mug of tea was very welcome. Tired from the journey, as there had been no rest since leaving JRHU, I tried to sleep, wearing everything I could pile on against the cold. It was not long before the Chinese welcomed me to the war with a few widely dispersed mortar rounds. I was very concerned at the explosions being so close at hand, but an old soldier with four months' combat experience under his belt told me, 'They are the safe ones, the ones you hear. It is those you don't hear that will kill you.' Sound advice, I thought.

Like my contemporaries, I had been brought up on a diet of cowboy films where the hero drops the baddy at 50 yards with a single bullet. I would find that war was not really the way Hollywood portrayed it. The first thing that surprised me was the sound of the 4.2-inch mortars being fired in retaliation to the enemy mortars. They do not go BANG!; the noise is more like tooooong … tooooong … tooooong, which is the only way I can describe it. I was woken while it was still dark and instructed to go to my stand-to position before first light. This would become my daily routine.

The Chinese usually attacked at night, I was told, but they could sometimes try something on as the sky lightened with the dawn. I could now see that B Troop was positioned in a narrow defile, with four large mortars pointed north. They were the first 4.2s I had seen, and their size surprised me. Mortars that I had seen in war films had been the small infantry variety, but these had barrels that were almost 6 feet long, and they were mounted on a mobile carriage for ease of movement in a hurry. Piles of brown boxes marked HE162 stood around for ready use, and loose bombs were piled by each mortar.

After receiving the order to 'stand down', everyone headed to the 'cookhouse' where the cook was making a brew and preparing breakfast. His domain was no more than a tarpaulin fixed across four stout, upright tree trunks, ready for a hasty move at any moment, whether to the north or to the south. After eating, I was shown from where to obtain hot water for a wash and shave. It seemed there was no pomp and ceremony, no morning roll call, as in barracks, all men being accounted for by their respective NCO. Mine was B Troop Signals NCO Bombardier Reader, who administered the Paludrine anti-malaria pill we had to wash down daily with our tea.

Next I was quizzed on the types of wireless equipment I had used. Reader was lost when I mentioned the large receiving unit at Lincoln, called an R208 set, I believe, but when I mentioned the 22 sets I had used at Rhyl, he knew what I was talking about. He showed me 19 sets, which were similar to the 22, only larger, saying they were for command post (CP) use, but in the hilltop observation posts (OPs) we would use American 31 sets, and when out 'swanning' with the infantry, the 88 set was usual. The 31 was carried man-packed on the back. The 88 was in two pieces, one being the transceiver, the other the battery pack, both carried on the belt. At least they would be lighter than the 22 sets I had dragged up and down the North Wales mountains. Then, as nobody was permitted the luxury of standing around with nothing to do, I was given the task of charging a large pile of flat batteries on a piece of equipment called a Chore Horse, which I was familiar with from Rhyl.

I had been informed that I would take my turn at OP duty with one other signaller, Dusty Miller. Although the wireless equipment was lighter than I had been used to, on OP duty I would also have to festoon my body with my personal weapon, a Sten with two spare magazines, binoculars, sometimes a field telephone, plus a water bottle at the belt. Then, with the OP officer, known as FOO (the forward observation officer), I would climb the nearest hill in the vicinity that provided the best view of Chinese-held real estate –

and Korea was wall-to-wall hills. So, I had arrived at my war, several miles south of Suwon, so the lads told me.

I heard that B Troop was soon to be reunited with 170 Battery, as our attachment to 116 Battery was coming to an end, and we could expect to start to move up to Suwon, and then to the Han River in our next move. There had been some intense fighting north of Suwon recently where there had been an enemy stronghold, and all available artillery was used in the action. Even the 40mm Bofors anti-aircraft guns of 11 (Sphinx) Battery were used, firing in a ground target role as extra-heavy machine guns. Soon we started our move up through Suwon to the south bank of the wide Han River, which flowed between Seoul and Yongdung-po.

How was it that 170 Battery had been selected to go to Korea, and to operate in an independent role for close infantry support? In August 1950, 49 Anti-Tank Regiment Royal Artillery, at Norton Barracks, Worcester, equipped with the splendid 17-pounder, was ordered to convert one battery to mortars. The designated battery would be posted to 29 Brigade. The battery chosen was 170, with two troops each of six guns. Short of personnel, the battery was brought up to strength by calling up men from the reserve, although none of the reservists allocated to 170 Battery had ever seen a 4.2-inch mortar. By the time the battery was ready to proceed overseas there were about 40 per cent reservists in total strength. National Servicemen were told they would only be taken to Korea if they volunteered.

In August 1950, 170 Independent Mortar Battery was formed, consisting of A and B troops. Training, and live firing was carried out at Sennybridge, South Wales. They were there for only two weeks. As the 4.2-inch mortar was still in the experimental stage in the Royal Artillery it was little enough time to prepare for war. From Sennybridge the battery moved back to Norton Barracks, where they were brought up to a war footing. It had been the intention to head for further infantry training at Stanford Training Ground, Norfolk, but the sailing date had been brought forward. After embarkation leave and other essentials, on 10 October goodbyes were said to Worcester. From there they departed by special train to Southampton, where they embarked the same day on HMT *Empire Halladale*. They sailed on the following day, together with 1st Battalion Royal Northumberland Fusiliers (1 RNF) and a Royal Army Ordnance Corps Field Park unit.

They enjoyed all the usual ports of call en route, possibly apart from Colombo, where instead of seeing the pleasures of strolling around among the coconut and pineapple sellers, or buying real ebony carved elephants, they had to endure a route march with the fusiliers because officers had suspected the men had become idle on-board ship, and they needed some exercise.

The lads told me they were pleased it was not a rifle regiment they were travelling with, as they would not have managed 140 paces to the minute in that sweltering heat.

They arrived at Pusan on 19 November 1950, disembarking the following morning. With the machine-gun platoon of Support Company of the Fusiliers, they marched to the rather grim looking train at Pusan Station that would take them north. At that time General MacArthur's Eighth United States Army in Korea (EUSAK) had driven back the North Korean Army from whence they came, and the war seemed all but over. After a very slow journey the battery arrived at Kaesong, just on the southern side of the 38th parallel, where they awaited the arrival of the vehicles and guns that were in convoy on the appalling roads. A man I came to know well, Bombardier George Philipson, who had been responsible for maintaining all vehicles on the road, was immediately promoted to sergeant for getting everything to Kaesong in good order.

The first task given to 170 Battery was the protection of the main supply route (MSR) to the north. By now the two troops had been reformed into three, to operate more efficiently as detached troops with the three infantry battalions of 29 Brigade. It was hoped that a few days could be spent in preparing the battery for action, but on the morning of 28 November, a warning order was received informing the battery commander (BC), Major T.V. Fisher-Hoch, that he was to proceed north, the advance party leaving on the morning of the 29th. The main party started out north on the 30th, and within thirty minutes they had crossed the 38th parallel for the first time. It would not be the last, although nobody expected to see it again so quickly.

The destination for 29 Brigade was Anju, about 50 miles north of Pyongyang. During the move north the men would experience their first taste of a Korean winter, with nobody believing it could get any colder. They were in for a shock. It could. And it did. The battery passed through Pyongyang shortly after first light on 1 December, but about 20 miles north of the city they were met with the astounding news that hordes of Chinese troops were heading south, and that the battery had probably already been bypassed on their flanks. Within ten days of arrival in Korea, it looked as though 29 Brigade was due for its first battle.

Defensive positions on either side of the MSR were manned, but there had been no sight of the reported Chinese hordes. When the first Chinese troops had been taken prisoner, General MacArthur was informed they were believed to be volunteers in North Korean units, but General MacArthur was in for a surprise. On the following day orders were received to start moving back to the south to a harbour area on the north-east outskirts of Pyongyang.

In the late afternoon the battery joined the entire Eighth Army on the first lap of a sensational withdrawal that would not halt until they consolidated in positions far to the south.

Travel on the almost non-existent roads, which were jam-packed with civilian refugees who were also fleeing from the Chinese advance, was very unpleasant. No doubt the people had seen the possibility of an escape from communism, and an opportunity to start a new life in the south, which many did manage, but not before suffering the most appalling hardships along the way. Traffic jams were continuous, with all vehicles heading in one direction, to the south, as fast as possible. After dark the battery took up a position in a frozen paddy field for the night, but moving yet again to another temporary position before settling in. At last light A and C troops moved to a position on an island in the Taedong River, north-east of Pyongyang, where they were to cover the withdrawal from the city as 29 Brigade formed a bridgehead. B Troop was placed under command of the Royal Ulster Rifles in a forward position.

Friendly forces poured past their position all day, all speaking of 'Chinese hordes just up the road', causing one wag to enquire, 'How many hordes to a platoon?' Still no Chinese were seen. It was hoped that all UN forces would be across the river bridge by first light on 5 December, and 29 Brigade started to withdraw at 0500 hrs. The last unit across was 170 Battery, and the bridge was blown after the last vehicle had crossed. Vehicles were required to tow two broken-down vehicles, casualties not of the Chinese who had not been seen, but of the totally unsatisfactory roads. The battery limped into Sinmak during the ensuing twenty-four hours, and there was still no sign of any Chinese. During the retreat from Pyongyang, everything that could not be moved rapidly to the south was destroyed by demolition or fire, mostly by US Army Engineers. The 170 Battery's own surplus baggage dump, established at Pyongyang a few days earlier, narrowly escaped the fire.

After two freezing days of comparative quiet at Sinmak, on 9 December the battery moved south again, with B and C troops joining their respective battalions. A Troop occupied a position near 29 Brigade HQ, where the battery commander established a command post. On that day C Troop fired the first British 4.2-inch mortar rounds of the Korean War. On 11 December the battery was again ordered to continue its progress to the south, crossing the 38th parallel again after eleven days in North Korea, and still there had been no direct sighting of the enemy. Another move on 13 December would be the last move for three weeks. The battery arrived in an assembly area about 5 miles north-west of Seoul, along the road from Kaesong, where they established themselves in and around a former rubber shoe factory. This was to be the battery's home until New Year's Day 1951, although experience in Korea to date indicated a long sojourn in one locality was very unlikely.

However, the withdrawal had at last come to a halt temporarily, and it was something of a relief for all to stop withdrawing before a still unseen enemy. By now the weather was bitterly cold. All trees were felled for firewood, US Army sleeping bags had been issued and as much US Army winter clothing that could be acquired by the battery quartermaster, BQMS Foreman, by fair means or foul, was piled onto cold bodies. It now seemed as though the battery would be able to spend Christmas in the comparatively comfortable location, although there were rumours in the air that the Chinese might commence a major attack on Christmas Day. In consequence it was decided by most 29 Brigade units that celebrations for the festive season would take place on Christmas Eve. So, thanks to the magnificent efforts of the BQMS and his cooks, a fine dinner of roast turkey, roast pork, stuffing, Christmas pudding and mince pies was enjoyed, and one bottle of frozen beer per man was issued. As a move did not materialize, the officers of the battery had their festive feast on the correct day.

During this 'peaceful' period many reconnoitres were carried out for the possible defence of the already devastated city of Seoul, and a great deal of training was put into effect, including firing the mortars, although some movements of the human body were difficult due to the weight and bulkiness of all the winter clothing. The sickness rate was growing alarmingly, causing a drop in battery strength, although only one case of frostbite was recorded – a sergeant who was returned home. Snow-proofed bivouacs were erected in an attempt to keep out the biting wind that blew straight down the Korean peninsula from Siberia, and fortunately straw was in plentiful supply, pulled from the thatched roofs of ruined village houses, but the problem of keeping warm was becoming a major complication.

At 0500 hrs on New Year's Day, just five hours into 1951, orders were received to standby to counter-attack on 1 ROK front, where the enemy had broken through. All three mortar troops had now been embedded with their respective infantry battalions: A Troop with 1 RNF, B Troop with 1 RUR and C Troop with the 1st Gloucestershire Regiment (1 Glos). The 29 Brigade was ordered to occupy a defensive position on high ground about 15 miles north-west of Seoul. Its task was to fight a delaying action while the bulk of 8th Army withdrew south across the Han River. As far as was known, there were now no other friendly formations to their front. It looked as though 29 Brigade was going to start the New Year with a battle.

The positions occupied by infantry and mortars were on high ground reached from two parallel valleys. About 8 miles of very narrow track had to be traversed from the main supply route, and it was advisable to take only minimum transport forward, a lesson that was to be learned slowly, and often painfully. The left-hand valley led to the Ulster position, and B Troop went into action in the battalion's forward positions. A Troop and 1 RNF's companies were on the right, and 1 Glos with C Troop in reserve in the valley leading to 1 RNF. The battery command post was deployed in 1 Glos area, from where it could cover 1 RNF's front. The battery commander set up a tactical headquarters (Tac HQ) at 29 Brigade HQ, a system that provided good liaison with 45 Field Regiment and the rapid transfer of information from forward observation officers on the battery wireless net to Brigade. In that way they upheld the Gunners' reputation of always being 'first with the news'. That would probably explain why only the cream of my intake had been selected for training as regimental signallers by the personnel selection officer at Oswestry. (I exaggerate, of course.)

The following day, 2 January, was spent in preparing defensive positions, and in registering likely targets, although no enemy had been seen. At 0500 hrs on 3 January, enemy activity had been reported on the Ulsters' front, and the fusiliers came under attack at 0630 hrs. It was seen by then that there was considerable enemy movement on 1 RNF's front, but immediate confusion was caused by the suspicion that the 'enemy troops' were actually South Korean soldiers. This was disproved very quickly, however. A Troop engaged their first target at 0715 hrs when the Troop FOO saw armed men moving in front of his position. His observation post party with 1 RNF came under continuous mortar fire between 0730 hrs and 0830 hrs. There appeared to be only one enemy mortar firing. It was engaged by A Troop. This mortar continued to harass during the morning, but it was eventually silenced by a bombardment from A Troop. By 1000 hrs, enemy movement was visible all over 1 RNF's front. The Chinese had penetrated between the infantry company locations and had attacked 1 RNF Support Company, who were bivouacked in and around a damaged school building. By this time, A and C troops' mortars were firing continuously in support of 1 RNF. So far the Gloucesters had not been committed. Targets fired on included many men in the open, as well as in two villages the enemy appeared to have occupied. For some time the battery OP was under direct enemy observation, all movement being answered by heavy machine-gun fire. Members of the OP party engaged rifle fire with a group of enemy dug into a deep ravine. The OP was engaged for a long time by a single mortar in an attempt to pinpoint them. Eventually the enemy soldiers crawled out of the ravine to obtain better cover for themselves. When they subsequently broke and ran they presented an ideal target for the mortars of A and C troops.

At 1230 hrs, the battery commander ordered the battery to redeploy in order to simplify movement in case of having to withdraw while continuing to give support to the infantry. C Troop was then withdrawn to a position about a mile down the valley towards the main supply route and the right section of A Troop moved to a position nearer the main dirt track to enable the troop to withdraw more easily when 1 RNF returned. At that time only two mortars remained in action, firing for about thirty minutes. As enemy infantry were massing to the front, the order was passed to the guns: 'Gunfire until ordered to stop' – a very unorthodox command. They were eventually ordered to stop. C Troop then occupied a position from where they could cover the withdrawal down the valley, although they were not called on to fire as the enemy chose not to follow them, possibly suspecting entrapment. A Troop continued to fire until 1800 hrs, most targets being on the reverse slope, and flanking infantry reported that the shooting was very successful. At 1750 hrs, Y Company of the Fusiliers had started to withdraw, and at 1800 hrs, A Troop was evacuated. All personal kit and some wireless batteries had to be left behind as the OP party had to escape on foot. A Troop withdrew at the same time, but C Troop had to remain in action under command of 1 Glos until 2200 hrs. They then followed the battery CP personnel and A Troop to a harbour area near Suwon, about 30 or so miles south of Seoul. In the eleven hours of shooting, all targets had been observed by the A Troop commander and his signaller. Both were Mentioned in Despatches for their conduct in this action. B Troop had enjoyed a much quieter morning, but they were destined for a very hectic night.

The infantry and A and B troops had been forced to withdraw, but returned to the positions later when their abandoned wireless equipment was found intact. During the remaining daylight hours there was little activity on B Troop's front, although the enemy were seen close at hand in a neighbouring ravine. At 2140 hrs, B Troop left its position under withdrawal orders from 1 RUR, but shortly afterwards the head of the troop column came under machine-gun fire, and the rear of the column was mortared. One vehicle, a gun tower, received a direct hit and ran off the track. It had to be abandoned. With the arrival of tanks of 8th Hussars and D Company 1 RUR, it was possible to restart the column, but not before an enemy patrol had infiltrated into B Troop position. The troop Signals NCO, Bombardier Reader, despatched one of the enemy patrol with his rifle. After a short move B Troop came under fire again, but the infantry deployed and the enemy appeared to withdraw. Thereafter the troop was able to withdraw in more or less good order, although one vehicle and trailer had to be abandoned. Two gunners went back to recover the vehicle. They managed to get it to move, but had to abandon the attempt due to enemy pressure close at hand. The gunners joined a detachment of 1 RUR, who fought their way out on foot and in universal carriers, but only one of the gunners eventually returned. The other, believed dead, was later found to have been taken prisoner by the Chinese. B Troop Commander Captain John Lane had stayed behind with the commanding officer of 1 RUR, after sending his OP party to rejoin the troop when his jeep ran off the track. Although Captain Lane was seen at a later stage, he did not manage to escape. His remains would be recovered when the position was recaptured in March.

During 4 January the battery reorganized at Suwon. Losses had amounted to one officer, one Other Rank, two mortars, three 15 cwt gun towers, one ammunition trailer, and one jeep and another trailer, all suffered by B Troop. The troop was now in a sorry state and was taken over by a new troop commander, Captain Tony Fowle, posted in from 45 Field Regiment. Some of the abandoned equipment would be found in March, but only a few mortar parts and nothing of value. The performance of the battery evoked much praise, especially from the infantry, who appreciated the close support of this new experimental Royal Artillery weapon. The commanding officer of 1 RNF, Lieutenant Colonel Kingsley Foster, went out of his way to address A Troop to tell them how effective their fire had been. The 4.2-inch mortar had undoubtedly proved itself in action in the hills of Korea.

It was only twenty-four hours before the battery was on the move again, this time occupying a position near Pyongtaek, about 20 miles south of Suwon. As 1 RUR had now been placed in reserve, to recuperate and rebuild the battalion, the embedded B Troop was positioned to the rear of the battery. The following week is acknowledged as having received the worst weather of the campaign. All three troops and the CP were in very exposed positions in a paddy field when the temperature dropped to 50° below freezing. No bivouac could keep out the cold, and bedding became encrusted with ice. The extraordinary numbing effect, both mental and physical, had to be experienced to be believed. Fortunately the enemy did not take advantage of the arctic conditions. They must also have suffered, probably much worse.

On 13 January, A and C troops and the CP moved forward into the village of Pyongtaek, where billets had been found in ruined buildings and the opportunity to thaw out was welcomed enthusiastically. February began with another move in freezing weather, this time north to Suwon. The ten days spent in that position were devoted to training, including live firing and small arms practice. The next move was into a position previously occupied in January, but the stay would be even shorter this time. One hour after arrival, orders were received that 29 Brigade was to move west for a major advance up to the Han River. The destination for 170 Battery was Pabalmak, north of Kumyangjang-ni. Traffic congestion on the completely inadequate dirt road was so bad that they had to pull off and harbour for the night about 5 miles short of their destination. The recce parties for this move found themselves in the middle of a battle at one time, but managed to extract successfully. Next morning the battery went into action again together in the fusiliers' area. At 0500 hrs the next day, C Troop fired defensive (DF) tasks when an enemy patrol penetrated the area occupied by the Gloucesters.

The next battery move came on 13 February, when they moved 1,000 yards north-east to cover the right flank. The battery CP was established next to RHQ 45 Field Regiment, about 800 yards to the rear of the gun position. A set piece attack on Hill 327 by 1 Glos was planned at this time. Hill 327 was a hill on the right flank of 29 Brigade, dominating the road, 327 being the height in metres. It was thought that a considerable number of enemy were dug in, and a three-day softening up programme was carried out by artillery and air strikes before the attack on 16 February. So many shells and mortar bombs fell on Hill 327, removing so much soil and rock from the crest that it would have been more like Hill 325 by the time the attack went in. The 170 Battery expended about 2,000 rounds of HE (high explosive) in support of the attack. The FOO and his party advanced with the attacking infantry up the hill. All objectives were reached, with only one casualty, Major Fisher-Hoch, the BC, struck by a shell splinter. He did not submit to medical examination until after the battle, when it was discovered that he was more seriously wounded than had been realized, necessitating his removal to hospital in Japan. He would not return to the battery until April.

The advance to the Han River continued, the three mortar troops leapfrogging forward to provide continuous support to the infantry battalions. A Troop was placed under command of 1 RNF again, who were operating on the left flank of 29 Brigade. On 19 February, the battery occupied positions within range of the river. The 1 RUR, who had been brought forward from reserve, gradually cleared the enemy from the hills up to the river, the battery firing a large number of rounds in support, although opposition was slight. An unfortunate accident happened in the battery on 20 February, when a round fired by A Troop exploded in the air after travelling only a few yards, wounding ten men in C Troop who had been in action alongside. Seven were evacuated, the others receiving treatment on the position. All except two men returned to the battery at later stages.

When 29 Brigade relieved 1 ROK on 23 February, the battery returned once more to Suwon, occupying positions on the outskirts of the town. B Troop was detached on 27 February for temporary attachment to 45 Field Regiment, who had remained in the line in support of 1 ROK at Yongdung-po. From the river position B Troop engaged some interesting targets on the north bank of the Han, including a Chinese cookhouse queue, which must have caused many enemy soldiers to go hungry that day. B Troop remained with 45 Field until 29 Brigade left the Suwon area on 5 March, two weeks after I arrived at the battery, while B Troop was attached to 116 Battery. Or had I been posted to 116 Battery? It would be the first week of May before the situation would be clarified. The 1 ROK reported they were greatly appreciative of our support.

At this time A Troop had departed to join 1 RNF, who were carrying out a deception raid on the Kimpo peninsula. They remained there until 7 March, but the operation was uneventful, so only Battery Headquarters (BHQ) and C Troop remained at Suwon. B Troop joined the battery there, where excellent accommodation was found in a large deserted school building. Battery training continued in pleasant surroundings and reasonably good weather. There were still the occasional light snowstorms, but the weather was improving daily and men began to believe that the worst of the winter was over.

At this time I was not the only new arrival, as there was an interesting development in the battery's training and operation. A number of Korean porters were engaged soon after arriving at the ruined school near Ichon, north-east of Suwon, not, as some veterans believe, Inchon, which is on the west coast. It was uncertain how best to employ them at first, but it was soon discovered that they might be useful in action, in addition to their obvious and more mundane use as labourers in gun and camp site areas. Using the native wooden carriers, known to us by their shape as 'A-frames', thirty-five porters could transport a complete mortar troop with forty rounds of ammunition. In a country with such few and very poor roads, really just dirt tracks outside of the few larger towns, this was a distinct advantage. They were later usefully employed in action. This experiment naturally had its humorous side. The porters were formed into an unofficial 'D Troop' under command of a newly arrived gun position officer (GPO), Lieutenant 'Paddy' Breene, and having as unofficial troop sergeant major (TSM), the battery interpreter, known to all as Lawrence, who had been attached to the battery at Kaesong. Lawrence, who spoke several languages, proved himself an efficient TSM, doubtless modelling himself on Battery Sergeant Major (BSM) 'Dudley' Davenport. The number of porters increased to almost 100 in later months, many becoming quite attached to 170 Battery, some sporting various types of military headwear, often with a Royal Artillery cap badge or a red and blue diamond that indicated Royal Artillery, and some with our tac sign '45' on it. Lawrence even granted himself the title 'Interpreter RA'. I recall seeing him on numerous occasions sitting in the jeep with the battery commander on the latter's visits to B Troop, dressed very smartly, in the warmer weather in pressed jungle greens, and wearing a yellow cravat made from the material of a field dressing.

Orders to move north were received on 29 March, following our advance across the Han, passing through the devastated and virtually deserted city of Seoul just two days after the Chinese had withdrawn further north. The move required rather more effort than usual, as due to the poor state of the 'road' north of Uijongbu, no 4x2 vehicles could proceed beyond that point. Reorganization was necessary and implemented; all 4x2 vehicles were left behind at B Echelon or at BHQ, and the gun troops were equipped with all available 4x4 vehicles. The battery duly moved and eventually arrived after an exhausting journey along one-way roads at a concentration area about 15 miles north-east of Uijongbu, where B Echelon was left. The next day, A and B troops were once more placed under command of their respective infantry battalions, who were all now in the line, occupying forward positions in the battalion areas. C Troop remained with the command post that was established in 1 Glos area, this being the reserve battalion at that time.

It was not long before the porters were in action. On 1 April, B Troop was ordered to move one section and half of the CP personnel and equipment on foot with thirty-five porters. The distance we covered was about 6,000 yards over very difficult country, completely devoid of any useable tracks, and the move took about three hours. Fifty-five rounds of HE were carried for each mortar by a shuttle system for the porters. The 29 Brigade was now holding a very wide front along the Imjin River, and the main activity was patrolling across the river, which at that time was fordable in two places, to the right and to the left of the brigade positions. During these patrols very few enemy were in evidence, although for a while roughly the same time each evening a mule train would briefly appear in a gap between two small hills. They would have been moving much needed supplies to the Chinese forward positions. Much as the British are known as animal lovers, it was essential to delay any enemy build-up of ammunition, and the mule train did make a good target. We had no idea if any were hit, as the sightings of them were so brief.

When we occupied the river positions 1 RUR and B Troop were on the right flank with 1 RNF to our left, and a Philippine infantry battalion of US 3rd Infantry Division (3 Div) in the centre. The latter battalion was relieved on 4 April by 1 Glos and C Troop. It was not yet known that it would be in those positions that 170 Independent Mortar Battery would fight in a historic battle before the month was out.

Chapter Four

The Imjin River Battle – A Gunner's View

In April 1951, we were dug in on a line of hills along the Imjin River for better observation of the hills beyond the river, where intelligence had gleaned the information that we were faced by the 63rd Chinese Army consisting of the 187th, 188th and 189th divisions, about 28,000-strong. Masters at camouflage, they were known to be in the vicinity, although light spotter aircraft piloted by Royal Artillery officers could find no trace of them in daylight. They must have been laid up during the day, moving only at night. Later it was reckoned they had been in laying-up positions about 20 miles north of the river, and when they attacked had force-marched those 20 miles and continued to cross the Imjin without stopping to draw breath under cover of darkness. It was widely known that the Chinese planned a major spring offensive, intending to drive the United Nations forces back beyond Seoul now that winter's freeze was behind us.

In B Troop with 1 RUR we did not stay on the south bank for long, moving across the river to occupy Hill 195. Our early maps, printed during the years of Japanese occupation, had given varying heights for this hill, some with 194, others with 196, but later US Engineer maps showed it as Hill 195, so I will stick with that throughout. It was not long before 1 RUR were withdrawn to reserve. We remained with the replacement infantry, the Belgian Capital Battalion attached to 29 Brigade, who inherited the well wired-in position left by 1 RUR. The Ulsters, unlike the other two battalions in the brigade, who had laid only thin aprons of barbed wire, had made sure their stronger defences would slow any enemy advance.

On my first observation post duty with the Belgians things were comparatively quiet; there was just the occasional incoming shell or mortar round, to which we retaliated with a few rounds from our own mortars, but we all guessed by now that something big was in the offing. At first the Belgians seemed a mad lot, a bit gung-ho, but we quickly found them to be first-rate soldiers, although we could not always converse with them. Conversations became a bit of English, French and Flemish, although the Belgian officers spoke some English. As some of our officers had schoolboy French, we managed to get by.

When volunteers for Korea had been sought, 700 men were selected from among those who stepped forward. Only the best were picked, mainly from among those with Second World War service experience, including commandoes and parachutists. The battalion had arrived at Pusan on 31 January 1951. Whereas British infantry battalions had four rifle companies, the Belgians had only three, including one platoon recruited in Luxembourg. I have read somewhere that one of their officers was a former Belgian defence minister.

While we sat on our hill, with our OP situated between the forward platoons of A and C Companies, the US 3rd Infantry Division to our right made a strong advance into enemy territory towards Chorwon, which put something of a bulge in the front line. We were separated from 3 Div by the northerly sweep of the Imjin. Recent inhabitants in the vicinity had seen only limited activity in recent weeks, the Chinese having apparently withdrawn from contact. They would not remain out of contact for much longer.

On 15 April there was some limited activity. Our A Troop had moved forward to a night position, while in B Troop we stood to at 0500 hrs. We had been notified that a long-ranging patrol would be carried out across the Imjin, although it appeared likely that only A Troop, who had borrowed four universal carriers from the fusiliers, would be involved. The borrowed carriers would be used to carry the mortars and forty rounds of HE in each forward on 'Task Force Foster', named for the commanding officer of 1 RNF. Another universal carrier was used to transport our battery commander, Major Fisher-Hoch (who had returned from hospital in Japan) and his party.

Task Force Foster comprised one company from 1 RNF, a squadron of Centurion tanks of 8th Hussars, and A Troop. The river crossing was accomplished with only moderate success, as the carriers continually bogged down in the soft going, and great difficulty was experienced in finding dirt tracks that were suitable for the gun towers, which had been brought forward and loaded with ammunition for the mortars. There were no tracks wide enough for their considerable width as paddy fields dropped away on both sides. Only narrow tracks had existed for the villagers to move from one village to the next. Bullock carts were the only form of transport for them. A wide patrol action was carried out, the task force roving at will up to 12,000 yards north of the river. A Troop reported no enemy seen, although night patrols nearly always encountered some opposition. Only one suspected enemy location was engaged by A Troop mortars. Our BC in his carrier was accompanied by 29 Brigade Tac HQ.

In B Troop we left our permanent position at 0700 hrs with six vehicles, finding a difficult road, although it was fairly firm. Our guns were partially dug in and camouflaged. We were ordered to return to our normal location at 1430 hrs. No enemy had been seen close to the river, but the stage was set for the Chinese spring offensive. As our three troops were widely dispersed it would not be possible to fire battery targets with all three troops engaging the same target simultaneously. Each troop was in its battalion area, with separate day and night locations. Ammunition was dumped liberally on troop positions, with reserves loaded onto vehicles at our battery CP, ready to move at short notice.

Attempts had been made to tow mortars with universal (Bren gun) carriers, but with only limited success. They were liable to bog down easily, the tracks digging in on soft surfaces. On one river crossing our BC was carried on a Centurion tank, and a trial was made carrying a FOO, mortar, static base plate and forty rounds of HE. I did not hear of the success or otherwise of this trial, but no more similar exercises were carried out using tanks. Due to the considerable width of the tanks they were not a great success in country where no tracks wide enough had existed. When the Oxford carriers could be borrowed from 1 RUR, which was only rarely, they proved to be the ideal mortar tower, both by reason of their superior performance and their load-carrying capacity. One hundred rounds and a mortar detachment of four gunners could be carried in each. If only the battery had been equipped with Oxford carriers at Norton Barracks. But as the 4.2 was still in the experimental stage, nobody could foresee the problems that would be encountered in Korea without a crystal ball.

The battery organization for the impending battle, which we knew was imminent, was a little different than previously. The second-in-command, Captain Waterfield, known as the BK (battery captain) in Gunner language, had to go into hospital in Japan for a non-wound operation, so some reorganization was necessary. A Troop Commander, Captain Waters, deputized for the BK, and Lieutenant Powell took over command of A Troop, with Lieutenant Lakes as Gun Position Officer. As Captain Wisbey was the sole officer in C Troop, embedded with the Gloucesters, WO2 Askew took on the role of GPO. The BC had decided that each mortar should be commanded by a sergeant, so sergeants who had been operating in other capacities were set a new task. Sergeants Hawkes and Witty became the Number Ones in A Troop. In B Troop there were other signallers with whom I shared OP duty. Bombardier Reader was Signals NCO, and my fellow signallers were Gunners Lowry and Dusty Miller. TARAs (Technical Assistants, Royal Artillery) would also be sent out with OP parties. Our TARAs were Lance Bombardier Lambie and Gunner McAuliffe.

When the Belgians had relieved 1 RUR on Hill 195, the Ulsters had been moved back to a reserve position from where they were on call if required. They had still not fully recovered from the serious mauling they had suffered in the January battle at Chaegunghyon.

From our OP position on 21 April, away to our left rear I noticed some activity taking place. A party of Royal Engineers had arrived with assault boats, into which a small number of fusiliers climbed. They appeared to be on a recce to discover why a great deal of smoke could be seen a short distance from the north bank. As I watched I heard a series of 'pops' coming from a group of enemy soldiers who had suddenly appeared on a low ridge to the fusiliers' front. A brief fire fight ensued, both antagonists firing from available cover, giving the appearance of a battle in miniature from my vantage point, although this was not a Hollywood film; this was for real. The fusiliers must have called for support from their 3-inch mortars, as puffs of smoke appeared on the ridge from where the enemy were firing. The fusiliers then beat a hasty retreat for the assault boats under cover of the smoke. It looked as though the Chinese had been laid up on the ridge, possibly watching our movements, and they had started the fire by accident. Although in our secure OP on Hill 195, nobody could foretell what was about to happen. We knew that at least some enemy soldiers were much closer to the river than had been realized.

I think everyone in the battery hoped that after months on the move it could be too good to be true that we might remain in the new locations for the foreseeable future. Those who had arrived in 29 Brigade the previous November had seen enough of continual movement, having crossed the 38th parallel three times already. Having become a member of one of B Troop's OP parties, which were a bit thin on the ground, I hoped that fortnightly rotations could be more or less maintained. With our camouflaged OP on the crest of Hill 195, our mortars were settled on a flat sandy area to our right rear, adjacent to the north bank of the river. When we called down targets, they would fire directly over our heads. We hoped there would not be too many 'drop shorts'.

Occasionally we might receive a copy of *Gunner* magazine, the journal of the Royal Artillery, which must have been airmailed from home as they were usually quite up to date. I found an interesting article in the April 1951 issue, written by a US Army general. He complimented British artillery units that had provided his division with 'quality support'. Referring specifically to our OP parties, he called them 'those unsung heroes whose steadfastness is so vital to successful artillery support'. I had already felt that, separated from the body of the troop, I was somewhat neglected, so it was nice to read those words of praise from the American general. But, although sometimes feeling neglected, I certainly did not think of myself as an unsung hero, and I am certain my fellow signallers did not either. We all had different tasks to tackle, whatever we had been trained for.

It must be remembered that although 29 Brigade was as well provided for as equipment tables allowed for in 1951, given the usual shortages, and the all too often obsolete material that the brigade was fighting with, in reality the brigade was but a small cog in a very large fighting machine. The brigade had been placed under command of Major General Soule's 3rd United States Infantry Division, one of fourteen divisions, United States and Republic of Korea, stretched across the 150-mile breadth of the country. And 29 Brigade, small though it might have been, was responsible for holding an 8-mile segment of it, with just three battalions and supporting arms.

For us on our hilltop, it was Sunday, 22 April when early indications were apparent that we could expect an imminent attack. As I had only experienced war while we had been in an attacking, advancing mode since I joined the battery, I was about to receive my initiation into a major defensive, withdrawing action. Reports had filtered in from right across the Eighth Army front of increasing enemy movement, coupled with a considerable build-up of their increasing use of artillery, which had previously been sparse. The capture of a Chinese artillery officer and his survey party yielded intelligence that the enemy's much heralded spring offensive was about to be launched. The combined Chinese and North Korean armies intended to sweep the entire United Nations before them in a massive assault that would carry them victorious all the way south to Seoul and beyond, with the avowed intention of holding a grand parade to celebrate May Day on Tuesday, 1 May, nine days hence. If I had been aware of that in advance, I might have been much more concerned.

The positions held by the brigade were straddling the centuries-old traditional invasion route used by conquering armies from the north, and we were now told that trouble could be expected. The Gunner grapevine had imparted the information that 27 Brigade, about 25 miles away to our east, was already involved in a major battle for survival, but as I was not directly involved, in the cynical way of the soldier, I thought: rather them than me. Generally speaking, although officers would have much more information on the overall picture, like all soldiers in the lower orders, I was concerned only with what was happening to my immediate front. There used to be a saying that 'a good soldier never looks behind him'. At that time I was not concerned with what was happening to my sides either. Certainly, what was about to happen would come from my front initially, and then from both flanks, but I was too busy with my own task to be overly concerned at first.

I am aware that in today's military environment, with vastly improved communications by satellite, all men involved have a much larger picture of what is happening around them. Today, infantrymen and attached personnel in forward locations are likely to be wearing headphones and microphones that will enable them to be in communication with those who control their actions. In 1951, generally only those who needed such apparatus – in the main, officers, signallers and CP people – had the facility to remain in contact with their control base, whether to troop, battery, regiment, brigade or division. Being tuned in on the frequency allotted to B Troop, I could flick to the battalion net, and also to A and C troops, each having unique call signs.

In the OP, when I noticed a group of enemy I would bring them to the attention of the FOO, who would decide if their presence warranted expenditure of ammunition. If a decision was made that they should be eliminated before coming any closer, while watching their movement through binoculars he would request, say, a troop target, which would mean four mortar detachments preparing to fire. I would repeat all orders called out by the FOO, and report back to him when the guns were ready. The FOO would have worked out the grid reference of the target area, which he would either pass to me or send to the GPO personally. In the CP the duty TARA would be busy with necessary calculations, so that the guns were brought to bear on the target. One mortar would send a ranging shot, corrections would be made to the right, to the left, to drop or add distances in yards, until the rounds were landing on target. Then the troop would be ordered to fire one or more rounds depending on the size of the enemy group. If no further corrections were necessary, the FOO would tell me to send 'target neutralized'. The next response from the CP would be a request for 'target description', which I would request from the FOO, to account for the ammunition expenditure. The target description might be something along the lines of 'ten men in the open'. And that, as they say, was all there was to it. Sounds simple? It does when you read it, but when you are engaging visible targets at close range, to say nothing of incoming fire from the enemy who might have calculated where your position might be – all adding to the cacophony of sound – it certainly got the adrenalin gurgling through the tubes.

During any quiet period in this position, either Dusty or I would have to walk back around the hill, crossing the skyline and down for replacement batteries, a jerrican of water, C rations, solid fuel tablets ... just about anything. A jerrican of water bears heavily on the shoulder after the first couple of hundred yards on that steep hill climb, but without water, there would be no brew, and it certainly sorted out the men from the boys. The Korean porters thought nothing of carrying two full jerricans on an A-frame. They were the men, we were the boys. And if on reaching the OP I found the FOO had forgotten to tell me to bring another urgently needed item, such as a supply of Army Form Blank (toilet paper), I would say, 'Well blow me, what a blessed nuisance,' or something very similar, and I would head back across the skyline again, hoping that the Chinese had not zeroed in on me when I had made my previous trip, and waited for me to show myself again.

I had noticed on that quiet Sunday that the lads on the gun site had been put to task by the TSM to start tidying up the gun position; others were filling sand bags to dam up a small tributary to form a swimming hole for when the weather improved. From our exposed hilltop we had spotted small groups of enemy, about 600 yards distant, on whom we had fired a few rounds to send them to ground, but little else happened to disturb the peace. The Belgians had opened up on them with their medium machine guns (MMGs) each time the enemy were sighted. It appeared that the Chinese were becoming bolder. These sightings of the enemy increased during the afternoon, indicating the possibility of an imminent attack. A Troop, with the fusiliers to our left rear, was also calling down fire on enemy soldiers who were appearing in front of them across the river. Reports had started to come in of increasing enemy activity right across Eighth Army front, and it looked as though a large-scale attack was imminent. Dusty, who had arrived the previous November, had seen much combat, and he could teach me a thing or two.

Prior to this quiet Sunday, the FOO had told me to gather up my equipment to accompany him on a recce with an infantry patrol to the village of Oridong, about 2½ miles west of our OP, as reports had been received from air observation that the Chinese were occupying the village in large numbers. On arrival on a ridge from where we could scan the village with binoculars, however, no sign of any occupation was evident – just a few magpies and stray dogs. We had returned to Hill 195 hoping to continue our peaceful existence as spring gave way to summer. Sunnier days were approaching and we looked forward to using the swimming hole when it was finished.

In the dark, late on the 22nd, it was eerie listening to the bugles and whistles, used by the Chinese to direct troop movements, growing ever louder. On full stand-to since last light, we were about to start calling down the first mortar rounds in an action that would continue unabated for the next eighty hours. First, to protect our position, previously selected DF targets were fired on, starting at 2130 hrs at the first dim sight of enemy movement close in to our immediate front. We continued calling on our mortars without respite until 0500 hrs on the 23rd. In all, eight DFs were fired on during the long night. Meanwhile, back at the gun position, all spare bodies were placed in a defensive role with personal small arms, due to enemy infiltration close at

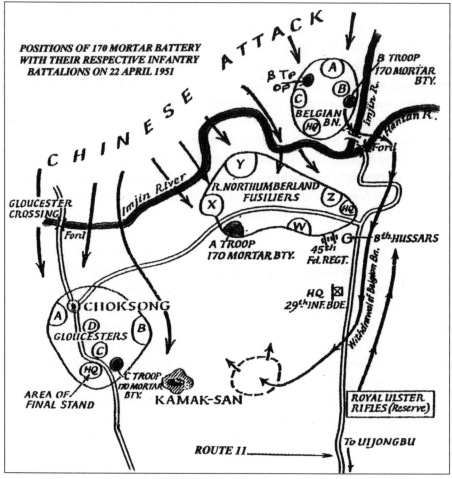

The Imjin River Battle 22–25 April 1951.

hand. The bugle calls were now coming from three sides, indicating that the Chinese were probably trying to isolate our hill, which was in a stand-alone position on the wrong side of the river at the confluence of the Imjin with its tributary, the Hantan.

The first indication of an attack came at 2215 hrs, concentrating on the fusiliers, with whom our A Troop was embedded, necessitating their mortars also to start firing DF tasks. At 0300 hrs on the 23rd, one platoon of X Company of 1 RNF was overrun, the remnants and A Troop having to withdraw under heavy small arms, machine gun and small bore mortar fire. The withdrawal was accomplished with only the loss of some kit and personal belongings before A Troop lost communication with the battery CP. Captain Waters was sent out at first light in an attempt to make contact with A Troop, in which he was successful, bringing the troop into action again at first light behind a battery of 45 Field's 25-pounders. In recent times, Bob Nicholls, a former paratrooper and K volunteer who had been a signaller in the OP, told me that he and his mate, Gunner McCaffery, killed two Chinese with their Stens before they were able to make an extraction with the fusiliers.

As I had a panoramic view all the way to the south-west right along the front line, beyond the hills held by the fusiliers, I could see that from distant gun flashes our C Troop with 1 Glos appeared to be under constant attack, although we were much too far away to appreciate how involved they were. At 2300 hrs I was sending target data back to the guns as fast as the FOO could identify the grid references, although due to the mass of enemy troops to our immediate front, grid references would not need great accuracy, provided the bombs were not landing within 100 yards of our OP.

Located between A and C Companies of the Belgians, our OP was shared with an FOO and his party from 45 Field. During the early hours of the 23rd, the FOO, Lieutenant Walsh, was struck in the face by a shell splinter. Although it was obvious he was in considerable pain and discomfort, and badly in need of medical attention, he continued to send target data to his 25-pounders until first light, when he finally succumbed to his injuries. It was several months later that I heard on the grapevine that his injury had been caused from one of his own shells, indicating how close in our targets had been. I also heard later that he had been decorated with the Military Cross for dedication to duty and leadership. Like me, he had been experiencing battle for the first time.

The 23rd dawned, St George's Day – normally a day of regimental celebration for the fusiliers, who had arranged for red roses (with which it was traditional to decorate headwear), real or artificial, to be flown in from Japan. But it now appeared that there would be no ceremony, no pinning on of red roses on that St George's Day. The fusiliers had found that the enemy in some strength were already across the river to their front. At the same time in B Troop it was all too visibly obvious that we were being attacked on three sides, and in danger of being surrounded.

By first light I could see that we were in a precarious position at the point where the Hantan merges with the larger Imjin, the latter forming our fourth side, the other three sides having been infiltrated by the enemy's advance troops. Things looked pretty grim. There was no time for breakfast. Dusty and I were told that we might have to extract on foot at any time. Also, there was no time for a brew, which was even worse. We continued to send target data to the guns virtually continuously. By then the Chinese were everywhere, tracers were flying, and bullets were cracking around us. By around 1000 hrs, some American 105s were also firing on targets to our front and, worryingly, by then also to our rear, where our escape route lay. And I had volunteered for this? If I had not been so busy I would probably have been asking myself how I had allowed Tiger Mitchell to talk me into being one of his 'fifty volunteers for Korea'. Of course, it was hardly his fault. I blamed General MacArthur and his 'home by Christmas' bragging. Which Christmas did he mean?

Early in the day, US Army helicopters had landed on the flat area to the rear of Hill 195 to evacuate wounded Belgians. By then the Belgians' vehicles started to leave by crossing at the juncture with the Hantan. Enemy troops were found to have infiltrated deep into 29 Brigade positions all along the line. The fusiliers' celebrations had been cancelled, and we and the Belgians would also have a rapid change of plan. That was to discontinue our OP operation and remove ourselves and our equipment from Hill 195 as rapidly as possible before we were overrun, but not before the mortars had vacated their location and exited across the river to go into action on our escape route, a dirt track known as Route 11.

It was evident to all that this major attack right across 29 Brigade front was the Chinese spring offensive that had been anticipated. Our three mortar troops were by then either firing or withdrawing by leapfrogging section by section continuously to the rear, although at the time in B Troop we could not move very far as we had the river to our backs and to the east. Our western side was already swarming with Chinese, who had already crossed the river to the fusiliers' front in considerable numbers. I believe a company of the Ulsters had been brought forward from reserve with orders to extract us and the Belgians, and make a safe passage across the river for us, only to find that the enemy had already crossed in some numbers, the lads taking many casualties in the process. But we saw no sign of them as we consolidated on the east side of the hill ready for a breakout, although we were well aware that a fierce fire fight to our left rear was under way.

During the morning, A Troop found they were engaging two, even three, targets at once – a GPO's nightmare not likely to be encountered at Sennybridge, where the firing had been on a much smaller scale and they had had no real enemy to kill as they practised before departing for Korea. Later, A Troop came under fire again from mortars and small arms. During a slight lull they were withdrawn another 1,000 yards south, again leapfrogging section by section in their effort to extract the fusiliers, the Belgians and us in B Troop, always having one section of mortars in action during the withdrawal.

Meanwhile, in B Troop we had discovered at first light that the two 'bridges' that had been our lifeline to safety back across the river, which 1 RUR had been sent forward to secure, were in enemy hands. With the Belgians we were cut off and exposed on three sides. As we attempted to withdraw we continued to send target data to our mortars, where at least one section was in action at all times. Many of the targets were by now so close they were under the minimum range of a mortar, but we were still visibly inflicting severe casualties on the enemy, who made little attempt to seek cover. This prompted the rumour I had heard from other units that they could have been drugged to the eyeballs on the marijuana that was grown in the villages to help the villagers forget about their poverty, for medicinal purposes, of course. The old men would sit smoking long bamboo pipes with a small brass cup. I brought two pipes home as souvenirs, only for wall decoration in my office, I assure you.

At 1000 hrs, our left section, two mortars, was turned around to engage enemy troops who were swarming over the high ground on the south bank above one of the captured bridges. We eventually cleared them by firing white phosphorous (WP) rounds to set the scrub alight. By 1400 hrs, a US Army Regimental Combat Team (RCT) of 3 Div that had been located on our right flank had been withdrawn, so now our position was completely surrounded, with large numbers of enemy actually infiltrating amongst us and the Belgians, making it difficult to distinguish friend from foe. Life had become awkward for us all.

Enemy medium machine guns, which sounded very similar to our Vickers, were making long sustained bursts, which were now falling about our ears. There were also the distinctive bursts from their sub-machine guns we knew as 'burp guns', from the sound made when the trigger was pressed. They were Russian-made, of Second World War vintage, and I understood fired a 9mm bullet similar to our Sten ammunition. There were, in addition, of course, single rifle shots cracking past our ears. Any infantryman will confirm that you only realize small arms fire is directed at you personally when you hear a sound like a whiplash crack as a bullet passes through the sound barrier close to your ear – just a sharp crack, like the snap of a whip. As we were hearing far too many whip cracks, Dusty and I tried to keep our heads as low as possible, which was not easy as we were now on the move in an attempt to consolidate. It was at that stage of the battle that B Troop had been ordered to abandon all equipment and attempt to walk out. Our troop commander was not at all happy about leaving mortars, vehicles and ammunition in Chinese hands for them to use against us. Captain Fowle notified the BC that, as the Belgians had decided to make a run for it, we would load as much of the ammunition as possible onto the troop vehicles and attempt to rush the nearest bridge, which had been found to be not completely demolished. An American tank then miraculously appeared from nowhere on the other side of the bridge, so Captain Fowle asked the senior NCO, the tank commander, to provide us with covering fire to enable our escape from Hill 195. But before that could be put into practice, I witnessed an action of another kind.

When the 45 Field FOO had been pulled out wounded, another officer had taken his place. He now called for a 'Plan George', which I knew was the code for an air strike. I was instructed to switch to brigade net, as 29 Brigade would authorize and control the forthcoming action. During the operation of an air strike all artillery fire plans had to be curtailed in the target area as no pilot has a desire to compete for airspace with shells and mortar bombs arcing through their trajectory. All that was required now was for one mortar to fire a WP round to mark with smoke the centre of most enemy activity, and then to cease fire.

The smoke round hit right on target. Then I heard in my headphones: 'Plan George effective imminent,' which meant aircraft were on the way. That was followed by 'aircraft inbound, figures two', which indicated aircraft were two minutes from target. The WP round had struck about halfway down the forward slope to our front. We waited for the action that was about to kill a large number of enemy soldiers. Within seconds three aircraft roared low over our hilltop position, dropping down into the valley and attracting small white puffs from enemy small arms in a vain attempt to shoot them down. After a practice run, the aircraft disappeared in a tight turn to our left. The next second they were back to deliver their message of death. The first aircraft roared overhead and jettisoned two silver cigar-shaped objects, which I knew were napalm canisters. As they impacted with the ground, nothing happened. The second pilot also released his canisters in close proximity to the first, and again nothing happened. No explosion; nothing. While we all considered that the igniters on the canisters of a jellied petrol compound might have been dud, the third aircraft hurtled low overhead, firing rockets into the centre of the area that had been splashed with napalm. Then the world exploded.

As the rockets struck the hillside where the napalm had been distributed, there was the most almighty 'whoosh' as they ignited the entire area in a single tremendous conflagration. I had seen napalm used from a distance, but never as close as this. In our position we briefly felt both the shockwave and the heat flash. When the thick black oily smoke had cleared a bit we saw that the entire slope to our immediate front was black and burning. The breeze wafted the smells of gasoline and death towards us. It did not do to dwell for too long on the fate of the enemy soldiers who had been annihilated in a split second, or who were dying a terrible death in front of us … not a pleasant thought, as I can still see it all clearly in my mind. But at the time it was a 'them or us' situation, and there were more of them, and plenty more where they came from. So we managed to raise a cheer for those pilots as one gave a wave in salute as they disappeared back to base. Today, the use of napalm, like land mines, is an emotive subject, but in April 1951 it was considered a legitimate weapon, provided it was directed at the enemy.

Following the air strike we fired a final 200 rounds into the valley in front to assist the Belgians in moving back from their positions, and to lessen the load with which we would attempt to extract from our hill and hope to rejoin our brigade further to the south. Moving out with one of the Belgian companies, we led the charge on the remaining, reasonably intact bridge, most of the troop vehicles reaching the east bank safely, in spite of small arms and small-bore mortars being directed at us from 200 yards. The Belgians hurled WP grenades into the dry scrub around the bridge in an effort to obscure our departure with smoke.

One of our trucks stalled on the bridge, and the American tank commander was asked to blow it up to prevent it falling into enemy hands. The resultant explosion so close at hand was quite spectacular, but unfortunately it had been the truck carrying my personal kit. That was goodbye to my camera, all my photographs, propaganda leaflets the Chinese had left lying around in the hope that we would surrender to them, a wad of North Korean currency 100 won notes I had found in an abandoned village, but which were worthless in the south, and most of my spare clothes. It had been a very busy day, during which B Troop had fired on a great many targets, the most remarkable being a solid mass of enemy that had congregated on open ground and who appeared to be listening to instructions or perhaps having a discussion with their company political commissar. The men made no attempt to move to avoid the devastating effect of our mortar bombs and 25-pounder shells falling among them, the fragmentation from which would have been considerable and must have wounded many.

Meanwhile, on 29 Brigade left flank, C Troop, with the Gloucesters, fired their mortars virtually continuously throughout the morning of the 23rd, having commenced their DF programme at 0500 hrs, reporting that all tasks had been completed and they were holding their position in spite of massed enemy attacks all around – very similar to our experience. Supplies of ammunition were being ferried to them unceasingly by the drivers of the Royal Army Service Corps (RASC) until they reported that the road to their rear, occupied by the enemy through infiltration, was now blocked as their only escape route. By 1000 hrs, our battery CP had moved south, close to 29 Brigade A Echelon, a better position to control our firing, although our three gun troops were too widely dispersed for the possibility of all mortars engaging a single target. The usual good wireless communications between troops were being maintained, in spite of all the difficulties each troop was experiencing.

In B Troop we continued firing on targets after first light on the 23rd as they presented themselves, and they were numerous and almost non-stop, barrel changes being made frequently as they became overheated, with the consequent loss of accuracy. There was little time for more than a perfunctory examination before cooled barrels were used again. Overnight from the 22nd to the 23rd, pressure had built up around us. A Troop, to our left rear, was now engaging many targets in support of both 1 RNF and 1 RUR, the latter attempting to escape with us. As we extracted to the east bank, courtesy of the American tank commander, we could see the last of the Belgians leaving the hill in two long columns, some in vehicles, and others wading the river, as the Chinese fired mortars into them. By that time it could be seen that the enemy were already occupying the positions we had just left. I wondered if they would put our swimming hole to use. The Belgians had managed to reach the south bank, where their Browning .30 calibre machine guns had been set up. They were being used with good effect on all visible targets, and of those there were more than enough. American artillery units and air strikes in the meantime were demolishing much of Hill 195. By then it must have been more like the size of Hill 194, or smaller, just as recorded on those old Japanese maps we had started out with.

In B Troop, having negotiated the river crossings, we had been ordered to continue our escape along the dirt track called Route 11, where we expected eventually to rejoin the battery in the continuing fighting withdrawal to the south. We were now passing so many Chinese dead that we could see how far they had infiltrated amongst and around us during the night, in an attempt to completely encircle us. There were also some of our own dead, who were beyond help; only the wounded had been taken to the rear. As ambulances continued to collect the wounded, we knew we were passing through an area where a fierce fire fight had taken place. Walking wounded were being advised to make their way to 26 Field Ambulance RAMC (Royal Army Medical Corps) for new dressings or to have dressings changed, and then they were given transport to the rear.

Ulster and Fusilier stragglers, some of the fusiliers proudly wearing bedraggled red roses in their headwear, were heading forever south, as British and American artillery and air strikes continued to pound the area they had evacuated. We were passing wrecked vehicles that had been pushed off the track to permit passage of others. We were still deployed in support of the Belgians and the Ulsters, the latter having moved into a fallback position on Route 11. While we continued to move away from the river, now aided by 7 RCT, a self-contained unit the size of a British brigade, we first halted close to Hill 289 on the extreme left of 3 Div. We were covered by 7 RCT while we abandoned that location, as it had become too hot to handle, and we withdrew once more to the south. Without 7 RCT's tanks and artillery fire we would in all probability not have extracted at all.

Progressing along Route 11 we passed many damaged and burning vehicles, some with obvious dead on board. They were beyond any assistance we could offer, having been killed by enemy fire, which indicated how close the Chinese had come. We still had no idea at that time if we would escape their enveloping movement.

Ambulances continued to collect the wounded, and trucks with any room on board were offering lifts to infantrymen who were hiking to the rear. Some wounded were placed on tank decks, close to the engine exhausts, but any lift was better than none. However, we had now become the target for enemy machine-gunners on the ridge above us to our left, close by Hill 217, with Sopyonch'an to our left and Hill 398 to our front. It was not possible to direct our mortar fire with any accuracy on the visible targets that were becoming more numerous, and now much closer. The enemy soldiers could be plainly seen running along the ridgelines above us, a scary position to be in.

The line we had been driven from had been named Kansas Line. We were now withdrawing to Delta Line, where we expected to consolidate. All we needed to do was to arrive there safely. I believe the next potential defensive line after Delta if we had been driven even further to the south was named Utah. Continuing to progress ever south, the Chinese were still running along the ridge to try to head us off. Infantry Brens were used against them, but where one fell, another appeared to take his place. They also seemed oblivious to the air strikes that were killing their comrades, who were taking appalling casualties from napalm and rockets. We could hardly refrain from thinking, 'poor buggers, what a way to die'.

Continuing to head south, passing between Hills 398 and 675, the latter one, Kamak-san on our maps, was the tallest hill in the vicinity, and we knew that the Chinese by then had bypassed 1 Glos and C Troop and were occupying the crest, from where they had a grand view of us and were directing fire onto us. My maps showed that Route 11 and the track from C Troop met at some further point, but there appeared to be few men walking that route. I guessed it would not be long before they would appear with us on Route 11. Later I would discover that was not to be. But right then we were more concerned with getting out ourselves. Dusty and I were seated in the back of a 15cwt truck that was loaded with about eighty rounds of HE, which would make a nice explosion if we were hit with any sort of rocket the Chinese might have. It still looked as though the Chinese were endeavouring to surround us as they were now coming down from the crests near Hwangbang-ni, with Hill 424 to our right front, most armed with a personal weapon, others just carrying stick grenades. When it looked like our position was becoming desperate, just at the right time a squadron of 8th Hussars Centurions appeared. They were instrumental in assisting our safe passage at that point, but they had already lost several of their tanks.

By mid-afternoon, around 1500 hrs, I suppose, we reached a point on the track where we were ordered to halt. Ahead, about 300 yards away, we could see at least two burnt-out Centurions that might have become disabled and destroyed by the Hussars to prevent the Chinese getting their hands on the secret of the stabilized gun. The Centurion was more advanced than any other tank in 1951. There were other wrecked vehicles to the left of the track. An officer came along the column of vehicles to order drivers to leave the road and follow tank tracks that were clearly visible over the dry paddies. We were told that a Chinese ambush party had been established in a small wood of several trees and scrub, where the track entered the first of three S-bends, and it was believed they could still be in two wrecked houses further up the slope to our left. The paddy, we were told, had been cleared of mines by the Sappers. Leaving the track I could see the two blackened, burnt-out Centurions, also a half-track vehicle, and it looked as though the remains of a jeep had also been piled into the wreckage. Everything was in a confused state, but my mind was reasonably clear on one thing: if we had been further ahead in the convoy of vehicles, we might have suffered the same fate from the ambush.

After passing the ambush, by which time it seemed that the Chinese were no longer in the two houses up the slope, and after passing by two more S-bends, we rejoined Route 11 further along the track, about half a mile from the ambush site. We continued until we halted where I assumed we would consolidate and dig in on a firm line, from where we might be expected to stop the enemy's relentless drive to the south. But there was no consolidating at that point. We would just draw to a halt, the guns would be unlimbered, ammunition would be unloaded from the vehicles, mortars would be brought into action, fire would be carried out at minimum range on observed targets and guns would limber up again. We would continue to head back along Route 11 before stopping once more to fire the mortars, until we reached an area allocated to us by 29 Brigade.

Route 11 was now clogged with men and vehicles, many of them stretcher-bearing jeeps and ambulances transporting casualties to safety. The occasional US Army helicopter carrying a stretcher pod on either side would pass above us on their mercy mission, even though they were being targeted by the Chinese on the ridges. Those chopper pilots were brave men.

We were by now filthy, hungry, thirsty and in need of a rest, but we did not know then, on the afternoon of 23 April, that luxury was still another two days away. While we were busy in the right sector of the brigade's fighting withdrawal, over to the west our C Troop, with 1 Glos, whose wireless batteries were just about holding up, reported that they had been compelled to vacate their gun position due to the close proximity of large numbers of enemy. Man-packing barrels, static base plates, dial sights, tripods and wireless equipment with them, they had no alternative but to leave mobile base plates with the vehicles in the 'wagon lines', a Royal Artillery expression carried over from the days when horses pulled the guns into action. C Troop moved into a tight perimeter with the Gloucesters, with whom they were ordered to operate as infantry. All men were reported to be in good spirits, but hungry. A relieving force of 8th Hussars tanks and a Philippine infantry battalion of 3 Div attempted to break through to them, but without success. In the narrow gorge the lead tank was blown sideways across the track by a powerful mine, completely blocking the way. The other tanks were unable to pass.

Several other attempts were put into effect during the 24th, but without success. The Chinese now completely surrounded the Gloucesters and C Troop in enormous numbers. In my headphones I could hear the Signals NCO in C Troop, Bombardier Ted Maryan, gradually losing contact as his batteries faded then eventually died. We expected the worst for our mates. The men of C Troop, together with those of 1 Glos, a number of Royal Signals and Royal Engineers, were about to undertake the longest hike they would ever walk in their lifetime, the long march of several weeks to prisoner of war camps far to the north, laying up by day, marching at night to avoid observation by United Nations aircraft. Many years later, Ted, who emigrated to New Zealand after his release from captivity, related to me the story of the final moments while he attempted to escape capture:

I was in the CP at about 0300 hrs when we were continuing to fire on targets as they presented themselves. The adjutant of the Gloucesters, Captain Farrar-Hockley, came to tell us we would have to evacuate if the Chinese got around the rear of B Coy. Some of C Troop were sent out to the far end of the wagon lines to establish a defensive position. Almost immediately, the adjutant returned saying, 'Too late, you will have to go now,' or words to that effect. There was total confusion for a while. I was concerned with the signals truck and my signallers. Moving out we took little with us as we thought we would be back by daybreak. My driver and I lodged hand grenades at strategic points on the vehicle, extracted the pins and moved away rapidly. As we made our way out of the position and across a stream bed, tracer was cracking overhead from B Coy position, which added wings to our feet. We climbed up through a stony stream bed onto a small hill adjoining Hill 235 to the south-west and tried to dig in there. I believe that was where the mortar sights were buried. That was Tuesday, 24th. Captain Wisbey (C Troop Commander) came round to tell us we were to be relieved by a Philippines RCT, and about that time we saw a row of figures on the ridge to our north-west. We all cheered, happy to be relieved, until we realized they were shooting at us. It was then that we realized our backdoor was well and truly shut.

As last light approached we up-anchored and moved onto Hill 235. We were sited along the top ridge, from where we could see both the gun position we had vacated and the hill to our west overlooking what was to be our final, abortive escape route. We dug shell scrapes and had our first food since Sunday evening, half a can of US C ration apricots each, brought by the Gloucesters' RSM, Jack Hobbs, who led a small party down to Battalion HQ to recover any more food in the light of flares and burning vehicles. Jack Hobbs was a mighty man. He had helped me and my line crew out of a difficult situation earlier in the campaign as well. A mate and I had a go at a Chinese machine-gunner who was firing at us from a ridge on the western side of Hill 235. We guessed at the range. I had a try at 400 yards and we probably silenced him as his tracer arced down and then stopped as if he had been hit.

Came the dawn, with air strikes going in all over the place and the 25-pounders going great guns, plus the US 155mm and 8-inch howitzers, etc. At about 1200 hrs Captain Wisbey came round to tell us, 'At 1230 hrs it will be every man for himself.' I did not find that very encouraging. At 1230 hrs we were away, sliding down the steep slope on the seats of our trousers. At the bottom we turned left, south, and headed along a narrow path beside a stream. Our little group was at the front of the main body. As we rounded a bend the Gloucesters' adjutant was telling a group ahead of us to stop and pack it in.

The Chinese were all around us. They could have slaughtered us if they had so wished. We ran on until we reached an escarpment. By this time we were about all-in. Halfway up the escarpment I met one of our TARAs coming down who told me there was a Chinese machine-gunner covering the ridge.

There was no way round him. With that we turned back to the main body, where a diminutive Chinese soldier who was a foot shorter than his rifle handed me a safe conduct pass. The rest, as they say, is history.

Throughout the day the Chinese were infiltrating deep into 29 Brigade positions, but seemingly now in fewer numbers. Had they lost so many that the fight had gone out of them? No chance. All that had happened was that the original units that had crossed the Imjin in the first massive wave had apparently been relieved so they could lick their wounds. They had been replaced by fresh troops brought across the river, who were now attempting to close the last escape routes that were left open to us. These fresh troops attacked with renewed frenzy, accepting appalling casualty rates in the process.

It was about this time on Route 11 that the fusiliers lost their commanding officer, Lieutenant Colonel Kingsley Foster, killed when his jeep ran into an ambush. Battery Sergeant Major 'Spike' Ellis of 45 Field, an Australian by birth, passing in another jeep, took it in turns with his driver to fire a Bren from the hip into the packed Chinese ranks who were looting the jeep, in an attempt to rescue the colonel, but it was already too late. Spike and his driver managed to shoot their way through, despatching many of the Chinese who were massing in the hills above us to their maker. After the battle, for his coolness in action, Spike was decorated with the Military Medal.

As we continued to withdraw, with Sangbi-ri to our left, we were now in full mobile mode, our CP in the back of a Bedford 3-ton truck, while Dusty and I were trying to operate from the back of a ¾-ton Morris. We were sitting on top of a pile of HE rounds and we had already had a few small arms rounds pass through the canvas canopy above us. Our wireless equipment was still operable, but by now all targets were visible, with no great need for accurate grid references. Somewhere in the truck we had in addition the OP's Browning .30 calibre machine gun, but we both hoped we would not have to use it.

Passing through a former gun position of one of the 25-pounder batteries, all that was left now to indicate their having departed rapidly were huge piles of empty ammunition boxes, displaying how many rounds they had fired. The entire area was littered with them. Three or four times our mortars were set up into action, firing on anything and everything, and it looked as though we might need the Browning after all.

The Chinese, now installed on the tallest peak, Kamak-san, were watching the entire withdrawal along Route 11, and they were able to direct their soldiers to the maximum effect. By now I wondered if some of our 'K-types', men with former service who had volunteered for a limited period, purely for service in Korea, were wondering if they had made a grave mistake. So was I. I knew there were three Scots lads in C Troop who had served in the infantry in the Second World War, had gone to the recruiting office on the same day, signed on the dotted line as K volunteers, were given consecutive service numbers, and were all taken into captivity with C Troop. Reservists who had served in North Africa against Rommel's Afrika Korps, the Italian campaign or even in Burma, said they had never seen so many enemy so close at hand as in Korea.

I had noticed that too many enemy soldiers were now pouring down from the ridge just above us, many without small arms, but carrying grenades, and they were hurling them against vehicles as they passed below them. It was time for Dusty and I to cock our Stens – just in time, as two grenadiers were running along behind us. Without a thought we opened fire and saw them go down. As there were rifle shots, Brens and other weapons all firing at once I would never know if either I or my mate could claim those two running Chinamen, but if they had tossed a grenade onto the pile of HE mortar bombs we were sitting on in our truck, I imagine that I would not be here today.

We both realized that we had fired almost a magazine each and, on checking, we had only one full magazine apiece left, so we would have to expend ammunition carefully. We passed a point where two Bren-gunners, one on each side of the track, called out to our driver to get the hell out of the way, as they were firing at a large number of Chinese who were almost on top of us. As another three bullets from an unknown source whipped through the canvas cover on our truck, missing us by inches and then exiting through the wooden side panel, I was thankful they had not been tracer rounds and did not hit the HE rounds that Dusty and I were sitting on.

Continuing on along Route 11, we reached a point where the Chinese had cut the road ahead of us and formed a roadblock that had been completely inadequate against Centurion tanks, which appeared to have just ploughed straight over the soldiers that had been manning it. The road and the bank on the left of it were a bloody mess of crushed human flesh – not a pretty sight, but warfare is not pretty to behold. Some of the Chinese must have moved in close in an attempt to blow off the tank tracks, but they had been unsuccessful. I noticed at this time that whenever we stopped, our own Bren-gunners, Gunners Harrison and Holland, one at each end of our troop convoy, were assuming the prone position and putting their weapons to good use against attacking Chinese, who were everywhere. Dusty and I were beginning to wonder if we were going to get out of this.

Our mortars were to the north of us on the track and there was some concern about whether they would manage to get out, as the enemy had cut the track in two places between us at the front of the troop column, and them at the rear. A Troop mortars were still supporting the fusiliers on their withdrawal, however, while B Troop was still firing in support of the Ulsters and the Belgians. The support from the American tanks of 7 RCT was most appreciated, as the Hussars had already lost two or three Centurions. They could not afford to lose too many more.

Overnight from 24 to 25 April we harboured twice, only to be ordered to limber up and continue our southerly withdrawal. When would the nightmare end? We realized we were still sitting ducks for new Chinese attacks, travelling in a truck loaded with HE ammunition. At least if our truck was attacked we would not hear any resultant explosion, recalling that advice I had been given on my first night with 170 Mortar Battery that 'it is those you don't hear that kill you'. When I had time to look at the devastation within my vision, I thought of the .303 rounds I had wasted on some target practice I had before this battle had commenced. Opening a box of .303 rifle ammunition, occasionally there would be a note from the girl packer in the ordnance factory asking for pen friends. Sometimes there would also be a note from the manufacturer advising the user to 'use this ammunition wisely, they cost seventeen shillings and sixpence'. That was for a bandolier of fifty rounds. Nowadays I understand that one round costs in excess of £1 sterling.

On the right flank of the brigade sector, the brunt of the attack now fell on Z Company of 1 RNF. A troop had been firing all night in their defence. Their troop commander, Captain Waters, was commended by the Z Company commander for performing valuable service to his company, until in the morning when he had to be evacuated in a state of mental and physical exhaustion. The fusiliers and A Troop had managed to hold firm throughout the night, eventually extracting safely in the morning. The Chinese continued to attack both A and B troops with renewed vigour. In B Troop at that time we were ordered to continue our support for the two battalions, the Ulster Rifles and the Belgians. We were still moving back one section at a time to permit A Troop to withdraw, then A Troop would cover our withdrawal through their position, and so on.

As one section moved back at a time, that section would hold firm, then the other section could move back in reasonable safety – not that any of us felt safe in our canvas-topped trucks. We could have put some of those Oxford carriers to good use for a start. They would at least have provided better protection against Chinese small arms ammunition. By the leapfrogging method we were able to continue our support to the infantry while still falling back along Route 11. During the afternoon of the 24th, Major Fisher-Hoch passed the information to the battery that, when we managed to free ourselves, Major

General Soule had ordered US 3rd Division to relieve 29 Brigade and that we would move back to Yongdung-po when the situation permitted. I think it is likely the general had finally realized that one brigade could not possibly have held such a wide frontage against a strong and determined enemy who had orders to eliminate us. He would now be moving in a full division, nine battalions and all supporting arms, and 29 Brigade appeared to have been on a loser from the outset.

On Tuesday, the 24th, we had our orders to withdraw to the south bank of the Han River, but prior to moving out, almost two full days into the battle that had started on the 22nd, without rest and with no time to stop for a good brew-up, we were still firing DFs in support of the Belgians and the Ulsters. Once again, early morning mist was causing some confusion in distinguishing friend from foe. When the mist cleared it was plain to see that the Chinese had infiltrated through or around us in the night, and with the Belgians we were completely surrounded once again. The enemy had occupied a range of low hills to our rear. Once more our mortars were turned through 180 degrees to engage a concentrated mass of enemy soldiers, causing a great many casualties among these new, fresh enemy soldiers, who apparently were dissuaded from following us as a way was forced through them, killing large numbers in doing so.

We commenced moving back again on the morning of the 25th on the remaining stretch of Route 11. But before travelling very far, once again our mortar troops were called upon to bring the mortars into action to fire on numerous targets requested by the infantry, who still had the Chinese snapping at their heels. At least, as we finally extracted ourselves, there were many fewer mortar bombs to carry to our fall-back position. Everything was loaded on the battery vehicles, as nothing useful could be left behind for the Chinese, who would have used any abandoned ammunition against us, possibly using C Troop mortars. But finally they seemed to have run out of steam. Their supply line had probably been stretched to the limit, and although the prize of recapturing Seoul was no longer possible for them, it was likely that they intended to consolidate on the ground we had relinquished to them, and they would try again at a later date. In fact, that never happened.

Units of 3 Div were moving in to occupy positions at the southern end of the long valley through which Route 11 ran from the Imjin River to the junction where the track from the Gloucesters' positions connected. Although starting to withdraw for the final time, once again we had to request fire from two Hussars tanks to effect our extraction, the enemy having completely encircled us for the third time and compelling us to make another fighting withdrawal with the help of the Ulsters and the Belgians. Where would we have been without them? Well and truly in the proverbial, that's where.

We approached the junction where the escape route for the Gloucesters and C Troop met with Route 11, but there were few men walking that track, and even fewer vehicles. We continued on, crossing the Sinch'on, a minor tributary of the Hantan.

More supersonic cracks whipped around our heads as we watched, fascinated, the streams of tracer arcing away from the Besa machine guns mounted on the Centurions, and listened to the mighty crack of their main armament, the splendid 20–pounder. That was some gun.

That was my last memory of the battle, which for B Troop was over. It had been a frightening experience for me and Dusty, as it would have been for all my colleagues, following complete encirclement on three occasions, although not one of us would have admitted to any frailty at the time. Eventually, A and B troops reached Yongdung-po after midnight on the 25th. The only men missing were C Troop, who I supposed were making a slow fighting withdrawal with the Gloucesters along the track to their rear. But on arrival at Yongdung-po we would soon learn that was not the case. I have read somewhere in a Korean War memoir that a troop of British 4.2-inch mortars was still firing at 0630 hrs on the 26th, but they were not of 170 Mortar Battery, the only British mortar battery in Korea. We had come out of action six and a half hours before that, and nothing had been heard from C Troop. They had been forced to bury their mortar sights, so it was certainly not their mortars that were still engaging targets at that time. It could only have been the 4.2-inch mortars of 3 Div that were still firing on targets in support of their infantry battalions after we had departed the scene.

During the period 22nd to the 25th, 170 Mortar Battery had expended in excess of 14,000 HE rounds and some smoke. The RASC drivers had performed splendidly, ensuring that none of our mortar troops were short of ammunition until the Chinese had encircled C Troop, cutting the road to their rear. Mention must also be made of the men and tanks of the 8th Hussars, and of 7 RCT, without whose valiant assistance in extracting us on three occasions would have meant we would almost certainly not have been able to leave Hill 195 in safety and escape along Route 11. Without them we might have been lost, together with another infantry battalion, the courageous Belgians, whose cheerfulness in adversity and their fighting ability earned them the United States Presidential Unit Citation.

After the battle, the Belgians were transferred to the United States 3rd Infantry Division, where they were re-equipped with standard US Army small arms and uniforms, handing over their British small arms, machine guns and ammunition supply to 29 Brigade. We said farewell to our colleagues.

On leaving 29 Brigade the original battalion commander, Lieutenant Colonel Albert Crahay, who had handed over his command and returned to Belgium, sent a personal letter to Brigadier Tom Brodie, 29 Brigade Commander, thanking all units for their support, with individually addressed letters to all unit commanders. The letter of appreciation received by Major Fisher-Hoch, translated from the original French, reads as follows:

20 August 1951

To Major T.V. Fisher-Hoch
Commanding 170 Ind Mortar Bty RA

As I am about to leave the 29th British Infantry Brigade, in the name of the Belgian Volunteers for Korea, I am keen to express the great esteem and friendship that we feel towards our British comrades. We have been fighting side by side with the brigade for almost five months. We felt that we were part of it and we have been proud to share the fame that it has acquired among units that were fighting in Korea. We will always be happy to meet up again with our former brothers-in-arms, either in Korea or in Europe.

Lieutenant Colonel A.E. Crahay BEM
44 Avenue de Broqueville, Bruxelles.

At that time we still had no knowledge of the fate of C Troop, as they had not arrived to join the battery south of Route 11, nor was there any news of the Gloucesters. It was beginning to look like they had been annihilated. The final weak wireless messages from C Troop as their batteries faded stated that they would consolidate with the Gloucesters on Hill 235, after which nothing further was heard. Spotter aircraft, the pilots risking their lives, reported that swarms of enemy soldiers were all over Hill 235 and its surroundings, and the situation was chaotic to say the least. It would be many months, October, I think, before we were shown photographs, brought to the battery positions by the International Red Cross, I believe, that showed a large number of British soldiers sitting on a hillside, surrounded by armed Chinese soldiers, so we were aware that some had survived. Men were asked to identify any they recognized, so that families at home could be notified that their men had been alive when the photographs were taken. I had not at that time met Ted Maryan; he had been just a voice in my headphones, and as our three troops were each embedded with a different infantry battalion, I knew none of the C Troop lads. I was told that the Gloucesters' RSM, Jack Hobbs, was easily recognizable in the picture, as were Bombardier Oliver, Gunner Mick Menaud and others from C Troop sitting right at the left front when it was taken.

It had been estimated that 27,000 enemy infantry were thrown against us in the first wave. To put that into context, call it about thirty battalions against the three battalions of 29 Brigade. It does not need a degree in mathematics to calculate that we were outnumbered by ten to one, massive odds in their favour. They had gained the territory we had reluctantly surrendered, but had not taken Seoul.

It was estimated that the Chinese suffered around 10,000 casualties in their effort to sweep us from our hills and continue all the way south to Seoul. They did manage the first part of the plan, but not the second. Total British casualties over the three days of the battle were 1,078, and 29 Brigade had held their positions long enough to destroy the Chinese master plan. The long-prepared spring offensive came to nothing. For the political commissars and military strategists in Beijing (which we were more familiar with as being called Peking, as its name change had only occurred in 1949) it was back to the drawing board.

Although our enemy had won the day on the Imjin River, it was sheer weight of numbers that had driven us from our hills, massed ant-like attacks, not so much as carefully directed artillery and mortar fire, although use was made of these latter weapons, including some American artillery pieces that had been captured by the North Korean Army in the early days of the war. If the Chinese had enjoyed air supremacy and the use of weapons such as napalm, the Korean War would have ended almost as soon as China had committed the People's Volunteers to assist their North Korean comrades. I believe their very long supply line, which stretched all the way back to China with limited use of mechanical transport, was a critical factor in ensuring that they could not drive us back any further.

In 170 Battery we had played our small part in the battle, and in true Gunner tradition we had not let the infantry down when our support was needed. The loss of forty-six men from the battery was indeed a sad blow, but Major Fisher-Hoch told us we should take pride in their achievement, which was later recognized by the President of the United States of America.

Our sadly depleted battery, now just A and B troops and BHQ, eventually limped into Yongdung-po at 0330 hrs on Thursday, the 26th, where BSM Dudley Davenport had found dry billets in the remains of a building that appeared to have been part factory, part prison. There were a number of holes in the roof, but to us it was the Waldorf Astoria.

After a welcome hot meal, the first since Saturday evening, and a hot mug of tea, we lapsed into proper sleep for the first time since Saturday night, dropping off into the sleep of the dead. It was only on waking, well into Thursday, that I realized the disgusting state I was in. Like everyone else, my clothes were filthy, hanging on me like a scarecrow's rags. Most of us had not completely removed our boots since Sunday; just loosened the laces a few times. In B Troop, like most of the others, I had nothing to change into, having lost all my kit to the American tank-gunner who had demolished our stalled truck in the hurried exit from Hill 195. However, BQMS Foreman was quickly able to kit us out with basic requirements. I can still picture him standing there alongside a large pile of clothing shouting, 'Who needs a shirt? Who wants trousers? Anyone want socks?' and tossing each item to whoever had responded, which was everyone. Then we swapped around until we found something that more or less fitted, and once more took on the appearance of British soldiers. We managed to collect the bare essentials, even razors and blades to replace those we had lost. After a wash and shave we looked like human beings again. That gathering in the factory building would have been for the lads who had arrived on HMT *Empire Halladale* the previous November, the first time since then that they would have seen again mates they had known at Norton Barracks in A and B troops and in BHQ.

What remained of Thursday was spent in reorganizing. A formidable list of equipment was required, including the four mortars and eight vehicles that had been lost. Over the following week some equipment arrived, although complete replacement would be some time coming. Due to the battery losses we now had only eight mortars and one spare mobile base plate. A new C Troop was started with the nucleus of two mortars and the spare base plate, reducing A and B troops to three mortars each, until new mortars arrived. C Troop was temporarily combined under B Troop Commander, Captain Tony Fowle. Over the following days some replacement personnel arrived, BCRs from JRHU in Japan, others transferred in from 45 Field Regiment, and some of our own walking wounded returned from 26 Field Ambulance, from 60th Indian Airborne Field Ambulance, and one who had enjoyed a few days in the Norwegian MASH (Mobile Army Surgical Hospital). When asked, he was adamant that he had seen female nurses at NORMASH, as it was known, although he could have been hallucinating.

Prior to all the recent activity, General MacArthur had been removed from his position as supreme commander by President Harry Truman, who did not see eye to eye with the man who some more or less thought of as the Emperor of Japan. He was replaced by General Matthew Ridgeway. There were many reasons why Truman had sacked the great man, one being that MacArthur had wanted to use nuclear weapons against North Korea, even across the northern boundary into China. Another was that reports claimed MacArthur turned a blind eye to the shooting by South Korean troops of civilians believed to be spies who had infiltrated from the north, without any form of trial. More than one such massacre had been witnessed by British troops, who had attempted to put a stop to it. They were criticized by President Syngman Rhee, who told reporters, 'The British troops have outlived their welcome in my country.' Further, he told an Australian Embassy representative, 'They are not wanted here any longer. Tell that to your government. The Australian, Canadian, New Zealand and British troops all represent a government that is now sabotaging the brave American effort to liberate fully and unify my unhappy nation.'

It was not long before those pronouncements reached 170 Battery. Bombardier Alan Humphreys was incensed, so soon after Syngman Rhee's capital and a large amount of real estate south of the 38th parallel had been saved from the Chinese only by units such as 29 Brigade on the Imjin River, and the Australian, Canadian and New Zealand forces in 27 Brigade, aided by tanks and artillery of the US Army several miles to the east on the Pukhan River. Alan wrote a letter of protest to the Foreign Office in London. As Alan's letter is in the public domain, I will summarize it here. Basically, what Alan objected to was the ungrateful attitude of President Syngman Rhee. Alan was a reservist recalled to the colours to fight in a war he thought, when his call-up notice arrived, was wrong. He also believed that it had been wrong to have crossed the 38th parallel, without any attempt being made by General MacArthur to end the war at that point. Rhee's objection was that British troops ought to be removed from Korea, after the South Korean president had made it quite clear that we were not welcome in his country. This, so soon after more than 1,000 British men had become battle casualties in four days in an attempt to stop his country from being overrun by the communists. Alan considered we could have been better used in another part of the globe, where we might at least have been welcomed by the president or government officials of the country.

At the time, I recall that Alan was called to account for his action, and it is possible he might have been threatened with being busted to gunner, although the likely publicity at home would not have looked good. In 1951 it was not acceptable for a serving soldier to write to the Foreign Office, or to the press. Today, disgruntled soldiers are free to air their complaints in *Soldier*, the monthly magazine of the British Army, or by writing to their Member of Parliament.

After kitting-out and having been sorted into different troops with the replacements, some of whom, like me on my arrival, would not have known a 4.2-inch mortar from a drainpipe, we started asking around: 'Have you seen anything of so and so?' That was when I discovered that my fellow National Serviceman and signaller, John Kilburn, who had been due to leave Korea within one week, had been killed by a direct hit on his OP with the fusiliers. Saddened by the news, I knew I had been very lucky. Thankfully, the other OP parties in A and B troops had survived, although only after the horrendous withdrawal with the infantry and armour of 29 Brigade.

One might ask, what was the driving force behind our enemy's method of attack? Advancing through the killing field of red-hot shards, bombs, bullets, napalm and rockets, they would have known that many of their comrades could not survive the maelstrom. Was it something in the oriental psyche?

As far as our enemy was concerned, we knew who he was, but in reality we knew little about him. We were in Korea because our government supported the United Nations' call to assist the Republic of Korea in the fight against their northern aggressor, and to prevent the spread of communism throughout Asia. The Chinese People's Volunteers, as Peking referred to their soldiers, knew the war as the War for Resisting Aggression and Aiding Korea, by which they meant North Korea. He would have been told that it was the American-aided South Korea that had started the conflict by attacking the peace-loving citizens north of the 38th parallel, and that the United Nations forces were there to oppress the common people, lackeys of the United States. And that was also the interpretation that was accepted by some Members of Parliament in Clement Attlee's government, also followers of the British Communist Party, some of whom had actually visited POW camps in the north, to come home and disgracefully report that British POWs were enjoying better food than the average rationed Briton at home, and that they were being well cared for by the People's Volunteers. I know some of my colleagues would have enjoyed getting their hands around their throats, particularly one man and a woman who were outrageous in their reporting. A journalist resident in Peking told one POW that he could have him shot for telling him a few home truths.

Whatever the People's Volunteers thought of us, it must be said that we had a grudging respect for the fighting will of the Chinese infantryman. Their bravery in action could not be faulted. When ordered into the attack on a particular village or hill feature, directed by the bugles and whistles in lieu of wireless sets, they did everything in their power to secure the objective by the method we knew as 'human wave'. Initially, a probing platoon might be sent in to test our strength and to find out our defensive locations. Next, when they had been repelled, a company-sized attack would be committed. If that also failed the objective, a larger group would deploy, until they might take the position attacked, or, if their losses were too great, then the bugles would sound a recall as they left many of their dead on the fought-over ground. In attack, as they came at us, they looked for all the world like a disturbed ants' nest, an unbelievable sight, never forgotten – which is why I was reminded of them in May 1982, when viewing on television the millions of mice chewing their way through the Australian outback.

That the Chinese soldier suffered great deprivation was certain. Poorly clothed and equally poorly shod, I have no idea how they managed to survive a Korean winter. At times we could see that not everyone had a personal weapon; some were armed only with grenades, such as the two that neither I nor Dusty claimed as our own. Others would stop to pick up the weapon and ammunition bandolier from a fallen comrade who had no further need for one. They would also stoop to collect the food bandolier from the dead. That one would hold meagre meals, each twisted into separate portions, which could contain cold rice or other cooked grain, maybe a small amount of dried fish or vegetable, soya beans, etc. Hot cooked food was a luxury for the volunteer, reserved for when the fighting stopped.

While we continued to rebuild 170 Battery in our new position on the south bank of the Han River, 8 May became an important day in the life of the battery. All of us who could be spared were trucked to the ruined school building at Ichon that we had used the previous March. There, we formed up on three sides of a square with representatives of all units in 29 Brigade, as well as others. The occasion was for the presentation of the United States Presidential Unit Citation to the Gloucesters and to C Troop 170 Independent Mortar Battery. Men sitting or standing on vehicles parked behind the parading troops obtained a good view of the proceedings, as the Pipes and Drums of the Royal Ulster Rifles played. Our battery commander, Major Fisher-Hoch, and Lieutenant Colonel Digby Grist, formerly second-in-command of the Gloucesters and now the new commanding officer, escorted by two armed NCOs, waited for Lieutenant General James A. Van Fleet to make the presentation, which was on a parchment scroll. The individual insignia consists of a piece of blue medal ribbon, the same as on the ribbon of the United States Distinguished Service Cross, contained within a small gilt anodized frame. Some men received their insignia on parade, others, like me, when they were handed out back at the troop position. None of us knew what to do with it, and that was something that would not be sorted out for some time.

For many years the original parchment of the citation was held in a place of honour wherever the battery served in its many different roles over the following sixty years. It is worded in its entirety as an appendix in this book. The language is rather more colourful than would be used in the United Kingdom, however; it must be remembered that when it was drawn up in Washington, it was believed that an entire infantry battalion and a Royal Artillery troop had been killed in action. Only later, when a small number of men managed to escape, was it known that most of their comrades had been taken into captivity after being overrun by enormous numbers of the enemy. It was reported that Brigadier Tom Brodie held himself personally responsible for failing to request a relieving force until it was too late. He was devastated at losing so many men from his command, even though the rest of the brigade had held firm long enough to deny Chairman Mao his grand May Day parade in Seoul.

Our steadfast colleagues, the Belgian Infantry Battalion, were also honoured with the same citation, 'For gallantry and professionalism in holding a crucial sector against the enemy, for inflicting thirty-fold losses, and for holding open the valley mouth that allowed the Rifles and Fusiliers to break free.' It had been an honour and a pleasure to serve with those tough soldiers.

Although sketchy reports indicated some casualties had been suffered over the previous week in Korea, it was not until Thursday, 3 May, eight days after the battle concluded, that London newspapers carried the first early reports indicating that more than 1,000 men were officially 'missing in action'. The same newspapers also reported that at the same time the British Government did not see that a British medal was appropriate for service in Korea. Clement Attlee's cabinet still preferred to refer to the Korean War as a police action. All I can say is, if that was a police action, precisely what was a battle?

Also covered in the reportage at the time was the astonishing news that 'Britain is still exporting strategic materials to China', without disclosing what the strategic materials were. But we were exporting them, whatever they were, to the very country whose soldiers had been doing everything in their powers to exterminate us the previous week. On the opposition benches, Winston Churchill was stated to be furious. The Speaker had to order him to sit.

Over the following days in early May, as censored news was considered fit for human consumption, details started to filter through of two major battles involving British and Commonwealth troops that had been fought in Korea, that 29 Brigade had fought its way out of encirclement and had blocked the southward drive of an estimated three Chinese divisions. There were in addition some reports attributed to an unnamed officer, rifleman or fusilier, that had been gleaned by an intrepid newshound who would have scrounged a lift from his luxury hotel in the centre of Tokyo, secured a place on a US Military transport plane to Seoul, and dashed by waiting jeep to as near to the front line as he was permitted, notebook in hand, to be the first to get Tommy Atkins' story first-hand. Some of the articles I read later in newspapers left much to be desired, making me wonder if the Tommy Atkins that the reporter had spoken to had actually been anywhere near the front line.

Early reports did indicate that the Chinese had been repelled after suffering huge losses, in the region of 30,000, they claimed, which made me wonder if the reporter had thought of a number and then trebled it. The first lists of named casualties, not particularly accurate, started to hit the headlines as the figures were released by the War Office as they considered the population could cope with them. In an attempt to salve the conscience of Brigadier Brodie, he received a letter of appreciation from Lieutenant General Milburn, Commander of I Corps, which was considerably more restrained than the wording of the Presidential Citation, reading:

> I want to congratulate your officers and men for their gallantry in action while defending the Imjin River line against greatly superior enemy forces. Subjected to exceedingly heavy pressure you did not falter and met his attacks with a fighting will and courage beyond his, as attested by the hundreds of enemy dead in close proximity to your position. As you disengaged you fought, and our common enemy has good cause to remember the 29th Brigade as a formidable opponent. We are all proud of you.

However, I think the *Daily Mirror* said it all when, under the headline 'WE LOST 1,078 IN RECENT KOREA STAND', its editorial column paid the following tribute:

> All who believe in peace and civilization and order in the world have a debt to acknowledge that they cannot repay. The heavy British losses in the Korean fighting are a reminder that resistance to aggression calls upon men for many sacrifices. There would be something wrong with us if we were not proud of these men, some of them young National Servicemen, who acted out for us to the end the best beliefs for which the British Nation stands.

Certainly, those three days and nights will remain in my memory for as long as I live.

While we had been busy with our own tasks, not really being aware of the complete picture that was now unravelling, I feel I ought to mention the fine action of 45 Field Regiment, without whose constant firing of their 25-pounders many more of us might not have been successful in our escape along Route 11. I heard that their barrels had run almost red hot at times, as confirmed in the regiment's history. A man who became a good friend over the years, Sergeant O.R. 'Reg' Kitchener, had been one of the transfers to B Troop 170 Battery from 70 Battery 45 Field to make up our losses in the battle. Much later, Reg found himself featuring in a painting by Terence Cuneo, commissioned by 45 Field. Reg is depicted traversing his 25-pounder, which was firing over open sights at 200 yards' range, on a mass of enemy pouring down a hill towards him, his fire directed by Captain George Truell. It is a very fine painting, typical of Cuneo, but there is one thing wrong. The painting shows the gun in action in bright daylight. The occasion, Reg told me, actually happened at 0200 hrs, in darkness.

On the subject of 45 Field Regiment, here is the citation for the decoration with the MC of the officer, Lieutenant Walsh, who suffered a head wound in the OP with us on Hill 195 on the first night of the Imjin River Battle, as published in the *London Gazette*:

On the night of 22/23 April 1951, Lieutenant Walsh was a Royal Artillery observer with the Belgian battalion attached to 29 Infantry Brigade. The observation post was on a hill occupied by C Company and some little distance from the remainder of the unit. During the night the enemy put in a heavy attack all along the line and especially on the hill, which they managed to surround. All that night and the following day, Lieutenant Walsh remained in wireless touch with the guns, and although wounded in the head, called down accurate artillery fire on the enemy, who at times were only a few yards from the Belgian position. Without his support it is doubtful if the Belgians could have held out. Lieutenant Walsh's coolness and devotion to duty not only saved a dangerous situation, but proved a magnificent example to his comrades.

The citation for the Military Medal awarded to BSM Spike Ellis of 45 Field, for attempting to rescue Lieutenant Colonel Kingsley Foster, is produced herewith, in abbreviated form, as the full citation is rather lengthy:

On 25 April 1951, 847297 BSM Ellis left the gun position in a jeep to take urgently needed wireless batteries to his observation posts with the 1st Battalion the Royal Ulster Rifles ... he stayed to help the OP parties who were coming out on foot ... the enemy got close to his position, and started to engage him with small arms fire ... at once he and his driver engaged them with their Bren gun … as they rounded a bend they saw two leading jeeps had been shot up … firing his Bren from the hip BSM Ellis drove at them … he stopped to try to give assistance to the ambulance halted at the road [Lt Col Foster] … Ellis's coolness and complete disregard of his own safety in a very hazardous situation are worthy of the highest praise.

I met Spike several times over the years at veteran functions. As far as I am aware he never returned to his native Australia, completing an illustrious military career in the rank of warrant officer first class. He was later admitted as an in-pensioner in the Royal Hospital Chelsea.

Immediately prior to the outbreak of hostilities in Korea, a party of men serving in various Royal Artillery units in Hong Kong had been given the good news that they had been selected for some relief from the worst of the oppressive monsoon climate suffered in the colony in July. Their orders were to report to the Royal Navy Base, HMS Tamar. There they boarded HMS *Jamaica* for a summer cruise around Japan, where *Jamaica* was to participate in a naval regatta. For the men it was a revelation to see how the others lived. As they watched Hong Kong disappear astern in the monsoon murk, they had no knowledge of the strife that lay ahead for them.

Shortly after North Korea invaded the south, the United States Seventh Fleet, based in the Philippines, was ordered to sail north towards Japanese waters. Several ships of the Royal Navy were similarly directed. Within days actions were being fought around the Korean coastline. At daybreak on 2 July, the cruiser HMS *Jamaica* and HMS *Black Swan*, a frigate, became the first of the British Armed Forces to become involved in the conflict. Initially, *Jamaica's* guns were directed to fire at oil storage tanks about 10 miles north of the 38th parallel, and at cliffs overhanging the coast road, in an effort to cause landslides to effectively block the advance of fast-moving enemy motorized columns.

On 8 July, a combined force of United States Navy and Royal Navy ships were attacked by four fast patrol boats that had been guarding North Korean landing craft putting troops ashore. One enemy vessel escaped, the remaining three were sunk by naval gunfire, with the Army personnel, who had expected a pleasant cruise, in the thick of it as ammunition handlers feeding *Jamaica's* Bofors guns. And on that day Britain suffered the first casualties of the Korean War when *Jamaica* was hit by a single shell from a shore battery. The direct hit killed one Royal Navy man and five of the Army personal, three of whom were Royal Artillery, a sergeant, a lance bombardier and a gunner. The others killed were two men from the Middlesex Regiment, and one from the ship's company. They were buried at sea with full military honours. In my archives I have a copy of the Captain's Daily Report (often erroneously called the ship's log) covering *Jamaica's* first two weeks of action, reporting this event. On that day nobody could have contemplated that the war that had started in Korea would continue with bitter fighting for another three years.

In the meantime, in Hong Kong, other gunners were being prepared for war. When the War Office was pressured to activate troops for Korea, the hastily assembled and under-strength 27 Brigade, consisting mainly of the first battalions of the Middlesex Regiment and the Argyll and Sutherland Highlanders, was ordered to proceed to Korea. As both battalions were under-strength it was decided that men would be taken from their support companies to enhance the rifle companies. That left the battalions short of anti-tank guns for use against the fast-moving T34 tanks of the North Korean Army that were leading their rapid advance south. To provide that cover, one troop of 27 (Stranges) Light Battery, recently retrained on the 4.2-inch mortar but also retaining nine 17-pounder anti-tank guns as secondary armament, six towed and three mounted on Valentine tank chassis, were ordered to remove four of the 17-pounders from mothballs, form a troop of men with anti-tank experience, and prepare to leave for Korea. Several years ago I spoke to the officer who took the troop to Korea.

Lieutenant J. Trelawney Williams retired to Sussex, where I contacted him. I enquired if he could give me some idea of the movements of the troop in Korea, or where I could find them. His reply was that he doubted much existed, as in Korea his 'Troop Office' had consisted of an ammunition box in the back of a jeep. The first gunner to be killed on land in Korea was Gunner Ronnie Mitchell of A Independent Anti-Tank Troop Royal Artillery, as the detached unit was titled. He would not be the last. As only the two famous infantry battalions had hit the headlines at home, virtually nothing is known of the Anti-Tank Troop. Nothing was published until *Gunner* magazine's issue for November 1950 had a piece that read:

Contrary to general belief, a unit of the Royal Artillery has been fighting alongside our infantry in Korea ... the troop reached Korea early in September and has since been operating with the brigade.

Nothing further was published until June 1951, three months after the troop had returned to Hong Kong. That report included a photograph of Lieutenant Williams, Lieutenant F. Fuller, the TSM, and two senior NCOs wearing US Army cold weather clothing. For the troop's support of 27 Brigade on the Naktong River line, they were awarded the Republic of Korea Presidential

Unit Citation, together with the infantry. The troop returned to Hong Kong in March 1951, as by then no more North Korean tanks had appeared.

The members of 27 Brigade were not the first British service personnel to set foot on Korean soil. They were beaten to it by five weeks, when a Royal Navy officer and a Royal Artillery officer stepped ashore near Pohang on the east coast. After reading a very brief account of their activities, which was to establish a wireless link with naval vessels to assist the US Army, I telephoned both gentlemen. Commander Law RN and Captain McQueen RA had been ordered to form a Combined Operations Bombardment Unit (COBU) at Sasebo, Japan. The COBU would direct naval gunfire onto shore targets. I enquired of the retired Major General McQueen which of them could claim to have been the first to step on Korean soil. He explained that, as he was outranked by the Royal Navy, he had stepped aside to allow the now retired Admiral Sir Horace Law, GCB, OBE, DSC, to be first. So the Royal Navy, the Senior Service, beat the Army ashore on Korean soil by one footstep.

I am well aware that in lighter moments the infantrymen refer to gunners as Nine-Mile Snipers, a title possibly gained in the First World War when artillery bombardments by a variety of heavy guns from well to the rear became the norm. Well, it would have been an undeserved title; in fact, we would have considered it to be an insult. At that time, in April 1951, the virtues of 170 Mortar Battery had been extolled by the commanders of all the infantry battalions with whom we were embedded, and who would not have wanted to be without us.

Not all gunners in Korea lived comfortably in tents several miles behind the forward infantry, as was conspicuously demonstrated on the Imjin River. A mate, Tommy Clough, a former C Troop POW with whom I have remained in contact, will reply to veterans from the lesser branches of the Army: 'Nine-Mile Sniper, was I? Then how is it I was taken prisoner?' Tommy was given a rough time after attempting to escape. His wrists were tightly handcuffed and he was placed in a small cubicle that had formerly been a toilet, and later into one of the wooden crates known to the POWs as 'the kennels', in which it was impossible to stand or stretch out, where his sole companion was a spider. Tommy, a former boy soldier, had enlisted on 8 May 1945 – VE-Day. Today, living in Gloucestershire, he is an 'honorary infantryman, almost an honorary Gloster'. The word 'Gloster' had now appeared, coined by a newspaper, in the headline 'The Glorious Glosters', as Gloucestershire probably took up too much headline space. Tommy's wrists still drop on occasion when he tries to hold something, as a result of his tight bonds. In 2011 he journeyed back to Korea, meeting up with Ted Maryan for the first time in fifty-eight years. Ted made the journey from New Zealand. They walked again on the precise spot where they had been force-marched across the Imjin by their captors in 1951. Tommy told me it all came back to him, a reminder that the freedom of the people from the Republic of Korea came at a high price for him and his comrades.

Chapter Five

Interlude in Japan

Following a very hectic end to April, throughout May only limited activity disturbed the peace in 170 Battery. All the usual daily military routines recommenced, which was quite a change. One thing seemed certain, however. It appeared that at least for the present we might have settled into one place – rather an improvement after the continual backwards and forwards movements of the past months. The Chinese had been held about 20 miles north of Seoul, and it was the avowed intention of Eighth Army that they should remain there for the present. Men started to head for five days' leave in Tokyo, and with a wet, humid summer forecast and about to arrive with a vengeance, some men were sent to the rear for a course in the prevention of malaria and other medical hazards that might be expected in a country such as Korea. RAMC personnel arrived with their long needles to ensure our typhoid, paratyphoid, tetanus, typhus and smallpox jabs were up to date, and to inoculate us against a whole new medical dictionary of dreadful diseases with unlikely sounding names. One very unpleasant form of paralysis that was known to be prevalent in these parts was Japanese B Encephalitis, which could be the result of a single sting from a mosquito, and that meant another truckload of serum would be rushed to the troop positions to be offloaded into waiting arms. We had been warned that haemorrhagic fever, which we heard was akin to bubonic plague, could be spread by bites from the fleas that infested the rats. We continued to take one tablet of Paludrine each day to combat malaria.

As we were now settled in reasonable safety on the south bank of the Han, we had been promised a free day on 14 May, when the battery had anticipated a day at the beach, in reality just a swimming hole in a training area near Inchon. But just like in England on a public holiday when a trip to the beach is planned, it poured with rain all day, non-stop, making it quite unnecessary to jump into the sea to get soaked. This enjoyable lull in the fighting came to an abrupt end for us on 23 May when, with all units of 29 Brigade, we were ordered to move to an assembly area on the north-east outskirts of Seoul. Good accommodation was found in some excellent college buildings that had been only lightly damaged, even though the war had passed through the city on four occasions. Our neighbour in these buildings was 29 Brigade HQ.

Our pleasure in these unfamiliar surroundings was somewhat dampened by two very heavy thunderstorms. On the night of the 27th, orders were unexpectedly received for the battery to move up with the infantry again to exactly the same area we had occupied at the beginning of April, over which so much blood had been spilled. Next morning, 29 Brigade moved back through Uijongbu and Tokchon, and after harbouring for the night, next morning we occupied positions in battalion locations along the Imjin River. A Troop joined 1 RNF, while the still combined B and C troops moved to a two-troop position in the former Belgian battalion area, from where we would again support them and the Ulsters. The position was about half a mile south of the former C Troop position in April. The battery CP was established near 29 Brigade HQ and RHQ 45 Field Regiment.

In those surroundings there was a great deal of the detritus of war. Human remains that had been there for four weeks were recovered, but only one could be positively identified, that of Sergeant Herbert Danes, who had been killed on the last day of the battle. For fifty years his family believed he had no known grave, until they were notified that he lay in plot 24, row 8, grave 1,783 in the UN cemetery, Pusan. We also found assorted military papers, pay books, pieces of equipment, discarded ammunition that would not fit Chinese weapons, and much else. Shattered fighting pits and shell craters were everywhere. On establishing ourselves in these new positions, safe in the knowledge that the Chinese had withdrawn to well north of the river, my troop commander decided to recce the south bank, to the precise spot where men in a listening post of 1 Glos on a small cliff above a ford had heard the first sounds of the imminent attack when the first Chinese had started to cross.

On arrival at the river Captain Fowle was surprised to discover in a sandy cove several damaged Chinese 75mm mountain guns, the old fashioned kind with wooden spoke wheels. Sights and ammunition lay around among the bomb craters, and several bodies remained where they had fallen, killed by shellfire and bombs dropped by the US Air Force. Captain Fowle decided that the least damaged gun would be a suitable souvenir of the memorable battle, and he arranged for Sergeant Pennifold to bring up to the river a vehicle suitable to tow the gun back to B Troop position. Cleaned up, and with new spokes made by a REME (Royal Electrical & Mechanical Engineers) armourer, eventually the gun was brought back to England. Over the years, wherever the battery has been stationed, the 'Imjin Gun' has stood in pride of place in front of 170 Battery HQ, all recruits to the battery being told the history of the battle fought by their predecessors in April 1951 and of the provenance of the gun.

Much of May was surprisingly quiet all along the front line, so all spare bodies were put to work in building defensive bunkers for the first time, and preparing for the wet season that could break at any moment. Drainage ditches were dug, gun positions and OPs heavily wired in by the sappers and the infantry, who knew best about that activity. The major task of digging and roofing over a partially underground CP had us thinking that we could be there for some time. A vast quantity of ammunition was dumped on troop gun sites, as it was considered that supply was expected to be a problem once the rain started, especially to A Troop, which was positioned along a treacherous uphill track with the fusiliers.

As it was apparent that this was to be a permanent defended line, steps were taken to make the position as comfortable as possible. Rough cookhouses were erected from local tree trunks, rocks and discarded ammunition cases, building a low protective wall around the base with sandbags. A Troop dammed a stream to make a reasonable swimming hole, essential now that the weather was hotting up. There were dreadful warnings of the almost incessant rain we could expect in July. There was, in fact, very little rain in June, but the humidity had risen considerably, making life unpleasant. Mosquitoes and other insects, the known and the unknown, were plentiful, which brought forward another squadron of medics who sprayed men, clothing, equipment, food and much of North Korea it seemed with their DDT guns in the war against pestilence in previously unheard of form.

One day I watched, fascinated, a very large grey fly, the size of a bee, which had landed on my naked forearm. About to brush it off, I felt something pressed into my skin as it had the audacity to sting me. It was not so much the sting but what it had deposited into me that had me concerned. Under the surface of my skin I could see something that had not been there before. I squeezed around the red mark that this awful insect had left, and out popped a small wriggling grub. In recent times I have been told it was probably something called a bot fly, which lays its grub on a warm-blooded host, from where it will wriggle its way to places you don't want to hear about.

In terms of action, at this time there was little, apart from regular river crossings to ascertain how far the enemy had withdrawn and, on 10 June, 170 Battery was ordered to also provide support for 28 Brigade on our right flank. This was covered by A Troop who, due to a map-reading error, had arrived to cross the river at a place where there was no ford. On 13 June excitement mounted when we heard that a BBC recording team had been charged with making a short audio tape that was supposed to kid listeners at home into thinking they were listening to a recording made during the Imjin River Battle. We fired fifteen rounds for the benefit of the BBC, and we were all told to shout and make much noise, like the soundtrack of a Hollywood war film, imagining the paddy field to our front was swarming with enemy soldiers in their thousands. We all said it would not have sounded at all realistic without the sounds of MMGs, Brens, rifle shots and burp guns, plus the Chinese bugles, but no doubt the BBC would add all that to the soundtrack by intense editing back at the studio. Why on earth the team was sent so far, and spent so much money, when they could have ransacked their Second World War archives back at Broadcasting House in London if all they wanted was a soundtrack of warfare, I can't imagine.

Around that time it was announced that as the British, Australian and Canadian infantry battalions were sufficient to form three complete brigades, and as there were three field regiments of 25-pounders to support them, an 'Empire Division' was to be formed. There could well have been opposition to the title 'Empire' from one or more countries, so its title was changed to the 1st Commonwealth Division before operating as such. The three brigades would be 25 Canadian, which comprised the 2nd battalions of the Royal Canadian Regiment (2 RCR), the Royal 22eme Regiment (R22eR), an all-French-Canadian unit, and the Princess Patricia's Canadian Light Infantry (2 PPCLI). This latter battalion had been fighting in Korea since the end of 1950. The brigade was supported by Lord Strathcona's Horse (LSH) Sherman tanks, and 2nd Regiment Royal Canadian Horse Artillery (2 RCHA) with 25-pounders. The brigade was complete with transport, medical and ordnance units.

The Canadian gunners had been unfortunate to lose seventeen of their number before leaving Canada. They were being transported by Canadian National Railways to a training ground over the border in Washington State when they met full-on the Vancouver-Montreal express on the single track in the mountains. Several coaches disintegrated into matchwood, some falling far into the gorge below, killing some instantly while others were scalded to death by steam. A commemoration parade is held each year by the Royal Canadian Legion at the point of the crash, where a stone cairn marks the spot.

The 28 Commonwealth Brigade comprised 3 Royal Australian Regiment (3 RAR), which had also arrived in Korea late in 1950, initially the Argylls (1 A&SH), who had remained in Korea when 27 Brigade returned to Hong Kong in May and were now replaced by 1 King's Own Scottish Borderers (1 KOSB), and 1 King's Shropshire Light Infantry (1 KSLI). The 29 Brigade remained as before with the Royal Ulster Rifles, the Royal Northumberland Fusiliers and the Gloucestershires.

Excitement mounted on 18 June when our troop commander told us that 170 Battery was to be relieved by a mortar battery from Hong Kong in the October/November period. Spirits were high, and I looked forward to spending my remaining seven months in Hong Kong, the place I had enjoyed briefly on my outward journey. The move there would apply to only about half of the battery, as K-types and reservists would continue on home, and some National Servicemen who would have almost completed their two years. For us there would be no horrific winter, for which I was thankful, as it had been described to me by men who had suffered it. Some married personnel were already completing the paperwork to have their families brought out from England to meet up in Hong Kong.

A steady flow of reinforcements was maintained, although there was a shortage of regimental signallers with experience on the types of wireless equipment that we operated. The 22 set I had been trained on at Rhyl was unknown in Korea, where it had been superseded by the heavier 19 set, some of which must have been originally intended for Russia, as the figures on the fascia panel were in Cyrillic script. For OP work the 31 set, man-packed on the back, was normal.

When 1st Commonwealth Division (1 Comwel Div) was formed, the commander was named as Major General A.J.H. Cassels. The general paid a visit to every unit under his command, bringing with him when visiting artillery the newly appointed Commander Royal Artillery (CRA) Brigadier W.H. Pike, as well as some members of HQRA (Headquarters Royal Artillery), all of whom took a keen interest in our mortars and their performance.

During the CRA's visit, he announced that a second mortar battery was to be formed by converting much of 11 (Sphinx) Battery, although they would still retain a troop of their mobile Bofors, which had proved very successful when operating as heavy machine guns in a ground role. The 170 Battery had been advised they were to train the necessary people on mortars. Several officers and men from 11 (Sphinx) Battery were attached to our troops for about two weeks to learn the basic essentials. Then three mortars were 'borrowed' from each of our troops to form the nucleus of a mortar battery.

As we were short of signallers, I was not surprised one day to be informed that I was being sent on an upgrading course to enable me to instruct new arrivals in the intricacies of gunner wireless networks in a combat zone. That sounded good to me; perhaps I would be provided with lance bombardier stripes. I waited to be told I was going back to Seoul, or wherever a training school had been set up, where I would spend my days in a nice clean classroom with a load of new recruits. You can imagine my surprise to be informed I was going to a newly formed Commonwealth Artillery Training Centre (CATC) in the New Zealand base camp at Hiro, Japan.

Japan? Well, that was completely unexpected. Maybe I would get to see something of the country this time, and arrive back in Korea in time to prepare myself for Hong Kong. I had wanted adventure when I faced up to Tiger Mitchell in RHQ Office at Lincoln, but this was beyond anything I had anticipated. But before that happened, together with men from 1RUR, the Hussars and 45 Field, I was taken to the site of the January battle between the villages of Chaegunghyon and Pulmiji-ri. We witnessed a ceremony, during which Brigadier Brodie unveiled an obelisk of polished Korean granite that was inscribed on three of its sides, one side dedicated to the Royal Ulster Rifles, another to the 8th King's Royal Irish Hussars, a third to both the 45 Field Regiment and 170 Independent Mortar Battery, each commemorating 'Those who have died in Korea, especially those killed near this place 2nd to 4th January 1951'. The fourth side was engraved with something along the lines of 'Those who have lived in darkness have seen the light'. After the war the obelisk was brought back to Northern Ireland, where it was first re-erected in St Patrick's Barracks, Ballymena, the depot of the Royal Ulster Rifles. It has since been moved to its current resting place – pride of place in front of Belfast City Hall.

On the appointed day, battery transport took me to the railhead at Tokchon. The last time I had been conveyed by military train from Pusan the railhead had been further to the south, somewhere around Pyongtaek. This train was much more comfortable. I had been given an upgrade from cattle class to lower third class. Wooden stretcher-bearing bunks had been replaced by wooden seats, which were an improvement. Slowly at first we headed south through Uijongbu, reaching Seoul around mid-afternoon. There was a lengthy wait in the capital, during which time American Red Cross girls served free coffee and doughnuts to us. The train was now mostly filled with US Army and Marine personnel, as well as some other nationalities, all travelling south for different purposes.

I was on my way, much faster now. Stops were made at Suwon, Taejon, Taegu, and other places, where personnel disembarked. As the war had not returned that far south, it was a revelation to see how quickly rice paddies and fields of crops were showing much green growth. Pusan was reached around 2300 hrs.

With other men from 1 Comwel Div units, I was taken from the station to a transit camp on the outskirts of Pusan, where a comfortable night was spent in tented accommodation. Next morning it was off to the docks for all Japan-bound passengers. I boarded HMT *Dunera*, which had discharged its

HMT *Empire Fowey*. (© P&O Steam Navigation Company PLC)

The 56th US Army Band, which played all troopships in and out at Pusan.

A 4.2-inch mortar firing at close range, June 1951. Note the acute barrel angle.

A 25-pounder of 16 New Zealand Field Regiment.
(© Ian Mackley)

An 8-inch howitzer of 17FAB 'The Persuaders'.
(© US National Archives 111–SC–368738)

Mortars of 170 Mortar Battery on Route 11 during the withdrawal, April 1951.

The famous 'Captain X' sign, Hill 227.

Military policeman on traffic duty, Imjin River, spring 1951. (© IWM BF10243)

Trial river crossing of a 4.2-inch mortar on a Centurion tank.

Bofors of 11 (Sphinx) Battery firing on Hill 327, March 1951. (© IWM BF373)

Major Fisher-Hoch receiving the US Presidential Unit Citation, 8 May 1951. (© IWM31745)

Smashed Chinese 75mm mountain guns, Imjin River, May 1951.

The least damaged Chinese gun, the 'Imjin Gun', at Woolwich Barracks, 1988.

A 25-pounder of 176 Battery, 45 Field Regiment, Imjin River, April 1951.

The New Zealand Base Camp, Hiro, Japan, July 1951. (© Ian Mackley)

Typical mortar position, Hill 187N, east of the Samichon River.

16 Field Regiment RNZA on the move, Gloster Crossing. (© Ian Mackley)

Mortar detachment. The man on the right is smoking a pipe in the gun pit.

'This Could Be You' sign, US Marine Corps area, summer 1951.

Detachment of 120 Light Battery in camouflaged position.

The much smaller American 4.2-inch mortar, US 3rd Division.

The author posing with a
4.2-inch mortar.

The author in Hong Kong, 1954.

The author waiting for the boat home, Hiro,
Japan, July 1952.

'Easy 3' E Troop 120 Light Battery in mobile mode.

Korean porters and camp helpers, B Troop 170 Mortar Battery.

**YOUR BUDDIES ARE DOING FINE HERE
IN A POW CAMP**

From Dickie Grenies to Mrs. Amanda Grenies of Ring Street, Howland, Maine dated February 25th 1951.
"I am in fair health and in high spirits. We are receiving excellent treatment."

COME OVER! Join your buddies here. You will go to the rear in safety and get home in one piece.
Leave Korean to the Koreans.

------ USE THIS AS A SAFE CONDUCT PASS ------

When you see a Korean People's Army soldier or a Chinese Volunteer soldier, lay down your gun and shout:

投 "TOW SHONG" 降
(Surrender)

We guarantee you safe conduct and good treatment.

THE CHINESE PEOPLE'S VOLUNTEER FORCES

Typical Chinese leaflet inviting them to surrender.

Chinese Christmas card left by their barbed wire defences.

Dear Soldiers,
It is Christmas and you are far from home, suffering from cold not knowing when you will die.
The big shots are at home enjoying themselves, eating good food, drinking good liquor, why should you be here risking your life for their profits?
The Koreans and Chinese don't want to be your enemies. Our enemies and yours are those who sent you here and destroyed your happiness.
Soldiers! Lets join hands!
You belong back home with those who love you and want you back, safe and sound. So we wish you............

MERRY CHRISTMAS
AND
A HAPPY NEW YEAR
FROM
THE CHINESE PEOPLE'S VOLUNTEERS

Reverse of Chinese Christmas Card, often left with small plastic 'peace' doves.

Pintail Bridge under construction, Ulster Crossing. (©IWM 33256)

'Flying mortar' being moved by US Army helicopter. (© IWM BF11098)

Gunner 'Snowy' Carter posing for the camera.

The Daibutsu Buddha, Kamakura, Japan.

Portrait of the author by street artist, Tokyo, November 1951.

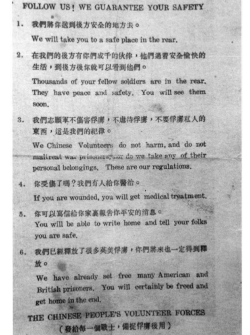

Another Chinese surrender leaflet.

The Chaegung-hyon memorial, re-erected at St Patrick's Barracks, Ballymena.

A 25-pounder at full recoil, 16 Royal New Zealand Field Regiment. (© Ian Mackley)

Chinese soldiers in front of their position on the first day of Peace, 28 July 1953.

Single mortar firing on DF target at night.

120 Light Battery truce position, Oridong, Kansas Line.

Captain Wisbey and the fit members of C Troop on release from POW camp, Woolwich, October, 1953.

HMT *Empire Pride*, 1942. (© Department of War Transport)

The currency with which
the British Armed Forces
were paid in Korea and
Japan.

The 'Ambassador for Peace' certificate
presented to the author in Seoul by Major
General (Retd) Tae-wan Chang, ROKA.

cargo of new replacements for British units, who were either travelling north immediately or were taken to the transit camp where they would occupy the tents we had vacated.

Sailing on the tide, *Dunera* was soon out of sight of the coastline and the islands of Japan appeared on the horizon, where our destination was Kure again.

Some of the infantry lads who had not disembarked at Pusan were heading for a battle school up in the mountains at Haramura to sharpen their infantry skills, or to where I had previously been billeted, the JRHU as BCRs. Accommodation on *Dunera* was on three-tier 'standees', as on the *Empire Fowey*, just for one night, and was far superior to that on the ancient *Po Yang*.

Kure had once been a major base for the Imperial Japanese Navy and was where the world's largest warships, the Yamato class battleships, had been built. The population had been roughly 150,000 before the United States Air Force firebombed the city prior to the dropping of the atom bomb on Hiroshima, just 14 miles away. By mid-1951, some rebuilding had taken place, but the buildings were mostly of timber, and they did not look very permanent to me. There was little above two storeys, apart from the British Military Base Hospital, which was quite a substantial building, and Kure House, a services club operated by the Australians. Kure railway station also seemed to be intact.

Kure itself was an unattractive place that had the advantage of nestling in a setting of natural beauty. Hills that became mountains in the near distance surrounded the vast harbour, where two of the Yamato class ships had been scuttled when Japan surrendered in 1945. One was the *Haruna* but I never learned the name of the other. Many men said it was actually the *Yamato*, but that ship had been sunk many miles away, south of Okinawa, in the closing days of the Second World War.

Together with four gunners, three from 16 RNZA, the other from 45 Field, I was taken to Acanthus Camp. It would be an easy walk over to the New Zealand base camp and then it was another easy stroll to the classroom each day. The instructors were a mix from all the Gunner units in Korea. My class included Kiwis and one Canadian, and our individual instructor was from 45 Field. He had been sent wounded to Kure, and had not returned to Korea. The CATC had been set up to ensure that all Gunner units in Korea used only standard Royal Artillery wireless procedures, as apparently some Americanisms had crept in, particularly among the Canadians, such as, 'Hey, you guys, I gotta fire mission for you,' instead of, 'Troop target, over.' Another reason was that potential instructors could be identified so that they could pass on all they had been taught when sent back to their units. This was great. My lance bombardier stripes and an increase in pay were just over the horizon.

I soon noticed that the classroom lessons were pretty basic. I had done it all before at Rhyl and Lincoln. But why should I curtail my time in Japan by telling them? Only an idiot would do that. When we started to go up into the hills to set up a wireless net with others who had been dropped off at various points all around the area, the sets we used were precisely the same equipment I had been using in Korea. Earning my stripe this way was going to be a doddle.

The weather was hot and quite humid down at Acanthus Camp but much more pleasant up in the hills, from where we could hear live firing from the battle school. After passing through some villages we would usually park up close to a large lake, possibly a reservoir, which was pure calendar art. The trees across the lake were usually mirrored on the water, without a ripple. The villages we passed through appeared to be in a nineteenth-century time warp. It looked as though nothing had changed since the days of the Samurai. Wood was the universal material used for everything. Houses were of unpainted timber, buckets were made from wooden staves, as in the practise of coopers and their beer barrels. Even shoes, called *geta*, were nothing more than a flat wooden platform raised above the dirt and mud by two chunks of wood beneath, with a strap across the toes to hold them on. They made an appalling clopping noise when walked on concrete. Village people generally wore traditional clothes, particularly the women and elderly men, but younger men usually wore western clothing.

When off duty I caught the free BCOF bus service into Kure, which also passed through the Australian married families' village, Niji Mura. We were told to use this service, not the civilian trams that plied the route from Hiro to Kure, as they were always crowded with civilians and were officially off-limits to us. I often used the trams, regardless. They were always packed with humanity, the people were always polite, making standing room for me, and the conductor would never accept my fare when offered. The tram rattled its way into Kure, where the final stretch was down a reasonably steep hill. The driver seemed to have a death wish about him, as the tram was allowed to freewheel and gather speed dramatically. I wondered if he was a leftover kamikaze pilot, as apparently some had been trained in the vicinity.

In town I spent many pleasant evenings in Kure House, where a good steak meal with all the trimmings cost three shillings and sixpence. That would usually be followed by a few bottles of Kirin lager in the Hikariso beer hall on Chome Nakadori (Nakadori Street). It was good beer.

On weekly pay parade we saluted the paying officer for our hard-earned cash, paid in British Armed Forces Special Vouchers – Baffs, the same currency we had been paid with in Korea. On receipt of our colourful notes we went to the next table to change one pound for 1,008 yen. We were expected to drop the odd eight yen into a Red Cross box, which was a good idea, and we knew it would be put to good use. In 1951, 1,000 yen was enough for a couple of good nights out painting the town red. Today, it will not even buy the paintbrush.

I spent three pleasant weeks at Acanthus Camp, picking up a few basic Japanese phrases from the girls who served our beer in the Hikariso. Once I was rostered for main gate guard, which was a good deal better than patrolling sentry. The latter had to patrol continuously between double rows of barbed wire about 8 feet high, which formed the perimeter of the camp. The problem with that duty was that they had to fend off local people who pestered them through the wire to sell them army clothing, and in particular blankets, which would end up on the black market as there was a shortage of good woollen cloth in Japan. I was given to understand that many illicit transactions were performed through the wire each night, the sentries turning a blind eye. After my course was completed I could sit back and wait to see when my stripes would be issued.

However, on roll call on the final Sunday morning, after the issue of Paludrine tablets, an important announcement was brought to our attention. We were confined to camp for the day. Disaster: no final steak meal at Kure House, nor a cold beer at Hikariso. When the assembled groans had subsided, an officer told us that the important announcement would be broadcast later in the day, at 1200 hrs, I believe, over the US Armed Forces radio service, 'Brought to you from Osaka/Nagoya, the twin cities of southern Honshu.' Those who had access to wireless sets told us the message was being repeated every thirty minutes. It appeared that all military personnel in Japan, and there were large numbers of Americans stationed there, were all confined to quarters.

The rumours started immediately: Eighth Army had been notified that an A-bomb was about to be dropped on Pyongyang, or even on Peking – on orders from President Truman; the truce negotiations that had just started at Kaesong had reached a conclusion and the war was over; and even that all British troops were to be paid the same as the Aussies (wishful thinking). And so it went on, all morning. Of course, as always, the barrack-room lawyers were hopelessly wrong, although money did come into it.

The important message, when it came, informed all United States and other military personnel in Japan that the US military scrip (payment certificates) they were paid in, like our Baffs, were being replaced by a new issue, and that consequently the current issue was obsolete and worthless. This was done to ensure that Japanese entrepreneurs who had managed to acquire massive illegal holdings of scrip could not benefit from their wealth. In camp we were advised that anyone who had scrip could hand it in against a receipt at 1200 hrs, and it would be replaced with the new minting at 1800 hrs. The only ones among us who ought to have any scrip were the Canadians, who were paid in it. They agreed to change any we might have. As the Japanese black marketeers must have lost vast fortunes, I imagine the suicide rate increased dramatically on that Sunday, in a country where in the past they would have thrown themselves on their Samurai swords.

The next day, my pleasant sojourn in Japan was over. It was time to say *sayonara* (farewell). I would have enjoyed a permanent posting to Japan, where I found a few basic words in Japanese had been easy to learn, but it was not to be. It was back across the water for me. Boarding an American military train at Hiro Station, we were told not to leave the train at any intermediate station before we reached a place called Sasebo, nor were we to try to sell our clothing to civilians along the way. With no map available we had no idea where Sasebo was, but the train was comfortable, spotlessly clean, being kept that way by the civilian cleaners who were on the go all the time.

We had been notified that we would be fed. Contemplating C rations, when it was our turn to head to the chow line, we moved along the swaying train to see what might be on offer. It was a proper hot meal, served on thick cardboard plates, and I have to say it was of a high order. We passed along the line of servers, each adding meat or vegetables, the final being a yellow vegetable I had not seen before, onto which a creamy sauce was spooned. It was very unusual, very colourful. I thought it must be an American specialty. It was only on tasting it back in my compartment that I realized it was canned pineapple and custard mingling with the gravy from the roast beef. Well, it saved on plates.

On my way to the feeding coach I had noticed a map of the rail system in another compartment. Finishing my meal, I made my way back there, excused myself to the seated Americans, and enquired if anyone knew where Sasebo might be. It was pointed out to me. When I returned to my mates I told them we would have to leave the train soon and catch a ferry, as our destination was on another island. Our train had been diving in and out of countless tunnels all day, so it was no surprise that after passing through Shimonoseki Station we rattled through an exceptionally long one. It was only on reaching Moji Station and daylight again that I realized we were then on the other island. That last very long tunnel ran right under the Shimonoseki Strait, which separates the islands of Honshu and Kyushu. It was a marvellous piece of Japanese railway engineering. Sasebo, I discovered, is a port city on the northern coast of Kyushu. In the 1950s it was a major supply base for the United States Navy and other navies operating off the Korean coast. As we would discover, it was also a jumping-off point for American troops on their way to Korea or rotating back home.

Collected from Sasebo Station, we arrived at an enormous tented US Army Replacement Depot, where two nights would be spent while being processed for the next ship leaving for Pusan. We were shown where our tent was, and also where to head for the evening meal, which was about to be served. As far as I can remember, we were the third sitting in this huge camp. Lining up, one of our sergeants enquired where the senior NCOs' entrance was, to which he was replied to by a mere PFC (private, first class), 'If you want to eat, hit the back of the chow line,' which probably did not go down too well. The meal, like the private, was first-class. There was a considerable choice of roast or grilled meats and a vast selection of vegetables, followed by as much apple, cherry or apricot pie or canned fruit and ice cream as a man could swallow. And this was the Army? Yes, sadly not ours. But it was at breakfast the following morning where the cooks really excelled.

'Revelly', as they pronounced it, was in the middle of the night, or so it seemed when we woke to hear the dulcet tones of a senior NCO in whose area our tent was situated. His voice hit my eardrums, yelling, 'OK, you guys, get the hell out of those cots and police the area before you hit the chow line.' I think he meant 'good morning'. By cots we knew he referred to the folding wood and canvas beds we had slept on, but 'police the area' was quite new. Did he mean check the barbed wire perimeter for any break-in during the night? It turned out to mean we had to patrol the entire area around our tent to pick up every scrap of paper, cigarette butt, piece of chewing gum, blade of grass or misplaced grain of sand that might annoy yet another senior non-com member of the United States Army. Where did they find all these 6ft 6ins master sergeants? Did they grow them? Our greeting for the day that lay ahead did not go down too well with some of the lads. Then it was a quick shower outside in the open, and a shave, after which it was time to head for the chow line.

I joined the end of the line, picking one of those compartmented 'aloominum' trays. It was self-service. I picked up a small carton of milk to pour over any of a wide choice of cereals, and passed along the counter. White bread, brown bread, plain or toasted – take as many as you wished – and then I had reached the hot press, where food was piled in glorious heaps, taking bacon, sausages and toast. A civilian cook enquired how I wanted my eggs. I thought, well, hopefully on my tray, of course. What he had actually said was 'howyouwanyouegg', or something very similar. I told him 'two, over easy', which were cooked to order and slapped on my tray. I headed for the coffee dispenser, having turned down a selection of various types of doughnut and other pastries. It was some breakfast. We all agreed that we would not see the likes of Sasebo again, not in our army.

Around mid-afternoon on the second day we were collected for the short journey to the docks, where our ship awaited, this time a civilian one that had at one time been a cargo vessel on the Japan to West Africa run. On descending to the depths I found that troop accommodation was not on three-tier bunks, but on wall-to-wall *tatami*, the mats of rice straw that traditional houses in Japan are fitted with. We were allocated one *tatami* apiece, which might have been fine for the smaller oriental form, but not for a 6ft soldier with all his kit. Men did sort of overflow onto the neighbouring *tatami*, getting to know fellow travellers rather well in the confined space. As in a Japanese house, we had to remove our footwear to avoid damaging the *tatami*.

Thankfully, the crossing to Pusan was short. I am unable to recall if we were fed on the voyage; probably not, but we had eaten well at Sasebo. An American had crawled over to say 'Hi', asking if he could look at my Lee Enfield. He was incredulous to find it was a single-shot bolt-action rifle, wondering how on earth we managed to operate the bolt without taking our eye off the target. There were also a few Belgian replacements, easily identified by their brown berets with crown and rampant lion cap badge.

Berthing at the familiar dock in Pusan, with the customary aroma still surmounting everything else, I noticed that the band was now fitted up with chromium-plated steel helmets, which gleamed in the sunlight. I spent one night and most of the following day in the transit camp, and then it was the short journey back to the station and train to the north. Like General MacArthur's famous statement in the Second World War on wading ashore in the Philippines for the benefit of the massed cameramen who had already arrived, after he had spent most of the war in Australia: I had returned.

Chapter Six

Static Warfare, Heat, Rain and Mud

Following a night and much of the next day in transit, I arrived at Seoul, where one of 170 Battery drivers, who had already rounded up two other lads returning to the battery after recovering from their April wounds, collected my kit and threw it onto the truck. Before I knew it I was back. The battery had moved to new positions while I had been in Japan, which explained why I did not recognize the scenery, assuming the driver was taking a new route to the old position.

Since the April Chinese offensive, their attacks had reduced considerably and talks of an armistice had commenced at Kaesong on 10 July. But on that day another form of fighting had commenced – a battle fought across the conference table, although there was no lull in the fighting on the hills. On that first day of peace talks, the UN Command reported sixteen killed, sixty-four wounded and fifteen missing in action across the front line. It was not yet time to pack up and go home. Infighting started on day one of the talks, with the communists refusing to concede any point that might make it appear they would lose face to the mainly Americans across the table, who were seated on lower chairs to give the communists equal height at eye level, and therefore equal status. Unbelievably, that fighting still continues at Panmunjom to this day, the village where the 1953 Korean Armistice Agreement was signed.

I remember being rudely awakened that first morning back in B Troop by the most almighty explosion. Waiting for the bugles and burp guns, I leapt up from my bedroll, wondering why I was the only one who had moved, although curses came from underneath the other mounds of bedding. Wondering why we were not at stand-to positions, I staggered out as another tremendous crack rent the air, and felt the flash and shockwave as one of the 8th Hussars Centurions fired its mighty 20-pounder away to the front. In the darkness the previous night I had not realized the tank was in a hull-down position right on top of our location. Tanks were not popular with us as they could fire and then reverse away a few yards below the ridgeline before retaliatory fire was returned by the Chinese. But it takes all sorts to fight a war.

Following the stand on the Imjin River in April, and one or two minor activities, the summer months were seeing much activity of a static nature right across the front. The wet season brought all the attendant hardships. Roads became impassable seas of deep mud, rivers overflowed their banks and a fair amount of digging and wiring was essential. I found several new faces had appeared in B Troop during my absence. New officers had moved in, but most of the old crew were still there. They confirmed that we were to be posted to Hong Kong in a little over three months. I looked forward to that with pleasure, as rats, lice and other abominations had now appeared, making life for the trench-bound squaddie only slightly less than bloody awful. Targets were being fired on whenever they presented themselves, and harassing fire (HF) broke into the sleeping patterns of us all.

As I had heard nothing about my promotion, when the battery clerk next arrived on site with the pay I asked him. He said he knew nothing but would get back to me. When he did I was shot down in flames; there was no stripe for this gunner, although my pay grade had been boosted to five-star. Whether or not that equated to lance bombardier rank I had no idea. I do not recall much about the star rating, but it could have been that one-star pay was awarded after passing out of basic training and then you worked your way up. I had no shop steward with whom to lodge a grievance. I thought, 'Oh, well, Hong Kong is just over the horizon!' I knew I would have extra pay there, as an overseas allowance was paid, although I never understood why it was paid in a peaceful station but not in Korea, where hardships were suffered.

By August it was plain to see that some major activity was planned, while we continued to consolidate our newly-dug positions on Kansas Line. Whilst the Imjin River Battle for us had been of a defensive nature, it seemed certain that a major offensive was about to be mounted in an attempt to take and hold territory north of the river. The barrack-room lawyers said it would not be long before we would be involved in this major advance, but apparently it was uncertain just how far back from the river the Chinese had settled. Light observation aircraft flew daily missions over the hills and valleys. The pilots reported that no enemy could be seen close to the river, but they were digging into a range of tall hills away to the north, as evidenced by the fresh earthworks they saw daily. Long-ranging infantry patrols forded the Imjin at night, usually with a gunner forward observation officer and his team accompanying them, often remaining over the river for three or four days to watch for enemy movement, and for an attempt at taking prisoners. I was co-opted onto several such forays with B Troop FOOs.

On a typical three-day, two-night assignment with a platoon-sized patrol with the infantry, I would be weighed down with everything bar the kitchen sink. If I had been an American, I would undoubtedly also have been carrying a couple of hand grenades, but I left those to my infantry colleagues. I carried quite enough kit to restrict movement as it was.

I followed in the footsteps of my officer, wading the dark river two hours before first light and heading into the unknown, pleased that the moon was behind cloud cover to obscure our careful progress and hoping no enemy were watching. Reaching the north bank, we changed into dry socks and made tracks northward, walking along the raised paddy bunds as we moved away from the river. I assumed that if I followed in someone's footsteps, if they did not explode a mine, neither would I. I wondered that, had I been the officer, would I have sent my signaller ahead of me, just in case? We occasionally slipped into the stinking ooze as we continued to our objective, which was to consolidate about 2 miles north of the river and then to lie up in cover for much of the next day.

Not knowing if the enemy would spring on us at any time, I expect we all carried our hearts in our mouths for the first hour or so, as we were well aware that the enemy preferred to attack under cover of darkness. Reaching our intended location, the only sounds were those coming from the bullfrogs in the paddies, whose continual roaring miraculously ceased before dawn, which was the origin of one of Korea's names – Land of the Morning Calm. I hoped it would remain calm, not just in the morning but for much of the next day as well. With a 50 per cent stand down at first light I had to admit I felt vulnerable sitting there amid a stand of stunted pines that would offer limited cover from prying Chinese eyes, and even less from shell or mortar fragmentation. But it all seemed eerily quiet as I heated a breakfast can of C rations on my Tommy's Cooker. This piece of kit was a small folding apparatus on which a solid fuel tablet that smelled of methylated sprit was placed, usually managing to singe my fingertips in the process of lighting it. I finished off such al fresco meals with a mug of lukewarm pseudo coffee, if there was enough heat left on the Tommy's Cooker.

Later in the morning, the FOO gathered me up from where I had been idly watching the paddies playing poker for cigarettes. I was told we were moving forward with a section of riflemen in a probing movement. Checking battery strength on my 31 set, cocking and applying the safety catch on my Sten (not that many men considered it a safe weapon), I followed dry-mouthed in the FOO's footsteps. In my mind I imagined the enemy was watching our every move from those distant hills, which were now not so distant. We passed by a partially destroyed village, where three civilians were spotted. An interpreter was despatched, probably to tell them to head south while they had the opportunity, as all hell could break out at any minute, and they would once more be engulfed in warfare at close quarters.

The first day passed reasonably quietly, although I did have to call on one section of mortars to engage suspected locations where the enemy might be likely to ambush us, but with no retaliation from the Chinese. We ate our lukewarm C rations, made more pseudo coffee and finally, after standing-to at last light, we gunners rolled up in blanket and poncho under an ominous sky. It was the wet season and it looked like it would rain. It did. In the small hours the heavens opened for about thirty minutes, soaking everything and everybody. Stand-to at first light saw us in a very bedraggled state, as another box of C rations was opened, and a breakfast of sorts was enjoyed. During the second equally uneventful day, still progressing slowly to the north, on two occasions I had to radio back target co-ordinates to the 25-pounders of 176 Battery of 45 Field Regiment, as we had advanced to well beyond the capability of our mortars.

Any shell-blasted dwelling, potential ambush or hiding place for an enemy artillery observer who might be silently watching our approach, received the benefit of the field gunners' expertise, before we moved forward again, the infantry advancing in what I believe was called extended line formation. Then, for the second time, we lay on wet earth, alert to the night sounds, hoping for some fitful sleep and an uneventful night. It was another routine night as far as our enemy was concerned, but it rained again, as expected. Our clothes, which had dried on us in a rare sunny period during the day, were once more saturated. But we knew that unless the Chinese had plans for us, we would, after removing three days' stubble, sleep more comfortably the next night at the troop position.

During the final day of this probing patrol, several shoots were carried out with no enemy retaliation. They could well have been sitting it out, watching us without disclosing their locations to us. The infantry sent half-sections forward at intervals, all returning to declare NTR (nothing to report): no enemy movements, no minefields encountered and, thankfully, no casualties. Two men brought back a family they had found wandering in no-man's-land, heavily burdened with everything they had been able carry as they headed, with hope, for the safety of the south. They were given some harsh treatment by the interpreter, who seemed to enjoy checking their loads. He said he had been searching for weapons, but he might have hoped to find a stash of money or valuables to extract from them. That he needed to be so tough on his fellow countrymen caused us to question his motives, but he said they could be spies from the north. After all, we were in North Korea. They were, of course, all of the same race, northerner and southerner alike, but it was a dangerous time, when brother was wary of brother. When I discussed these operations over the river with a late colleague several years ago, we reminisced over another excursion when he and I were trapped on the north bank from 2 to 6 August due to heavy flooding further upriver. That time we had the Belgians to our right. The Imjin rose an incredible 14 feet during the day, a raging torrent that swept everything in its path. We were cut off and at the mercy of the Chinese if they heard a whisper of our predicament. There were other infantry on this probing sweep over the Imjin, who were on our left flank, possibly the Canadians. We had not anticipated the sudden flooding at the time, or we would have been better prepared before starting out.

On our final day on the wrong side of the river, we had run short of rations and someone, it must have been the Belgians, to our right, arranged for an air drop by helicopter. It was more or less successful, the majority of the containers landing close enough, but we went hungry on that unplanned extra day as the loads when unpacked contained ammunition, which was useful, of course, but no food. Supplies did reach us later that day, by either Royal Engineers or US Army Engineers, by ferry. The Belgians fired on targets on two occasions. Eventually we were taken back to the south bank by the ferry.

Although there was almost continuous rain for the remainder of August, it was still confirmed that our enemy had not moved from his line of defence away to the north. The narrow dirt roads had become seas of mud, some up to 80 feet wide, as drivers drove further and further away from the original line to keep out of the deep mud. I did see signs erected by the Royal Military Police, reading, 'KEEP OUT OF THE RUTS. MAKE YOUR OWN TRACKS'. Many telephone lines were carried away at this time, giving signallers a muddy time when making repairs.

Since the April battles on the Imjin River and on the Pukhan River at Kapyong there had been departures and arrivals within the Commonwealth brigades. The 27 Brigade, the first British troops in Korea the previous September, had been replaced by 28 Brigade from Hong Kong. The 1st Middlesex were first to depart, relieved by 1st King's Shropshire Light Infantry, who had landed at Inchon on USS *Montrose* on 13 May. The 1st Argyll and Sutherland Highlanders were replaced during the battle at Kapyong by 1st King's Own Scottish Borderers. The 28 Brigade had been renamed 28 Commonwealth Brigade, due to its mix of British and Australian infantry and the New Zealand artillery regiment. The tanks of 8th King's Royal Irish Hussars (8KRIH) continued to provide their excellent support wherever it was needed.

The task of 1 Comwel Div was to defend the area fought over in April, and now extending further to the west to include the Samichon River valley. At this time, while the peace talks that had continued at Kaesong had reached stalemate and were abandoned, it was known that the Chinese armies were using the lull in the fighting to regroup, resupply, improve their artillery capability beyond anything encountered to date, and construct massive defensive works in the hills they occupied about 4½ miles north of the Imjin River. In 170 Battery, most of August was used advantageously to strengthen our defences, as it appeared that the front line had also reached stalemate.

We had to dig in and wait to see what our enemy's next move would be. Divisional artillery now consisted of three field regiments with seventy-two 25-pounders in total, two mortar batteries and a troop of 40mm Bofors. We could also call on the magnificent heavy artillery of the US Army artillery battalions. More or less attached to 29 Brigade was Battery C, 17th Field Artillery Battalion (17 FAB), known as 'The Persuaders', which was painted on the barrels of their superb 8-inch howitzers.

During August all men in 170 Battery who had arrived the previous November and who had not been on R&R were advised to give their names to the BSM, or they would miss the opportunity before our replacement battery arrived in November. I had not arrived until March and I decided the BSM would find me extra duties if I enquired about five days in Japan. Now it looked as though we would not occupy our newly constructed defensive bunkers, communication trenches and fighting pits for very long. All that hard work might go to waste. Rumours abounded that during the month the entire United Nations forces would commence a general advance once more right across the Korean peninsula. The rumourmongers had it right this time, as we were ordered to start preparations for a major advance north of the Imjin, and our well-dug defences would be a fall-back location if we were forced to abandon the plan and return to our defences on what would become Kansas Line. We wondered what lay ahead. Intelligence reports considered that the Chinese Army occupying the territory to our immediate front that had replaced the 63rd Army, which had suffered catastrophic and probably unsustainable losses in April, was now better equipped. To that point they had relied almost entirely on full-scale use of infantrymen ordered into an attack, seemingly with no regard to casualties. From August 1951, all that would change. Would the next major battle be like those in April, or would it be much worse? Time alone would tell.

During the summer our patrols had established that the enemy did not permanently occupy positions close to the river, although observation excursions under cover of night right down to the river were possible. Their permanent positions were still in the line of tall hills, about 8,000 yards further north. The 1 Comwel Div was tasked initially with advancing from Kansas Line to a new defensive line about 4 miles distant that would be called Wyoming Line. Both 25 Canadian and 28 Commonwealth brigades, with attached artillery and other personnel borrowed from 29 Brigade, would be involved. The move was titled Operation *Minden* and 1 KOSB were to remain on the river to cover a US Army Engineer unit that was building a permanent bridge across the Imjin at the ford that had become known as Gloster Crossing. The bridge was needed for supplying 1 Comwel Div once the new defensive line on Wyoming was occupied. All available armour, artillery and engineer units would be utilized in Operation *Minden* and a section of 60 Indian Field Ambulance was moved to the north bank to attend to anticipated casualties, which could be heavy. The three troops of 170 Battery were once more with their respective infantry battalions, while 29 Brigade would loan units to the selected advance troops. In B Troop we would support our old friends 1 RUR, and C Troop was once again with the newly reformed 1 Glos. B Troop and 1 RUR were to occupy the ridges above Chagundu-il and other features marked on our maps as Parak and Noru-gul to the right of the brigade positions. In the centre 1 Glos and C Troop occupied ridges running to the south-west of 1 RUR, and on the left flank 1 RNF moved to Hill 112 and a ridge feature known by 1 KOSB as Edinburgh Castle.

To the right of 29 Brigade, 25 Canadian Brigade had established itself with US 1st Cavalry Division to its right. On our left was 1st ROK Division. It was revealed to us that the move to Wyoming Line would not be our home for long. It would only be the starting point for a further offensive move forward to the hills occupied by the Chinese after they had been removed from them by a strong infantry assault, supported by all the available artillery and armour.

The river was too deep for fording due to flooding caused by heavy downpours upriver. Some pontoon bridges had washed away or were otherwise unusable. Meanwhile, the high-level timber trestle bridge at Gloster Crossing, now referred to as Teal Bridge, had been completed. (The three main crossings of the Imjin in 1 Comwel Div area were named after different species of wild duck.) A further bridge position was being surveyed for another crossing that became Pintail Bridge, immediately in front of the location where the Ulsters had been sent in the abortive attempt to extract us from Hill 195. Thus B and C troops were deployed in adjacent defiles with the reformed Glosters, with A Troop in a position from where they could cover three companies of the fusiliers. Later, a third river bridge was constructed at the Samichon River position called Widgeon.

While we sat on Kansas Line waiting for the move to Wyoming, occasionally we would be trucked to the Mobile Army Bath Unit on the Imjin, which was marvellous in the hot, sticky weather. It comprised three large marquee tents fixed end to end. The first tent was where all our disgusting clothes were dropped, the second was rigged up with one long overhead pipe that dispensed hot water through shower heads, and the third was where we wiped dry and changed into clean clothes from the skin out. We felt like new men as we left the bath unit. However, as we did not enjoy that facility very often, I had located an isolated trickling stream at the bottom of the other side of the ridge we occupied. I thought it would be an ideal place to enjoy an invigorating wash-down. The water, from an unknown source but which appeared to be coming from a spring higher up, would definitely not be for drinking without using sterilizing tablets, but was fine for cleansing the body. I investigated further until I came upon a place that looked as though it had been used by the village ladies to wash clothing, which they could then dry in the hot sun on two large flat slabs of rock. I had the entire valley to myself. Drying off one day on one of the rocks, slapping away the flies, my pleasure was terminated by an unmistakable sound. You have one second, two if you are lucky, no more, to prostrate yourself instantly on hearing it. The whirring, followed a second later by a soggy explosion in the adjacent paddy sludge, told me I had been the target of a small-bore mortar bomb. Assuming that it was not one of ours and that I had been the target of an unfriendly Chinaman, I grabbed my trousers, pulling them on at the run. I was racing back to the safety of the ridgeline when another explosion sounded from the position where I had been sunning myself. As least I was not bracketed as I headed through the barbed wire, which had been flattened by person or persons unknown.

Reaching safety, I felt a sharp pain in my left leg, behind the knee. I clamped a hand over the affected area and it came away bloody. I wondered how I would explain that away. But it was all right, no Chinaman could claim having eliminated me that day; I had merely jagged myself on the barbed wire. I still called it 'my war wound' until February 2009, after which my knee was not there any longer. I almost collided with a young RUR officer who must have come to see what the explosions had been about. He asked me who I was and where I had come from, wondering why I was half-undressed. I told him I was from the mortar troop and I had also been attracted by the explosion. I am sure he did not believe me, and probably thought dress standards ought to be tightened up in the mortar troop. I got away with it, but after that episode I stuck to using the official bath unit.

While in that position we very occasionally had a visit by a mobile NAAFI 'shop'. Most of the time the driver was unable to reach our position as the vehicle was in no way suitable for Korean dirt tracks, and to me it always seemed to be top-heavy. There was little on sale that I had a requirement for, apart from orange squash, which made a big improvement to our heavily chlorinated drinking water supplied by the Royal Engineers from available streams. However, I splashed out one day on the largest bar of Cadbury's finest. Thinking I would eat some of the chocolate the next day I put it on an alcove I had dug out of the earth at the side of my bunker for my personal belongings. Next morning it had gone. All that remained were scraps of aluminium foil and rat droppings. I really ought to have known better. How the rat climbed 3 feet up a sheer dirt wall was beyond me. That was the last food item that I saved to consume the following day. The rats had become a menace. And the fleas they carried were even more of a menace.

During our advance from Kansas to Wyoming Line there were a number of officer changes in the battery, including the departure of B Troop Commander, Captain Tony Fowle, who himself had been posted in from 45 Field to replace Captain John Lane, killed at Chaegunghyon. Our new troop commander was Captain Warren. Major Fisher-Hoch, our BC, had been relieved by Major Lewis. We now established a battery tac HQ at 29 Brigade HQ, about half a mile south of Choksong, the first village to be overrun by the Chinese in April at the start of the Imjin River Battle.

On Wyoming Line our existence was relatively peaceful initially, except for minor patrolling action on 1 Glos and 1 RNF fronts. After our move there followed the usual consolidation period, identifying new targets to register, such as enemy OPs, FUPs (forming-up points) and the location of newly-dug communication trenches that connected deep bunkers, as well as DFs to protect our positions if it appeared that we were about to be overrun. On 16 September, after having spent little more than two weeks with us, the newly arrived Captain Warren was killed while operating as FOO on a 1 RUR patrol. They had been ambushed near Hill 179, a favourite Chinese ambush location.

By mid-September it was plain to see that another big move forward, Operation *Commando*, was in the late planning stages. The name for the next defended line we would move to, about 6,000 yards to the north, was Jamestown Line. Originally it was intended that 29 Brigade would carry out a diversionary raid on Kumhwa-ri, and then return to Wyoming Line. The 170 Battery would take part in the raid and join 28 Brigade on the extreme right of 1 Comwel Div front. On 24 September, two companies from 1 RNF moved to Hill 169 to cover recce parties. They came under heavy small arms fire from the north and north-west. Our battery recce parties found suitable gun positions in the area, but due to only light enemy retaliation the diversionary raid was considered unnecessary.

There were two dominant features on Jamestown Line, the capture and occupation of which had been assigned to 1 Comwel Div. They were named on our maps as Kowang-san and Maryang-san, known to us as Hills 355 and 317 respectively. Aerial reconnaissance had reported that both high points were the subject of massive earthworks, tunnels and bunkers, observation posts, communication trenches and possible ammunition stores deep underground. The Chinese gave every impression that they intended to stay. Dislodging them would be no picnic.

Military strategy of the period dictated that an attacking force should ideally outnumber entrenched enemy defenders by a minimum of three to one. It looked as though we would have plenty to keep us occupied as our numbers were very much in the minority given the breadth of the Chinese defensive lines. Our enemy, in well-fortified positions, was reported to be of two-division strength, about 18,000 men, almost all of whom were infantry soldiers. With two divisions dug in on the area of our objective, we were faced with the certain knowledge that we would once again be greatly outnumbered.

For the advance to Jamestown Line two augmented Commonwealth brigades would participate – 1 RUR from 29 Brigade was attached to 25 Canadian Brigade while 1 RNF and 170 Battery were moved over to support 28 Brigade. The plan was for 1 KOSB to attack and hold Hill 355, 1 KSLI would take Hills 210 and 227, and 3 RAR on the right flank had the more difficult Hill 317 as their objective. The loaned battalion, 1 RNF, had been allocated the task of taking Hill 217 to the west of Hill 317. The initial plan for 170 Battery was to provide a creeping barrage of white phosphorous to obscure the advance of 1 KOSB. I had wondered why huge quantities of smoke rounds had been stockpiled on troop positions since our arrival on Wyoming Line.

But first the Chinese positions were the subject of the heaviest barrage yet laid down by 1 Comwel Div artillery since the start of hostilities in Korea. At 0300 hrs on 3 October, more than 120 guns and mortars, including US 1 Corps 8-inch howitzers and 155mm, both towed and self-propelled, commenced firing on known or suspected enemy artillery locations, machine-gun emplacements and FUPs. The infantry started to move up as the creeping barrage continued, supported by tanks of the ever-faithful 8th King's Royal Irish Hussars. On the Canadian front the main objectives were Hills 187 and 159 for 2 PPCLI, a second hill also numbered 187 for 2 RCR, while the attached 1 RUR was given the task of taking and holding the ground between the villages of Yongdong and Chom-mal. First into action was 1 RUR, and by mid-afternoon they reported that they had managed to secure their objectives.

By 5 October, both 2 PPCLI and 2 RCR had signalled success. To the right of the Commonwealth attack, 3 RAR had the most difficult task. The ground they had to advance across was wild country in the extreme, with overgrown dry rice paddies that could have hidden mines. It was heavily timbered and the battalion had to cross several ridges and small hillocks. To their immediate front lay the pyramidal peak of Hill 317. It was imperative that both Hills 355 and 317 should be in United Nations hands, to protect the vulnerable left flank of US 1st Cavalry Division (1 CAV).

At 0300 hrs on 3 October, the Australians commenced their attack, but due to unexpectedly strong defending by the Chinese, their objective had not been secured by last light. Only after putting in an attack on an adjoining feature the following morning, and then continuing straight up Hill 317 after taking many casualties, were 3 RAR in occupation on Maryang-san. Later, the name of that hill would be emblazoned as a battle honour on the regimental colour of the Third Battalion of the Royal Australian Regiment, and the Battle of Maryang-san passed into Australian military folklore.

With friendly forces to their immediate right, and under our continuing smoke-screening, it was not long before 1 KOSB completed their task, having successfully secured Hill 355. Attacks supported by the Hussars tanks were made against other hills in the area, notably those that had been designated Baldy, Brown Knoll (known to the Aussies as the 'Brown Bastard') and The Hinge. For 170 Battery to support 28 Brigade it had been necessary for us to move by a very circuitous route from the extreme left of 1 Comwel Div positions to the extreme right. As the direct route was in full view of the Chinese, a number of detours had to be made. In part, that was a diversion tactic to mislead the enemy as to where the attack would commence.

On 1 October, A and B troops had moved to a hide after crossing a fording point known as Whistler. On arrival it was found that fording was not possible for anything smaller than a 3-ton truck. The actual river crossing was eventually made in boats of the US Army Engineers. The following day, 2 October, I went out with a recce party to find a suitable position that was within range of our objective, Hill 355. Later we were joined in that position by C Troop. At last light on 2 October, full recce parties moved forward to prepare the positions. We moved off at 2359 hrs and reported that we were in action at 0600 hrs on 3 October. As our position was now in front of the infantry, one company of R22eR covered the battery until 1 KOSB and 1 KSLI had moved through. As soon as practicable we moved to re-entrants (small ravines) on the north side of a track between the river ford and the village of Ukkowang-san.

On 3 October, from 0730 hrs to 1600 hrs, we continued to pour smoke rounds onto the target hills, and this was called for again on several occasions on 4 October. By now A Troop had been ordered to test the tracks running north on either side of Hill 355 for the support of the fusiliers.

In B Troop, together with C Troop, we similarly attempted the route north from the village of Kangso-ri as far as Kojanha-ri. It was discovered that the route was usable only by jeeps and tracked vehicles. At first light on 4 October,

I went with the GPOs of B and C troops on a recce forward to find and prepare a position for our mortars at a point about a mile south-east of Hill 317. We reported that the track seemed passable now for all battery vehicles, allowing the combined troops to move through. It was found later that all the Oxford carriers had either broken down or were bogged down in deep mud.

Movement forward was by the bed of a stream, the banks having been found to have been mined by the Chinese and were awaiting clearance by the Royal Engineers. On 5 October, both troops found a joint position in the stream bed. Meanwhile, A Troop had not succeeded in finding a passable track, having to go into action near Kowang-ni, from where they were just able to range with HE on 1 RNF's final objective. It would have been difficult to use white phosphorous, as smoke had a reduced range compared with high explosive.

It was in that location that B Troop commander, knowing his guns were short of HE, asked BHQ to provide him with as many rounds as possible from the echelon that was holding supplies for ready use. We sent a truck back to load the rounds as we were too low to do much good if the Chinese counter-attacked and made a complete withdrawal necessary. On the return journey the truck was forced to give way to a heavily-laden Canadian vehicle to allow it to pass downhill. Our vehicle struck a powerful mine on the soft shoulder, demolishing the truck and killing two mates, Gunners Bob Dowkes and Harry Breakwell, and seriously wounding Gunner Peter Gore. The ammunition was transferred to another truck and brought up to the troop position. Peter Gore was removed initially to NORMASH (Norwegian Mobile Army Surgical Hospital), and then to a military hospital in Pusan, where he made a complete recovery and later returned to the troop.

By 5 October, 1 RNF reached Hill 217, but they were held up by heavy machine-gun fire. Further efforts were made against Hill 217 and The Hinge, but once again they were unsuccessful. Hill 217 and a nearby feature called United were finally taken on 5 October. That night the infantry company on The Hinge was heavily counter-attacked, necessitating all 170 Battery troops to fire many DF tasks, which were controlled by the infantry FOO, due to our FOO, Lieutenant 'Paddy' Breene, having been wounded. A Troop, whose route was completely under observation, were shelled as they came out of action. Sergeant Evans and Bombardier Moran were wounded. One mortar and one truck were damaged. Lieutenant Breene did not rejoin the battery until it had arrived in Hong Kong.

On 7 October, enemy artillery became very active for the first time. As the Royal Engineers had now cleared the stream banks of mines, B and C troops moved temporarily into re-entrants. By 8 October, the position had been made firm and no further advances were made. That left 170 Battery in an untidy state. A and B troops were with the wrong battalions, requiring a move by A Troop to join 1 KOSB and B Troop to move into a position in close support with 1 KSLI, who had taken over Hill 355.

Operation *Commando* was declared a resounding success. A letter of appreciation was received by 1 Comwel Div HQ from the American General 'Iron Mike' O'Daniel, Commander of I Corps, of which we were a part, reading as follows:

It was a masterful manouver [*sic*] skilfully combining aggressiveness and complete detailed planning, resulting in the taking of key terrain features with a minimum cost in manpower and the exploitation of firepower. The capture of critical terrain was conducted in a manner fully in keeping with the finest traditions of the military service and is a tribute to the courage and professional skill of officers and men of the division.

Following Operation *Commando*, 170 Battery had just one month to serve in Korea before we sailed for Hong Kong. I eagerly awaited details of where the battery would be stationed in the colony, as one or two lads who had been posted to Korea from there reckoned we were likely to find ourselves in tented accommodation close to the border with China. That sounded fine, as long as the Chinese there were friendly. I still had seven months of my National Service to complete. What I had seen of Hong Kong on the voyage from Southampton had looked good to me.

Operationally, the month was spent in improving defences for the relieving battery. Occasionally, A and C troops moved forward to engage HF targets from positions that collected a considerable amount of incoming shelling. On another occasion in B Troop, we moved forward to cover a patrol that was going into action close to Kowang-ni. As the track between B Troop position and that to which we moved was under constant observation by the Chinese, we moved before first light and returned after a successful day in close support of the patrol after last light, thus avoiding any direct enemy reaction. During one of those days in the forward position a trial was made with an experimental type of smoke round called BEDS (Base Ejection Discarding Sabot), which had a longer range than WP, almost that of HE. The trial with BEDS proved to be quite effective, but I don't recall seeing further supplies of them brought up to the gun positions. Not long to go now … like everyone, I was counting the days, although I did not make a calendar to mark them off as some of the lads had.

While we started to prepare for the move to Hong Kong, still located in the stony stream bed, I was filling sandbags one day to strengthen our defences against escalating Chinese firepower. Scraping away some shale I suddenly realized I could see a standard issue US Army belt buckle. Removing more shale to the left and right, I saw a shirt and trousers, indicating I had found the remains of an American soldier who had been killed very recently and, unusually for the Chinese, buried under a light covering of stony soil. He was about my age, no more. I fetched one of our officers, who contacted the Graves Registration Commission people, and they came and removed his remains in an attempt to identify him. I guessed that a family in the United States who may have already been notified that a son or brother was missing in action would now be informed that he would not be coming home.

Within days of the successful completion of Operation *Commando*, when it was considered safe for a small group of journalists to be brought up to B Troop position, a reporter from a long since defunct London newspaper was given a free hand to talk to us. Approaching Dennis Bedwell from Leicestershire, the reporter enquired how many rounds he had fired during Operation *Commando*. Perhaps suffering from 'mortar gunner's ear', Dennis may not have heard him correctly, but having heard from somewhere that 170 Battery had fired 11,000 rounds, Dennis increased that figure to 14,000. A couple of weeks later a copy of the newspaper arrived in the mail from home. And there was the blazing headline: 'FOURTEEN THOUSAND-BOMB BEDWELL TELLS HOW HE CLOBBERED THE CHINKS'. Well, you can imagine how that went down. And how on earth the reporter imagined one man could drop that many bombs down the tube, I do not know. From then on Dennis was referred as 'Fourteen Thousand-Bomb Bedwell'.

The days passed, bringing the boat for Hong Kong nearer. With a few days left to mark off on homemade calendars, Chinese shelling and mortaring increased considerably, and reports of enemy movement became more frequent. Probing patrols were attempting to penetrate any weak points in our defences. They were quite visible in the open as though they were goading us, and it started to look as though something was about to happen. Perhaps they were going to attempt to take back the ground they had recently lost. Most activity was in the region of Hills 355 and 317. This was happening just as the advance parties of 29 Brigade replacements started to arrive. The original 29 Brigade units were being relieved. The 1st battalions of the Royal Leicestershires, Royal Norfolks and the Welch Regiment were replacing 1 RUR, 1 RNF and 1 Glos. It was then that I was called to the Troop CP, where the troop commander dropped a bombshell. I was going nowhere. Together with other National Service signallers, TARAs and miscellaneous others who had more than six months to serve, I would remain behind when the battery departed. We would stay behind with 120 Light Battery. And I thought he was about to hand me my lance bombardier stripes. Well, as they say, you could have knocked me down with a feather. I found it hard to believe, but there it was; I was staying behind.

Unbelievably, it had transpired that the generals in the War Office had decided that my valuable services could not be dispensed with. Obviously they had agreed around the conference table that, for Gunner Jacobs, front-line service was beneficial for his continuing good health: it would do him even more good if he stayed behind with the relieving unit, 120 Light Battery. (All mortar batteries had recently been renamed Light.) I supposed that as the recalled reservists were leaving, there must be a shortage of men with my skills, and I hoped for a good explanation from Whitehall. It did not arrive.

I had already written home to tell my parents I would soon be leaving, and I would send them my new address when I knew it. I guessed that my troop commander considered it was not necessary to inform a mere gunner of War Office decisions. The true reason was never explained to me, and it took me almost fifty years to uncover it. It had been decided by faceless individuals that, as there was a considerable shortfall in volunteers for regular service, a man could serve for a maximum of eighteen months in Korea, provided it did not include two consecutive winters. And as Britain still garrisoned most of the known planet, National Servicemen had to contribute their last drop of blood to the cause. At least word of the extremely harsh winter conditions when living in self-dug holes in the ground had penetrated their brains, so nobody had to endure two consecutive invigorating winters in all their glory.

I was reminded of just how cold a Korean winter could get when talking some years ago at a veteran reunion in Woolwich with my late mate George Philipson. We were discussing those final days before 170 Battery departed. Conversation moved on to Troop Sergeant Major Kerr. George told me the story of an event that had occurred in the frozen wastes around Pyongyang before the 'big bug-out' had begun. The mortars were located in a paddy field with a reasonably soft surface when the troop had moved in, but overnight the temperature had dropped astronomically. There was an inherent problem with the 4.2-inch mortar, excellent close support weapon that it was, as the mobile base plate tended to sink into soft ground. Normally the base plate could be lifted out by two strong gunners using the issued levers to haul it onto its wheels, but it was not always that easy, remembered George.

Because of the acute angle at which the mortars fired when engaging the enemy, detonation thrust was downwards, forcing the base plate into the soft ground. On this occasion the base plate of one mortar had sunk into the mire and frozen in before it had been possible to move it a few feet away and under-fill a new location with shale. TSM Kerr was responsible for locating suitable positions.

To move a deeply frozen base plate the first requirement was a TSM with a loud voice. Luckily in B Troop they had just the man. A loud voice was essential in a mortar troop, as most of the gunners had lost some hearing ability because it was not often possible to clap hands over ears after releasing a bomb down the tube, and there were no such pieces of equipment as ear defenders in 1951. Some men thought mortar gunners were excessively polite when every word spoken to them was responded to with: 'Pardon?'

The first indispensable priority to our TSM was to reverse a gun-tower – a 15cwt 4x4 Morris of Second World War vintage – in close to the base plate and attach a steel cable to the towing eye. A shout of 'Right, go forward, slowly' took up the strain, while the gunners who were looking on sensibly ducked as a twang like a violin string being plucked indicated the cable was about to part, with the likelihood of decapitating anyone it wrapped around. Nothing happened. The base plate remained stuck firm.

The driver was ordered to stop pulling before he jerked the Earth off its axis, our TSM yelling, 'Get me a 3-tonner.' Down came a heavily laden Bedford QL truck, which had greater pulling power and better traction. 'We'll do it this time,' said the TSM to the large crowd of onlookers. And we might also see flying pigs, was the general consensus. The same procedure was adopted, but all that happened was that the towing hook on the truck was almost straightened. Now, the TSM was not a man to give in easily. It was soon sorted. 'Fetch me a can of petrol,' was the next command. After the gunners had removed the barrel, static bipod and everything else that was not nailed down, the petrol was doused liberally over the base plate, a match was thrown in and a spiral of black smoke ensued, which probably caused the infantry apoplexy, but it did the trick. The blackened base plate no longer looked like one of the Royal Artillery's finest; the dark green paint and red and blue No. 45 logo with which it had been splendidly decorated at Norton Barracks was all gone. The base plate was levered out and moved to a nearby location. A new paint job would have been attended to later. The lads who had witnessed the proceedings said there was a certain entertainment value, which had brightened up a freezing cold North Korean morning.

The infantry were usually generous with their praise for our mortars, the reason being that they could rely on a quick-firing, rapid response weapon after the first fall of shot had been observed. When 'on target' was reported from the OP, all that was required at the gun position was setting 'charge one' if called for, depending on the proximity of the enemy, simply by removing two of the six secondary propellant charges from within the blades of the fin, before dropping the requisite number of bombs into the 68-inch smooth-bore barrel. Due to the high trajectory taken by the bomb, which in flight is fin-stabilized, occasionally a dozen rounds would be put up, arcing towards the target, before the first bomb detonated. With a virtual 25-yard radius spread of hot steel splinters from the 20-pound bomb, which has an almost vertical descent, they were a weapon not to be treated lightly, causing fearful damage among closely packed groups of enemy soldiers. The recommended maximum rate of fire was twenty rounds for one minute, fifteen rounds per minute for the next three minutes, followed by ten rounds per minute for maintaining sustained fire. Sometimes these rates were exceeded for brief periods, caused by necessity.

The American M2 4.2-inch mortar fired a spin-stabilizing shell from the 48-inch rifled barrel, providing a slower rate of fire; five rounds per minute for the first twenty minutes, then only one round per minute indefinitely. Originally, the intended use was for chemical (smoke) rounds, HE shells were a later development.

Although a US chemical mortar company had been instrumental in assisting 3 RAR on the Pukhan River in April, there had been no further sightings of them since the formation of 1 Comwel Div.

Chapter Seven

Life on Jamestown Line

After receiving the deflating news that I was to remain in Korea with 120 Light Battery, I began saying my goodbyes to good mates while they were still around, as some had already departed with an advance party. But before the main party left for Pusan, another problem with the Chinese was brewing. The advance party of 120 Battery had arrived and the new battery commander Major L.G. Wilkes and B Troop's new troop sergeant major, along with a few others, had been flown from Hong Kong ahead of the main party and the battery's heavy equipment, which would arrive on HMT *Empire Pride*. Commander Major Lewis of 170 Battery said a collective goodbye to those few of us who were staying, wishing us well, and then he was gone. The new TSM in B Troop, WO2 'Curly' McDonald, probably wished he had not arrived so soon. As he was familiarizing himself with the B Troop gun site, a stray incoming mortar round wounded him, and he was shipped across to Japan after having spent only a few days in Korea.

While details of the handover were being discussed among the officers, the something big I had mentioned that could happen did happen. We had noted that the Chinese were appearing once more to show aggression, and already their artillery had increased to a level that had not yet been encountered in Korea. At last it might have dawned on the military planners in Peking that even with China's enormous population, they had already spent a lot of men's lives assisting their North Korean allies. Perhaps they had met with unexpected resistance on the Imjin and at Kapyong.

As the battery handover continued I found myself with my usual 170 Battery FOO for the last time, with 1 Norfolk, who had relieved 1 RUR. The Norfolks had many young conscripts in the ranks, a very different crowd from the reservists that had formed a large proportion of 170 Battery and the Ulsters. In fact, about 40 per cent of the original 29 Brigade had been reservists.

Following Operation *Commando* we had settled into our positions on Jamestown Line quite well, making ourselves as comfortable as possible as it appeared we would be staying there for the immediate future. If that meant the longer term, it would mean winter-proofing our newly-dug holes in the ground before the full power of the weather struck. But first, something other than the weather was on our minds. During quiet periods overnight, from our OP we could hear sounds of digging coming from the enemy line, and during the day sightings of soldiers in the open became more frequent, providing targets for the Norfolks' machine guns and our mortars. Large numbers could be seen passing through a communication trench on a left-hand slope to our front. It was almost as though they intended to demonstrate their superior manpower to us. As soon as our firepower was unleashed on them, they would go to ground, then continue on their way again. It mattered not how much of their earthworks we damaged, it was always repaired by morning, regardless of the illuminating flares sent up by the infantry mortars overnight.

The enemy was definitely becoming more brazen. One afternoon, while watching through the periscope binoculars, which we called 'donkey's ears', I noticed a party of five enemy soldiers who appeared to be watching our line through binoculars. As I had never seen the Chinese using binoculars I thought they could be high-ranking officers. They were clearly exposed from about chest height, and I was surprised that they did not realize they were perfectly visible from our vantage point. I brought them to the attention of the FOO, who decided to check whether I could be hallucinating and took over my donkey's ears and microphone. Next I heard him call up the field regiment for two rounds of 'Victor Tare' (VT, for variable time-fused shells, in the phonetic alphabet of the day). The top of the hill would already have been 'registered', so all necessary data to come on target would have been logged. Within a minute or so, I heard the usual express train sound of a 25-pound shell passing close overhead, followed instantly by the crack of the shell detonating above the heads of the curious Chinese. Whether they had been killed or not I would never know but I myself would not care to be splattered with red-hot steel shards from a 25-pounder bursting above my head. The second shell that roared overhead was rather superfluous. No more Chinese appeared in that shallow trench while I was on that OP duty. Whether they had deepened it for future protection could only be guessed at.

As the final days of October passed, 120 Battery became aware that Korea was going to be very different to the firing ranges of Hong Kong, and it was going to be a darn sight colder. The trouble that we knew was brewing did not take long to present itself. On 4 November, at about 1600 hrs, 1 KOSB were assaulted. Our A and B troops had moved forward to Chunggo-jon and Maktae-dong respectively, and in B Troop we moved our OP to Hill 199 on the extreme right flank of 1 Comwel Div territory, from where we gained a fine view of the reverse slopes of Hill 355. B Troop mortars were positioned just below Hill 355 to provide covering fire for 1 KSLI, the Shropshires, if requested. As the dirt track between A and B troops was under observation by the enemy, we were permitted to move only at night. At that time the BEDS smoke rounds we had trialled were back-loaded, as they had been found to be inferior to the smoke rounds of 14 Field Regiment, who had started to relieve 45 Field in the current series of replacements.

When the Chinese attack came, it was an all-on frontal attack. This time they started with an intense bombardment that began at about 1600 hrs, the like of which nobody had yet seen in the war. They seemed to have discovered that in modern warfare they needed artillery before sending in the infantry. An incredible avalanche of shells, mortar bombs and rockets fell mainly on 1 KOSB positions at the rate of about 6,000 per hour. It was evident that the battalion was about to be attacked in the enemy's attempt to recover Hill 317, which had been in UN hands since the previous month. After a creeping barrage (which the enemy had apparently discovered was the most effective method) they started up the hill, quickly overwhelming the forward platoons in hand-to-hand fighting. It was one of those occasions when men would say afterwards that many of the enemy soldiers appeared to be drugged as they advanced, heedless of the shell and mortar rounds from all available artillery and infantry medium machine guns that fell among them. As men fell, others took their place. It was like the Imjin River Battle all over again. By then our barbed wire defences were in a complete tangle, and it had little effect on advances made by the enemy. They used explosive charges called 'Bangalore torpedoes' and pole charges to destroy the wire.

The forward slopes of Hills 217 and 317 were swarming with attacking infantry, and at about 1730 hrs, Hill 217 had been retaken, as had the hills named The Hinge and United, with small parties of KOSBs making their way back to the comparative safety of other company positions. In A Troop a rapid withdrawal was necessary to avoid the mortars being swamped. By that time, 1 KOSB were being hard pressed, fighting in the trenches with fixed bayonets, but unable to hold firm, and they had started to move to fall-back positions.

Before last light Hill 217 was overrun, the survivors having made a fast exit. Night was falling and the entire area was illuminated by flares from the infantry's 3-inch mortars, against which the enemy were silhouetted. The infantry mortars using HE were having a good effect in attempting to stop the unstoppable. The enemy was still advancing in waves and before long, Hill 317, which had been taken by the Australians with considerable casualties the previous month, had to be abandoned. At that time one KOSB company had lost contact with battalion HQ, possibly as some wireless sets had been lost, but not before a Victoria Cross had been won by Bill Speakman, a Black Watch private attached to 1 KOSB, as had the unique award of the Distinguished Service Order (DSO) to a National Service officer, Second Lieutenant Willie Purves, also of 1 KOSB.

It now looked as though Hill 355 might be the enemy's next objective, and one of our troops saved the position of one company of 1 Leics, who had been immediately thrown into battle in 28 Brigade area, losing several killed, with others wounded and taken prisoner. A Troop, now in their fall-back position near Kangso-ri, served the infantry admirably with close-in mortar fire, for which event Lieutenant Monilaws, A Troop FOO, was later decorated with the MC.

Many years later I came to know a man who had been in 1 Leics Corps of Drums, Corporal Joe Kenworthy. Joe told me that a report came in to the effect that several of their men were lying wounded at a position where the enemy had ambushed them. In action the Drums Platoon are used as stretcher bearers and medics. Joe and some of the drummers were sent out to recover their wounded. On arrival at the ambush site, they were themselves ambushed, the Chinese having not left the scene in the knowledge that men would be sent out to recover the wounded. The Leicesters had been in Korea little more than two weeks when Joe was taken prisoner, spending the remainder of the war in POW camps in the north. He survived his period of incarceration quite well, although he admitted to a few problems in later life.

During the height of the Chinese attack we were kept constantly busy in our OP, calling down mortar fire on all perceived enemy movements, which were continuous, as well as on known and suspected FUPs. Continuous tracer streams arced away to our front from the close-at-hand infantry MMGs. By now we had been relieved of all surplus 'foreign' military clothing and equipment that we had managed to acquire in 170 Battery, often through barter with the Americans for beer. That included my US Army issue .30 Garand M3 carbine, my American winter parka, and the Browning .30 air-cooled LMG we always took to the OP, just in case. Now they had gone, like my promotion to lance bombardier, by the look of things.

The event I was involved in before the last of the 170 Battery lads departed from B Troop could have resulted in a court martial. It all started one afternoon when one of the reservists told me to throw my line repair kit on a truck as we were going to repair a broken line. Of course there was no broken telephone cable, but for him and two of his mates it was time to say goodbye to their friends in 162 Battery, 16 New Zealand Field Regiment, whose gun position was about 1 mile to our rear. Arriving with the Kiwis, I was greeted like a long-lost friend even though I was new to them, and out came a case of gleaming Asahi beer from under a tarpaulin in the back of the truck. It was not long before the Kiwis also found a bottle of rum. There were six of us and the idea was to say a final farewell in the best possible manner. I was not used to knocking back so much alcohol in such a short time, so I was soon left behind.

To cut a long story to reasonable proportions, it was when time to go beckoned that the fun started. The driver, who would have blown about 150 on the Richter scale on any breathalyser, climbed into the cab and released the handbrake. The truck shot away down the steep slope, straight across the main dirt track like a rocket, and embedded itself deeply in the paddy sludge on the other side. He climbed out, stepping straight into the mire, knee-deep. Both driver and truck were plastered, in different ways. I wondered how we were going to get out of this, but the Kiwis soon sorted it out by bringing down a GMC 6x6 truck with a winch. Our vehicle was quickly back on the track and headed for home, but was covered in very smelly mud.

On arrival back at the gun position, explanations were required from us all regarding why we had taken so long to repair a broken line, and why the truck was in such a state. Although alcohol fumes must have surrounded the driver like a swarm of bees, he got away with it by saying he had been cut up on the narrow track and ended up in the paddy. Nothing further was mentioned.

One of the NCOs who would recall this episode was Sergeant Jones, one of the number ones. I attended the annual Korean Residents Festival at Kingston-on-Thames in 2010. After the Korean Ambassador had presented me with a Sixtieth Anniversary medallion, I was approached by a man also wearing a Royal Artillery cap badge. He enquired which Gunner unit in Korea I had served in. I told him both 170 and 120 Batteries. He next asked if I remembered the incident when TSM Curly McDonald had been wounded shortly after his arrival. I said that I did. He enquired if I remembered who had replaced Curly until he came back from hospital. I replied, 'Yes, a shortish Welsh sergeant,' to which he replied, 'You are looking at him.' Today, Taffy and I keep in contact by email.

Another event occurred as soon as 170 Battery had departed from Korea. I was approached by the new GPO, Second Lieutenant J.J. 'Tug' Wilson, carrying a clipboard. He said that according to records he had inherited, it appeared that I had not yet been on R&R. I confirmed that indeed I had not. He then told me to collect my kit and get myself to BHQ in the morning, as Tokyo was where I was going. Well, life was looking up. Tug's parting shot was, 'And get a haircut while you are there.' I thought it best not to mention that I had enjoyed three weeks at CATC in July. If he had seen it on my records at all, it could well have just been recorded as 'Signals course at CATC', without mention that CATC was in Japan. I was told by the 120 Battery lads that Tug had a thing about haircuts.

The next day I would find out if all I had heard from the lads regarding R&R was correct. I cadged a lift on the ration truck to find a small group of lucky lads who were also on their way to Tokyo. The BSM checked us off, told us to check our heavy kit into the Q stores tent, sold us one bottle of Asahi apiece, and we settled down for the day. We discussed what we had been doing in the April, October and November battles, the latter now known as the Guy Fawkes Battle due to its proximity to Bonfire Night. The following day we were on our way, along the track until we joined the main supply route that generally followed the route of the single rail track. Just outside Uijongbu the MSR crossed to the other side of the line. There were no railway crossing gates as at home, and it was plain to see that some drivers had tried to take on the Tokchon–Seoul Express and lost, evidenced by a mess of metal that had once been a jeep and a rusted, twisted pile of wreckage that had previously been a GMC Deuce and a Half cargo truck.

Arriving in the much demolished Seoul, our driver pulled in at FMA (forward maintenance area), a damaged brick building with a seemingly untouched Korean shrine or temple to the rear. There we would spend the night. I wondered if we would have only four days in Tokyo, but my mind was set clear. Leave did not commence until signing in at Ebisu Leave Centre. We would be taken to Kimpo the next day for our Tokyo flight. When the time came for our great adventure we climbed up the steps into a Douglas DC4 Skymaster of the USAF. There were no conventional seats as in modern passenger aircraft, just bucket seats with canvas straps to fasten ourselves in.

Then we were off. Caught up in the excitement of our first-ever flight, we all tried to look cool, using the language of the day, giving the appearance of seasoned travellers. After a couple of hours we began to descend. Tokyo so soon? No. We were told we would be shortly landing at Komaki to refuel, and then travel on to Tokyo. I had no idea where Komaki might be, but later discovered it was a USAF base between Osaka and Nagoya, on the main Japanese island, Honshu. Refuelled, we were away again for the short flight to Tachikawa Air Base, west of Tokyo.

Debussing into a BCOF minibus that was waiting for our arrival, we soon passed through a jumble of suburbs that all looked alike, with no distinguishing features, and finally arrived at Ebisu Leave Centre. We checked in and lined up for clean, pressed uniforms, which were standard UK battledress as it can become quite cold in Tokyo in November. Taken to our rooms, we selected our beds, which had spotless white sheets and blankets, and were told we did not have to bother with making them up in the morning as there were room maids for that. A long hot shower came next, and then we went across to the meal hall and generally got to know our bearings.

Even by the morning we were not yet used to the idea that we could have as many showers as we desired. We breakfasted from real china plates – this was living! We checked out the Kookaburra Club, which had originally been the canteen for Australians in the occupation forces. It was operated jointly by ladies of the Australian Army Canteen Service and our own Women's Voluntary Service (WVS). Newspapers and magazines were available to read, records could be requested on a gramophone, and there was a notice board advertising trips out to various places of interest. But with only five days in which to 'do' Tokyo, time was short. With a mate I followed a street map I had picked up to find Ebisu Station, from where frequent electric trains ran to Tokyo Central.

On arrival there we thought it would be a good idea to find a toilet before heading out into the great unknown. The only one I could see was one where only women were entering. I stopped a passing US marine, to ask where the men's room was. He pointed to the entrance into which the ladies had gone. And that was it. One entrance: men to the right, ladies to the left. How about that? Unisex toilets in 1951! Our next stop was to the Imperial Palace, an edifice with the appearance of having been constructed by ancient craftsmen, when in fact much of it had been damaged in the bombing of Tokyo before the Second World War finished, and was subsequently rebuilt. We passed a large building with important looking US military police on either side of the entrance, in very smart uniforms, chrome-plated steel helmets and multi-coiled lanyards. There was a small crowd of Japanese milling around, so we guessed they must be waiting for something to happen. A large US Army staff car bearing a flag on the bonnet and red plates with four silver stars on front and rear bumpers pulled up, and out stepped a very important looking man in US Army uniform. The MPs saluted, and he disappeared inside. It was General Mathew Ridgway, we were told. The building, the Dai-Ichi (great one), had previously been HQ for Japan's most important insurance company until it became HQ for America's most important general – MacArthur, in person.

Next we headed to the Ginza, Tokyo's famous shopping street. There did not appear to be any evidence of the USAF bombing there either, unless it had all been cleared away and rebuilt, like the palace. We had a couple of lemonades in a beer hall just off the Ginza, and visited the Tokyo PX (Post Exchange), the American version of the NAAFI but much better. Finding our Baffs were not accepted there we had a look around anyway. I was surprised to see so many GIs buying expensive sets of golf clubs. From their shoulder patches I knew they were from units that were in Korea, and I wondered where they would play a round of golf over there on Kansas or Wyoming Lines. Then I realized they were placing orders to have the golf clubs, and many other luxury goods, shipped home, and they would later be used in places such as the 'real' Kansas and Wyoming.

When we decided to call it a day and head back to Ebisu, I looked at the notice board to see what trips were available, noticing one to Kamakura and another to the Nippon Brewery. I put my name down for both. But before setting out anywhere I decided to get that haircut Tug had threatened me with. I think I could have had it seen to in the leave centre, but there was a small barbershop on the way to the station and I thought I would test that one out. The barber was with a customer. I said '*Ohayo gozaimasu*' (good morning). He returned the greeting, bowed deeply, and with '*dozo*' (please) ushered me to a chair and pointed at a pile of magazines I could look at until he had finished. I picked up an American *Life* magazine, rather similar to our old *Picture Post*. On the front cover was a picture of a US marine, with his story inside.

When the barber had finished with his customer, I was offered the barber chair. He threw a cloth over me and looked at me expectantly. Nothing ventured … I picked up the magazine, pointed at the marine's crew cut and, in my best Japanese using words picked up while I was at CATC, I said '*Watashi wa crew cut kudasai*,' to which he replied, '*Ah, so ka? Karu katu desu ka?*' I confirmed that I did indeed need a *karu katu*, the Japanese people being unable to get their tongues around 'crew cut', and he got to work. I was unaccustomed to having the neck shave and shoulder massage – the whole shooting match – after the cutting was completed. It was all included in the small price of the haircut. My time with the barber cost me very little and I knew that Tug would be pleased.

The visit to Kamakura, a pleasant minibus ride accompanied by one of the WVS ladies, was very interesting. The chief reason for anyone paying a visit to Kamakura was to view the superbly maintained park wherein sits one of the giant Daibutsu (Buddha) monuments that are scattered around Japan. The Kamakura Buddha is not the largest, but is very impressive in every sense. Standing 44 feet high, it was cast in bronze in about 1250 AD. It is hollow so that visitors can walk through it. We had been advised to be reverent, as it stands on hallowed ground for those of the Buddhist religion. I could not imagine how the Japanese had acquired the knowledge to cast such a large object in bronze 700 years previously, and there were no signs of any joins. Clever people those Orientals.

Our visit to the Nippon Brewery in one of Tokyo's suburbs ought to have attracted a great deal of interest, but it was made clear that no free samples would be handed out. That wrote off the Aussies, then. There were just five of us plus the WVS lady. We were given the full guided tour of the plant, seeing the stages of manufacture from raw materials through to brewing, bottling and labelling. Then we were taken to a side room. There on a table was a veritable flood of Nippon Brewery's end results, enough drink to raise the Imjin by a couple of feet, plus soft drinks, various snacks, peanuts and the like. We had an enjoyable couple of hours testing this new brew, while the WVS lady had a soft drink. Listening to the welcoming words from the brewery officials I believe the idea of the brewery visit was an attempt to get us to encourage whoever negotiated the contract for Asahi Brewery to supply all beer requirements for 1 Comwel Div to switch to Nippon, but there was no chance of that. The mention of 'no free samples' on the notice board must have been to keep the numbers down.

Most days my mate and I took a train to anywhere that looked interesting, but one afternoon we just wandered along the main shopping street in Ebisu. There was a shop selling gramophone records, and the means on which to play them. A loudspeaker at the entrance played the latest Japanese hits to attract customers inside. As we stopped to listen, the tune suddenly changed to *Warship March*, the quick march of the former Imperial Japanese Navy, and then, as soon as we moved on, the previous tune was reinstated. I said to my mate that I thought it had been done deliberately. We tested it again, stopping at the door, and, as before, *Warship March* was instantly repeated. I reckoned the owner of the shop had been in the Japanese armed forces during the Second World War, and he was letting us know.

All who served in Korea will recall the song *Shina No Yoru* (*China Night*), played all over Japan. I was given to understand the tune was most popular during the Japanese conquests in North China in the late 1930s. The lyrics tell the story of a young girl who awaits the return of her husband or lover. I brought a copy of the record home but it became rather scratched from playing and was disposed of many years ago. Today the original version by Shirley Yamaguchi can be played any time on YouTube. The uncouth lads would sing '*She ain't got no yo-yo*' to the opening words.

My days in Tokyo passed all too quickly. It had been five glorious days of sleeping in a proper bed, showers at any time of day and meals served on plates. As we were being bussed back to Tachikawa, we were told there was a technical delay before our aircraft would be ready, but we could 'chow down' in the Airmen's Mess. We chowed down to a very palatable meal. The R&R programme was carried out by the United States Military Air Transport

Service (MATS, often referred to as Might Arrive Tomorrow Sometime). We arrived back at Kimpo safely, from where we were taken once more to FMA to await battery transport. Back along the MSR to the north, after a while I thought our driver had taken a wrong route as I did not recognize the scenery, so I asked where we were going. He replied that 120 Battery had moved to new locations while I had been away. Approaching the 38th parallel we crossed the Imjin over the new Widgeon Bridge, west of the Samichon River. There I discovered B Troop was in a fairly exposed location in a re-entrant.

The Commonwealth Division had moved to the south-west from our previous position close to Hill 355, to the ruins of P'anbu-ri, where we were now supporting 1 Welch. Battalion HQ was just over a ridge from our gun position. The battalion had brought to Korea the regimental mascot, a white, long-haired, curly-horned goat, in the charge of a corporal given the honorary title Goat Major. The goat, Taffy IX, or Taffy the Ninth, was probably initially viewed by the Korean porters as fresh meat on the hoof for the battalion commander. I understand that today's mascot goat is named Billy.

Our new position was in a fairly quiet part of the line, probably to give the Welch lads time to settle in. There was limited action for them apart from the normal night patrolling. That we were in a quiet zone actually suited the purpose as far as 120 Battery was concerned, as there was a serious shortage of 4.2-inch mortar ammunition in Korea. After using up most of the available stock in the Guy Fawkes battle, someone probably slipped up back at some dreary base depot and the paperwork to indent for more ammunition supplies had become lost. We could only hope that communist spies had not notified the Chinese of this shortfall. We were not at P'anbu-ri for long, but while we were there everyone was pleased that although the winter weather was severe, it was nowhere near as bad as the previous one, and we had all been issued with the new British winter clothing, which I thought was superior to the US Army winter clothing that had been taken from me when 120 Battery arrived. The outfit could not have been imagined by men who fought in cold climates in the Second World War. However, due to the usual shortage of cash for Britain's Armed Forces, we were issued with only one set of outerwear, which quickly became grimy from day-to-day contact with the dirt walls of our bunkers. It was not long before we must have looked the scruffiest troops in the United Nations Command.

Very soon we were on the move again. This time the battery moved to the north-east, to a position near Hill 159. Close by were the two hills that the Canadians had fought over, both numbered Hill 187. As one was slightly to the north of the other, to avoid confusion, they were to be known as 187N and 187S. It was in that position on 6 February 1952 we were informed that

King George VI had died. I had not heard that he had been ill. I do not recall having been called together to hear the news, as on arrival in Korea our new troop commander, Captain Hicks, after taking a group photo of the troop, had told us that it would be the last time we would congregate together, as one carefully placed Chinese shell landing among us would remove half the troop in one fell swoop.

Other interesting news arrived at this time. Due to favourable reports that had filtered back to the War Lords, the use of the 4.2-inch mortar by Royal Artillery batteries in Korea was being expanded. Together with 120 Battery on arrival from Hong Kong was 42 Light Battery, who had switched to mortars from a light anti-aircraft role in the summer of 1951. In Hong Kong both 42 and 120 Batteries had each consisted of three troops – A, B and C. Now we heard on the grapevine that a third mortar battery was to be formed, initially by taking one troop from the two existing batteries. Three mortar batteries could provide better close support for the three brigades in 1 Comwel Div. By so doing, each battery was reduced to two gun troops, the borrowed ones forming the new 248 Light Battery. The three mortar batteries created 61 Light Regiment, operational from 12 February 1952, the only Royal Artillery regiment ever formed with the 4.2-inch mortar as its main armament. A new 15 Locating/LAA battery had basically been formed at Woolwich. RHQ 61 Light Regiment and BHQ 15 Battery arrived in Korea in late January. This new battery would also have sound-ranging capability for the early detection of enemy guns and mortars. On 12 February 1952, the regimental line-up was:

- 42 Light Battery, being senior gun battery, retained A and B troops
- 120 Light Battery's troops were re-lettered D and E
- 248 Light Battery's troops were G and H
- 15 Locating/LAA Battery was formed from the two C troops removed from 42 and 120 Batteries, plus the Bofors of 11 (Sphinx Battery).

Nos. C, F and I troops were formed in the regiment initially, allowing for expansion to three gun troops in each mortar battery if the need arose at a later time, an event that did not happen. Meanwhile, 15 Battery also had J and K troops, and had responsibility for operating the sound-ranging equipment, to record from two widely separated hilltops the sound of enemy mortars firing, and pinpointing their precise location by trigonometry so that a counter-bombardment could be launched. Lieutenant Colonel H.S. Calvert MC was first to command 61 Light Regiment.

I know that it was somewhat confusing at this time when troops were being removed from batteries, there were new arrivals, and regimental control assumed much of the operations previously done at battery level. But over the years I have met mortar men who refused to accept that 248 Battery ever existed. I also came in contact with other veterans who swore they had been in 170 Battery in Korea, when they had not even had their call-up papers by the time the battery had left Korea.

So I was now in D Troop 120 Light Battery. We continued to fire on targets as they presented themselves, which at that time were few and far between. It was the quietest I had known it, particularly as far as OP work was concerned, where we spent countless hours peering through the donkey's ears until one tree, one bush blurred into the next. The remainder of February passed, and then in March we were once more on the move, this time forward and returning to the north-east to the same re-entrant that had been the last location in which I had said my farewells to the lads of B Troop 170 Battery.

The recent occupants, the 3-inch mortar platoon of one of the non-Commonwealth infantry battalions, had not been good at gardening. In fact, the entire site was in a shocking condition. It was in a small valley off of a dirt road that ran roughly west-north-west from Ukkowang-san to Hill 227. As we arrived at the location, the existing inhabitants were sitting on the left-hand ridge, waiting for transport to their next hill. But before leaving they would be fed. A truck arrived; two men jumped on board and started throwing food at the hungry warriors. They would have an alfresco meal. Oranges were tossed at them, as were chicken parts, loaves of bread and others items now forgotten. The loaves were torn in half and passed around. Food items that missed hands were allowed to remain on the ground. Then they came down to collect their daily half-litre of rough red wine. Lunch over, they departed, calling out 'OK Tommies, we go', which was all the English language they offered.

But what had not gone with them was going to cause endless problems. Where food had not been caught – over a couple of weeks by the look of things – it was rotting on the ground, making good pickings for rats. We looked for their latrine pits. There were none. To say the hill we had inherited must have been the most unhygienic in Korea would have been an understatement. The entire place was disgusting and crawling with rats. We were first put to the task of cleaning up the site, then digging in. First to be dug was a CP bunker, then officers' bunkers, and finally our own living accommodation. The dirt that was excavated was spread all over the hillside to cover over much of the filth, and then we set fire to everything else.

Did we manage to rid the place of rats? Not on your life. The rats there were king-sized – not that I considered myself to be an expert on Asian rodents, but I would not wish to see any that were larger. I had to find a way to kill them. There was one way. A British hand grenade of the period, the standard 36 Mills Bomb, had its detonator in the base, but after unscrewing the base cap the explosive material therein could not be removed. Now, the American hand grenade was a whole new ball game, and boxes of them had been left behind. The handle, spring device and detonator were in a single component that merely needed unscrewing to display the flaky yellow material that was the killing component. With my spike bayonet I scraped this out, replaced it with petrol, screwed the detonator assembly back on, and there you have it – a mini napalm-type bomb; a rat exterminator par excellence.

I know we are supposed to be animal lovers, but I could never see why some people bought rats for their kids – black, brown, white or piebald. With my petrol bombs I would locate a rat hole, clear some of the foliage away, pull the pin, toss it in the hole, and flaming rats would run all over the hillside. It worked perfectly, until the day a running bonfire almost set fire to the whole damn hillside. That ended my reign as King Rat Exterminator of North Korea.

As February rolled into March, 29 Brigade went into reserve for a period. The 120 Battery was allowed back for seven days, the only period a mortar battery had been withdrawn from the front line since the war had started twenty months earlier. The Royal Artillery had organized a rest camp in a former Catholic girls' school somewhere on the Kimpo peninsula, where I enjoyed a break from my normal routine. At that time RHQ 61 Light had decided that individual troop CPs were an unnecessary luxury, so personnel were lost to enlarged Battery CPs. In D Troop we were just left with a bunker where our GPO, Lieutenant Tug Wilson, one TARA and two signallers, with all the wireless paraphernalia needed to maintain listening watch, and we rotated signaller duties with the OP. Living in such close proximity with Tug, I hoped Stan would be able to keep my Tokyo crew cut in some semblance of order with his razor, comb and nail scissors. But I had no need for concern, as a Korean barber turned up from somewhere, with an ancient pair of clippers that looked as though sheep had been in mind, not human heads. That barber would have won gold at the 1952 Olympics, if there had been a category for shearing heads. He was mustard with those hand-operated clippers. Tug seemed happy, which lifted a big weight from my mind.

As 29 Brigade infantry joined us back in the line Captain J.A. 'Jerry' Harrison became our new troop commander. We had taken over the right flank of 1 Comwel Div, with Hill 355 as the dominant feature to our front, together with the ridges to the north of it and Hill 159 and the 210 ridge to our left rear, where 61 Light also maintained OPs. Captain Harrison informed us that TSM Curly McDonald had been awarded a Mention in Despatches for courage when he had been wounded shortly after his arrival in Korea.

The 'road' between D Troop position and Hill 227, an almost straight stretch with just a couple of mild doglegs, was under enemy observation along the entire length. Whichever infantry battalion was in occupation at the bend in the track as it passed, our gun position was required to post a sentry to warn the few drivers that needed to go forward beyond that point to take note of the sign by a small sandbagged sentry post. As during a hot dry spell the track was nothing more than thick, deep dust, the sign warned drivers: 'SPEED LIMIT 15MPH. DUST DRAWS SHELLS'. Obviously the slower a driver progressed, the smaller the plume of dust, making it less likely the Chinese would target the vehicle. I lost count of the number of times I saw a driver start out at 15mph with good intentions. But as soon as some Chinese mortar man had spotted him, he would accelerate faster and faster in an attempt to get ahead of the bracketing mortar bombs landing around him. I saw several jeeps abandoned, which must have been collected under cover of night. There was once a tank stuck in a paddy there for two or three days before it was dragged out by a recovery tank during the night.

At the far end of this stretch, known as 'Mad Mile', the Shropshires were in occupation on Hill 227. A sentry at their checkpoint probably had to record details of all vehicles that had reached him safely. A jeep arrived one day at his post, driven by a US Army captain with one passenger. He was shown the 15mph sign at our sentry post and continued along Mad Mile. Reaching the sentry at the far end, without stopping he continued on his way, quite oblivious of the fact that there were no more friendly faces beyond that point. As the Chinese Army was in occupation beyond the 1 KSLI checkpoint, the next meal the captain and his passenger consumed would probably have been rice. Possibly cold rice. The Canadians later renamed the infamous stretch of dirt 'the bowling alley'.

It was not long before we heard the news that the good captain from a US Army artillery battalion had been sent forward to recce for a gun position, with another grid reference that would be the target. The story had it that he had confused the two, and drove on towards the furthest of them. Within days a sign appeared at the checkpoint, painted in red and black lettering on a white background, reading: 'FRONT LINE. REPORT TO CP. CAPTAIN X DID NOT AND IS NOW A POW'. I have a photo of that one in my collection of Korean art; it has amused many veterans who have heard the story without knowing if there was any truth in it.

During this period of comparative quiet along the front line, away from the forward areas Korea had broken out into bloom, with some places looking quite beautiful, although we might not have appreciated it at the time. There were few tall trees apart from the poplars that grew along the streams where villages had been, now demolished by war. The Japanese had used Korea as a source of charcoal for heating their *hibachis* (fire bowls) in the home. Any usable timber had gone into roofing-over our bunkers, and the Royal Engineers no doubt had a use for some. In the villages where the rice paddies had not been flooded for the spring planting, there would be no crop in 1952; neither would the bright red chillies be picked from the vines that year, or the next. Before the war had wrecked the lives of the inhabitants, they had eked out a meagre existence in those quiet valleys, having been virtually self-sufficient, with enough left over to barter with other villagers. Stepping into a ruined home, there was always a smoky smell, which I have been reminded of every time I have caught the whiff of a backyard bonfire over the years. That, and the other fragrant aroma that veterans will always associate with Korea, has never left me.

In April, targets were mostly few and far between, although we sometimes assisted infantry patrols that had got themselves into difficulty. Other days would see frantic activity when all spare bodies were put to work opening boxes, each containing two bombs, which we passed into the gun pits as fast as possible. On one such frantic occasion a padre arrived at the troop gun site just as we were all feverishly breaking open boxes and passing bombs to the gunners. He stood watching for a few minutes with fingers in ears before hurrying back in the direction from which he had arrived in his jeep. We never saw him again; I guess he thought a mortar troop was a noisy place to be on a sunny morning. The infantry continued to send out listening posts after last light, returning to company positions before first light. The Royal Engineers continued to build bridges, lay minefields and try to make something out of the dirt tracks by bulldozing half a hill into a paddy field, and grading it into a passable surface. They did a great job. Then, on 1 May, there was another surprise waiting for me. I was asked a particularly stupid question. As it was almost six months since I had been on R&R, would I like to go again? Would I? Wild horses, and all that. I was waiting for the boat home at the time, as it was already overdue, but I guessed the boat would wait for me while I enjoyed the Tokyo scene one more time. I felt privileged to have a plane waiting for me at Kimpo.

This time I found that larger aircraft had been allocated to troop movements in theatre, and I boarded a DC124 Globemaster of the US 65th Air Wing based at Tachikawa, which for its day was a very large aircraft. Troops were crammed in on two decks. But crowded or not, Tokyo waited for me. Landing again at Tachikawa, followed by the bus ride to Ebisu, I lined up for clean clothing. It was summer now and I believe we were able to obtain fresh shirts and trousers every other day. If I am wrong, my phone will be ringing from veterans who remember this differently. Tokyo was quite hot in early May, so it was 'shirt-sleeve order' for us. The Occupation of Japan was apparently over, and we could now be arrested by civilian police for drunkenness, theft and certain other serious misdemeanours.

As soon as I had cleaned up I headed out past the fire station and the barbershop where I had been served admirably the previous November and on to the station for a train to Tokyo Central. I recall walking past the Ernie Pyle Theatre wondering who Ernie Pyle was and how a theatre named after him came to be in the centre of Tokyo. In recent times I have discovered that he was a well-liked Second World War correspondent, who spent much time with the island-hopping US Marines in the Pacific Campaign, where he was killed. The Ginza shopping street was given the once over, as was the PX. Back at base I scanned the notice board for minibus trips, but there was nothing I had not already done on my fist visit. I noticed it was possible to visit the Commonwealth Cemetery at Yokohama, and thought it would be a nice run out into the Japanese countryside. How wrong could I be? I had not realized that the entire Tokyo/Yokohama conurbation was one enormous built-up area consisting of homes and factories jumbled together apparently with no thought given to town planning. The cemetery is where men were buried who had died during the occupation years, and others who had not survived wounds in Korea after the most professional surgical and medical teams at the Commonwealth Military Base Hospital at Kure had done everything possible. The only other place I visited was the Higashi Honganji Temple, a place of quiet, the fragrance of joss sticks in the air disturbed only by a heavy bell or gong struck at regular intervals by a Shinto monk.

The only other tour on offer was a visit to Tokyo Zoo at Ueno, but it had no appeal. I had spent altogether too much time in bunkers to want to spend the afternoon looking at animals similarly incarcerated. The record shop at Ebisu still switched from *China Night*, or whatever else was popular in 1952, to *Warship March* as I passed. I pretended to continue walking on by, but ducked back quickly to catch the proprietor in the act, just as he was switching back to the Japanese ballad, and without giving him time to return to the march of the Imperial Japanese Navy. I just stood in the doorway looking at him, saying nothing. We both smiled; he knew I had caught him at his little game. I wondered how many times he did that in the course of a day.

By 1952 there were many locally made cars and trucks on the roads, but it would still be some years before Japanese products impacted on the European and United States markets. Unfortunately, both time and money were in short supply, so I did not stray far from the central Tokyo scene. As expected, my five days' leave were over too quickly, but now I had the boat for home to look forward to in the near future. However, the excitement was far from being over. Boarding another Globemaster, on the upper deck I strapped myself in on a seat that faced across the fuselage to where I could look out of one of the small windows. It was a smooth departure, then the pilot headed initially east to overfly central Tokyo and on out over Tokyo Bay. The lights of the city came up sharply as a slow left turn stopped suddenly when a large flame shooting from the outboard engine startled those of us seated where we could see the port wing. A crew member wearing a 'Mae West' survival jacket running down the central aisle did nothing to ease our worry, and then an increase in engine tone indicated to us novices that something was amiss. The crew member had to yell to make himself heard, but the gist of it was that the outer port engine had flamed out, had been extinguished, and the inner port engine had been stopped for safety reasons. For the present we would be heading many miles out to sea, to circle while fuel was jettisoned. There was no problem at all, we were told, but on arrival back at Tachikawa, the runway was edged with fire appliances, just in case, and they followed us back to the apron. Then the best news of the evening came: we were told that as there was no spare aircraft, we would have to suffer another night in luxury back at Ebisu. Next morning some of the lads must have been shaken by the experience, as they declared they would never fly again, and they demanded a sea passage to Pusan. Needless to say, they boarded a relief aircraft, another Globemaster, like the rest of us. Our flight to Kimpo went off without incident.

On arrival back at D Troop, the dustbowl weather had everybody sweating at their allotted tasks. I enquired of the battery clerk when I would be leaving now that I was past my demob date. He said he had heard nothing, and I would just have to wait. The next day he came up on the field telephone to say my name was on a list of conscripts whose two-year service had been voluntarily extended by two months, and that my TA service would be reduced by that amount. Nice of them. Many years later, when I was able to obtain my service record from the Data Protection Cell, Army Personnel Centre, under the Freedom of Information Act, it read: 'Whole time National Service voluntarily extended. Provisionally eligible for bounty.' I wondered if I had agreed to working overtime when I had signed some paperwork in Tiger Mitchell's office at Lincoln. Had he conned me?

On my last visit to the mobile bath unit on the Imjin, Stan and I were hiking back in the dust, raising a thumb to each vehicle that approached from the rear, but there was nothing doing. Eventually a jeep could be heard fast approaching. Up went our thumbs, but it continued on ... although not for long. Screeching to a halt about 20 yards further on, we raced down to the jeep. The first thing I noticed was that the driver was wearing a Balmoral cap. Good, I thought, KOSB. He'll be going our way.

Then I noticed the driver had red tabs on his shirt collar. Wait a minute. I looked at the driver. There was no mistaking him. This was no KOSB; it was the commander of 1 Comwel Div, Major General 'Gentleman Jim' Cassels in person. He always preferred to pilot the jeep himself, his signaller, a sergeant in the Royal Canadian Signals, sat in the back wearing headphones. 'Sorry, Sir,' I said.

'No, jump up, there is room for two,' was his response. With that Stan climbed in the back, and I took my place in the front seat. 'Gunners, eh!' he said, having noticed our cap badges. 'Where are you going?' I told him the 4.2 mortar troop to the south of Hill 355. He said, 'It is a bit out of my way, but it will give me a chance to see the mortars.' I thought he might have been going only as far as the Kiwi Gunners' BHQ, and we were located some way beyond there. 'Where are you from?' was his next question. This was my kind of general.

I said, 'Portsmouth,' which I told everyone, as they might have heard of the city, but not Fareham.

'Pompey, eh!' said the general, 'they are doing very well this season,' as indeed Portsmouth FC were. Next came, 'Are you regulars or National Service?' I told him we were both conscripts, and both due for home, to which he said that our families would be pleased to see us. Arriving at D Troop gun site, who would be standing there but Tug Wilson? He semaphored a Sandhurst-style salute. The general dropped us off, and without further ado shot off back down the track again, calling 'Goodbye' over his shoulder, and he was gone.

Speechless, Tug managed to ask me what the hell we thought we were doing, bringing the division commander unannounced. He also wanted to know what we had spoken about. What did he think? That he asked us how to bring the war to a conclusion? The reason we had not realized it was the general's jeep when we had stopped him in his travels was that the red plates bearing two silver stars on front and rear bumpers were totally obscured by the thick dust. If I had seen them I would not have stuck up my thumb. But he would have stopped anyway. He was that sort of general.

While I was waiting for news about my RHE (repatriation to home establishment) the battery moved again, this time to the Samichon River valley, where we had the US Marine Division to our left. Out tracing a line for a break one day, I came upon a marine sitting on a rock, playing with his carbine. On the other side of the track was a notice that read 'This could be you. Wear your helmet', topped off with a bullet-holed standard US Army steel helmet and a human skull. The sentry would not let me pass as I had no steel bowler on. I told him we had not even brought such a thing up from our B Echelon, where our heavy kit was dumped, but he was adamant: no helmet, no right of way. I turned back, knowing I would have to lay a new line over the ridge, bypassing the sentry point. As far as he was concerned I was just another Limey who could have his head blown off.

Another sign in that area, erected by the Marines, read: 'YOU ARE NOW ENTERING THE WORLD-RENOWNED SAMICHON VALLEY PARK. ADMISSION BY HELMET ONLY. DO NOT FEED THE ANIMALS.' They had a thing about helmets, those Yanks. They even wore them on the dock at Pusan, John Wayne-style with the chin straps dangling, real combat men, at least 200 miles from the nearest angry man.

Before leaving Korea, I recalled a peaceful week guarding the Division Ammunition Dump near Yongdung-po, a task that all units could expect to undertake. We were a mixed group of gunners, infantry and Canadians from 2 RCR. The ammunition was protected by a high double-wire fence with floodlights at strategic points. Our guard commander, a 2 RCR corporal, read out our orders. They were relatively simple: 'If anyone breaks in, you shoot them.' Well, that seemed simple enough. We were also warned not to go to certain places as we would snag tripwires that would send illuminating flares skywards. We had a quiet time during the daylight hours, but at night it was a different ball game.

Idly watching the Canadians skin our blokes alive at poker, suddenly a loud 'plop' and a bright light on the canvas of the tent told us someone had tripped a flare. One shot rang out, and it was all over. Civilians were running everywhere, disappearing through a large hole in the wire. A trail of blood indicated that someone had been hit. As nothing could be repaired until daylight, a sentry was posted at the hole for the rest of the night. The Canadian Provost Corps (military police) investigated next day, saying it was a common occurrence. They filled in paperwork, the guard commander signed it, and nothing further was heard. The Provos said the infiltrators had been after the round canisters in the middle of each box of No. 36 Mills grenades that contained the detonators. They used them on homemade bombs for fishing in the Han estuary. Hungry people, desperate for food, will resort to desperate measures.

On the subject of food, when we were in a permanent position, and it appeared that we would be staying for a while, we would be on Composite rations, known as Compo, which were really pretty good, but some of the fish varieties were not popular and there was not a lot the cooks could do with them. A member of R22eR (the famed French Canadian battalion known as the 'Van Doos', as *vingt-deux* – twenty-two – took some getting our tongues around) drove up one day in a jeep towing a trailer. He and our cook went into a bearded huddle, the Van Doos' beard, that is, and shortly afterwards our cook was seen to load all the unwanted fish in the trailer. They disappeared down the track together.

After about forty minutes they were both back again, the trailer still fully loaded, the cynical among us thinking the Van Doos had told our cook what to do with his lousy fish, probably in French. But on unloading the trailer we saw what a good deal the cook had made. We saw food the likes of which we did not receive in our rations: large tins of peanut butter, honey, grape jam, maple syrup, fresh coffee, sacks of flour and cartons of Hershey bars. There were other items, now forgotten. I tell you, our cook was worth his weight in Compo rations. And we had thought he had been about to sell the fish to enhance his bankroll for when he went on R&R.

We had some characters in D Troop that I would miss, like Ginger, a Londoner, who caused a company of infantry to stand-to one night by blazing away with the .30 Browning. When questioned as to what the hell he thought he was doing, Ginger said he had been firing at 'those Chinamen with lighted cigarettes coming through the wire'. What he had seen were not enemy soldiers about 40 feet away, but fireflies dancing in front of his face. He had probably dozed off, woken suddenly and thought we were under serious attack. I never heard if Ginger was court-martialled, as I was on my way home within days. We had men who, after a fire fight, reckoned they had dangled an arm over the parapet to get a wounding that would not heal – broken arm, smashed shoulder blade, something simple, they said – so they might be taken to NORMASH to discover if there really were 6ft, blue-eyed, blonde nurses there. I understand they did have nurses that were about 6 feet tall, with blond hair and blue eyes, but the majority of nurses were men.

Then came the day I had waited for. My RHE notification had arrived at BHQ. I would be leaving D Troop in three days. But before I left, with one day to go, I had to take a small group of new arrivals back down the track to demonstrate how our telephone lines were laid, to show them how easily many lines could be carried away on the soft shoulder by two vehicles passing on the narrow track. On hearing the most almighty bang close at hand, followed by an express train roar passing overhead, every man crouched low on the assumption that we were being attacked. Standing upright again, they felt a little foolish when I explained it was just a Kiwi 25-pounder firing outgoing, not Chinese incoming.

Like me on my first day in Korea, they had a lot to learn. They would soon find out that death in battle is not often the clean, clinical way of the movies. Most men did not die from a single sniper's shot in the forehead. Most men in Korea were killed by shell or mortar bomb, and it was not a pretty sight. A direct hit by shellfire is horrendous, leaving a chaos of limbs torn off, the body mangled beyond recognition, and only identifiable by someone who happened to know that it was 'so-and-so' who had been standing there one second before.

But there was little I could tell them, apart from those words of wisdom I had been told on my first day in the line, which now seemed so long ago: 'They are the safe ones, the ones you hear. It is those you don't hear that will kill you.'

Chapter Eight

Homeward Bound

A s I said my goodbyes to good mates that I knew I would never see again, I picked up a copy of *Crown News*, a single-sheet information paper printed at 1 Comwel Div HQ and circulated to all units. I put it in my pack to read later. All these years later, I still have it, yellowed with age. Most of one side of print is a message from Major General Jim Cassels to all ranks in his division, reading:

> This division may not be only the first but also the last Commonwealth Division, for in any future conflict it is likely that each country would make up its own divisions. It is only the circumstances peculiar to Korea which caused this division to be formed, but for those who ask does such a division work, the answer is in the record.
>
> Such a question is best answered by stating the simple fact that the division can claim that it has never failed to carry out its allotted task. In every engagement it has acquitted itself with credit. This record had been achieved because the officers and men who have been privileged to serve in the division have found that although they may belong to different armies, this fact is only incidental.
>
> It had been learnt that nearly all Commonwealth ideas, conceptions and techniques of war are virtually the same. Where there have been differences it was always possible to find a solution to the problem acceptable to both schools of thought.
>
> Everyone is struck by the way that every Commonwealth unit seems to have the same aim in life, namely to be a credit to the Commonwealth and the division as a whole, as opposed to its own particular army.

Certainly I had been privileged to have been among men, good mates whom I could rely on in a tight corner. Now I was going home I knew I would miss the *esprit de corps*, the comradeship, that something the Aussies call mateship, something that was never achieved in the same manner over the following forty years of my working life in civilian employment.

Very little is remembered of my departure from 120 Light Battery, but I can conjure up the likely scene: climbing over the tailgate of a Bedford

QL 3-tonner, hauling my packs on board, shouting out last goodbyes to the best of mates as the driver pulled away. First stop was BHQ, where I had to display that my personal weapon had no rounds in the chamber or magazine. I was back on the Lee Enfield again as the Sten had been OP kit. At BHQ I met the other lads who were also going home, including one who I had travelled out with, who was also two months late for demob: he must also have 'volunteered'. He had been in A Troop 170 Battery, then E Troop 120 Battery, and in all that time we had only met once, when a much reduced 170 Battery had arrived back at Yongdung-po on 26 April 1951, and we had been given the shattering news that C Troop had not made it.

Then came the long dusty road over Pintail crossing, and on past 1 Comwel Div HQ and Fort George airstrip, where the light spotter aircraft were based. We were heading south on Route 11, where with 1 RUR and the Belgians we had made our fighting withdrawal. It was still a dirt track, but widened to take two-way traffic. Well, almost.

Away to our right was Kamak-san, from where the Chinese had directed fire down on us. I could not identify the ambush site where we had needed to follow the tank tracks across the paddy, as the S-bend where I had seen the burnt-out Centurions had been almost straightened by the Royal Engineers. Then we were at Tokchon, now the railhead for Commonwealth traffic, where there was a NAAFI shop where urgent supplies could be bought. We continued south on the MSR. I had to kick my heels at FMA overnight, and then next morning it was a short journey to Seoul Station, where I was quickly seated. No splintered bunks or wooden seats this time. I would be travelling in some style aboard the crack flyer of Eighth Army, the EUSAK Express.

In no time at all the train picked up speed, and the ruins of Seoul were left behind. There were stops at Suwon, Taejon, Taegu and other places to offload or collect military personnel, and after a reasonably comfortable journey Pusan came up on the horizon. I have no recollection of how long it took, but it was certainly much faster than my first train ride on Korean railways.

Next day, after a fairly comfortable night on a folding camp bed, I was told that my ship would not be taking me home direct from Pusan docks, but I was to travel across to Kure, where a few days would be spent before boarding the same ocean liner from there. That was a pleasant surprise. With all this extra time in the Army I began to wonder if the barrack-room lawyers had it right when they said that a National Serviceman had to be paid one pound for each day served beyond his two years. I doubted it, but I would have to wait until I reached Woolwich to find out. So, another day to kick my heels, then it was Japan again, and then I would be on my way home.

I asked the regimental policeman at the guardroom if I was allowed out. I was, by signing myself out and telling him where I intended to go. So I wandered along the road, through a small village, and on to an airfield where US Air Force planes were landing and departing. When I had seen enough I started back to the transit camp. I had hardly begun when a jeep driven by a US Army major pulled up. After telling me to jump in, he asked me where I was going. I told him the Commonwealth transit camp. He then told me I ought not to be out walking in that area, particularly through the village. 'Two of my boys were castrated right here in this village last week,' he told me. I was pleased to be riding back to camp, as I had no desire to leave any souvenirs behind me in Korea.

Before dropping me off he surprised me by asking if he could look at my glasses, asking if they were standard British Army issue. I confirmed that they were. He asked if I had a second pair, and I told him I had just the one pair, to which he enquired how I would have managed in the front line if they had broken, something I had never given a thought to. Handing back my spectacles he also handed me a card on which was printed his name and rank, and that he was something like, from memory, the resident ophthalmologist in a nearby military hospital. If I came to his hospital the next morning he would have me fitted up with two pairs of 'GI glasses'. I had no chance to take him up on his kind offer as I was leaving for Kure early in the morning. It was another demonstration of American generosity.

My voyage across to Kure was by another of those ancient tramp steamers, this time on the *Wo Sang*. I knew there was a sister ship, the *E Sang*, and I had already travelled on the *Po Yang*, so a Hong Kong shipping line was making good money from the Korean War. The voyage was uneventful.

It was good to be back in Kure again, although I could not drive from my head the thought that I ought to have been demobbed already. During previous times there I had come to know my way around quite well. On arrival at JRBD (Japan Reinforcement Base Depot), just along the way from the New Zealand Base Camp, I found that little had changed when I forayed into town. Kure House still served decent Australian steaks for three shillings and sixpence, and Hikariso was still serving ice cold beer at 180 yen a bottle. I whiled away two pleasant evenings at Hikariso.

It was now possible to take a ferry to Miyajima, or a train ride to Hiroshima, but I had insufficient time as my transport for home had arrived in port that morning, and already incoming drafts for the battle school at Haramura had arrived in JRBD. I spoke to a couple of young gunners who had just arrived and wanted to know what it was like 'over there'. I expect my E Troop mate and I shot them a war story or two, and I asked what HMT *Empire Pride* was like, as that was the ship for my sea excursion to Liverpool, via all those fascinating parts of Empire along the way. They told me it was not bad, provided I got the hang of slinging a hammock.

That evening, my last in Japan, before heading for Hikariso I walked as near to *Empire Pride* as possible. It looked a bit of a tip, and a fresh paint job would do it the world of good, but it was going in the right direction. I had listened to *China Night* once more, and regretted having lost the camera I had bought in Tokyo. It had been buried under an avalanche of mud in the wet season, although I did manage to save a few photographs as well as some of the souvenir Chinese safe conduct leaflets they fired at us in non-exploding mortar bombs, or left around our defensive wire. I was ready for home. I had also managed to bring with me a Composite Pack from C rations to show the folks at home a small sample of Uncle Sam's ingenuity.

It was 6 June 1952 as our homeward-bound draft called out a chorused 'You'll be sorry' to the sentry on the gate, already two weeks past my demob date, before I had been 'volunteered' to stay longer. I thought I might write to Tiger Mitchell after I had my feet under the table at home, and then promptly let it ride. I had a nice sea voyage ahead of me, even though I knew that *Empire Pride* was the slowest trooper on the UK to Japan run, taking forty-three days to reach her home port, Liverpool. Built in Glasgow in 1941 – not in Germany, as the rumours had it – she was subsequently used by the Department of War Transport for military stores and troop movements. I had already been told there would be no comfortable three-tier bunks for us steerage class passengers – just hammocks.

Directed to our troop deck, just above the keel it seemed, we dumped our kitbag and packs in a former cargo hold and grappled our way back up several decks to be issued with hammocks on which to rest our bones each night. Nobody was impressed. Back down to the depths with our portable beds, we were faced with the message stencilled on a bulkhead: ACCOMMODATION FOR 120 PERSONNEL. No problem, I thought, until one bright spark, probably a Royal Signals corporal, carried out a rough headcount. He made it that about 160 bodies were crammed in down there.

Knowing that a dreadful mistake had been made, and considering that forty men would have to be moved to another cargo hold, he took it upon himself to act as spokesperson. Proceeding up to the office of the ship's commandant, he told the duty officer that someone had screwed up, or something similar in 1950s' language. The Royal Signals corporal reckoned the whole ship could easily cope with a thousand troops, and only about 200 had boarded that day. He was soon put right.

The duty officer agreed that today there was plenty of room, but after virtually an entire infantry battalion boarded in Hong Kong next week, and another load of home-going men in Singapore, we would be riding very low in the water for the remainder of the voyage. I can tell you that the forty men who were slowest in grabbing a pair of hammock rings that night would be sleeping on the deck, or the mess tables, all the way to Liverpool. But most men agreed they had slept on harder surfaces in Korea.

Departing at around 1500 hrs that afternoon we slipped away from Kure, past the huge superstructure of the battleship *Haruna*, which many men still insisted was the *Yamato*. *Haruna*, built in Kure shipyards, was, I believe, of the Yamato class, but the actual *Yamato* ship had been sunk by the Americans south of Okinawa just before the war with Japan ended.

I had survived a testing period in my young life. Still only twenty, I would return to the peace of Civvy Street. But prior to Liverpool I had six weeks of adventure ahead of me. It would be as well to enjoy all this foreign travel while I had the opportunity. Forgetting thoughts of the overcrowding that would not be permitted under today's health and safety regulations (and probably broke regulations such as they were in 1952 – the shortage of hammock rings, not to mention the atrocious food), life was made a little more acceptable as some men still marked off 'days to go' on their homemade calendars.

I would suffer the overcrowding like a man, looked forward to Hong Kong five days ahead, and this time hoped that nobody contracted smallpox before we reached Singapore. Would there be the route march in Colombo that I had heard mentioned? If there was, I had already decided to skive off by reporting to the ship's MO, if I could think of something, like sunburn. But that was no good; I would be put on a charge for self-inflicted injuries. I would have to think about it.

With Hong Kong only a little over two days away, disaster struck. Passing through the Formosa Strait with the coast of China to starboard, suddenly the coastline disappeared in heavy rain. A typhoon hit us with all the power it could muster. Our floating home was stopped dead in its tracks. I think the nautical term might be 'dead in the water'. Whatever, we were certainly not making headway. I was informed that the word 'typhoon' is an approximation of '*tai fung*' or 'big wind', as the People's Volunteers would say. And it was not only wind; the waves were tremendous. Each time the bow dipped into the next enormous wave the stern came up clear of the water, the screw turning aimlessly before hitting the water again as the bow came up, sending such horrendous vibrations through the ship I hoped those shipbuilders back in Glasgow had made a good job of the riveting. I almost expected the ship to break in half.

And you never saw such seasickness. The entire ship was painted with part-digested meals. Not that anyone felt like eating. Loudspeaker messages warned us not to go out onto the open decks until the massive waves, incredibly strong wind and torrential rain ceased. That condition lasted for about twenty-four hours. The following day you would not have known a typhoon had passed. The sea was almost as calm as a millpond for the remainder of the journey to Hong Kong and, surprisingly, we did not appear to have lost any time – or if we had, it had been made up in the night. Such is the fickleness of the world's oceans.

Our arrival in Hong Kong was greeted by derisory shouts from the squaddies in Lye Mun Barracks at the eastern entrance to the harbour, to which we replied like for like. We enjoyed a really good day ashore, and then it was on to Singapore, where this time, as nobody had gone to see the ship's doctor with spots that looked deserving of quarantine, we saw the sights. Then it was on to Colombo where, despite the rumour, there was no 10-mile route march. Aden hove-to on the starboard bow, shore leave was taken, and the know-alls still insisted it had not rained since 1936. On the bank of the Suez Canal we shouted out our 'get your knees brown' comments to the squaddies stationed there, as we progressed slowly through in convoy to Port Said. There was no shore leave there for us, so we did not have to fight off the locals who insisted we could not arrive back in Blighty without their postcards, clean and dirty, fly whisks, imitation photo albums or Egyptian Turkish delight. Then we were on the home stretch … only nine more days to Liverpool, and home.

Watching the North African coastline slip by, Malta was passed, and then Gibraltar, and there was only the Bay of Biscay to attack us before the English Channel was entered. England was just ahead now, somewhere over the horizon. I was almost home. What an adventure I had volunteered for. I was pleased that I had not refused Tiger Mitchell's kind offer to join the other forty-nine volunteers for Korea. But I did wonder if I ought to follow up that bit about also volunteering to extend my period of enforced conscription by two months.

Chapter Nine

Obligation Fulfilled

With everyone straining their eyes to be first to sight the lighthouse off Land's End, in the late evening it became visible. Passing by, I saw the coast of Cornwall, then later the Welsh coast on the starboard side, with lights of towns clearly visible. I imagine I was not the only man standing on that deck who experienced a whole range of emotions, and memories. Those of us who were National Servicemen – at least one year older and, I like to think, wiser for the experience – would be looking forward to discharge from a service environment. As I had already passed my official release date I guessed I would not be held onto for very long, unless good reason could be found for the retention of my undoubted military skills.

I recall walking out on deck quite late, gazing at the lights ashore, my thoughts returning to the men I had left behind. I probably thought of John Kilburn, a conscript who ought to have left for home in one week's time, but was killed in an A Troop OP before he had the opportunity to pack his kitbag, remaining in Korea forever with a grave marker in the cemetery at Pusan. Also Captain Warren, my new troop commander, who had been killed after only two weeks in Korea, Bob Dowkes and Harry Breakwell, both killed in Operation *Commando*, or the lad who had been burned to death in his petrol-soaked sleeping bag before he had time to get out, and whose family would have been notified 'killed in action' without details provided.

I might have given thought to the men of C Troop, taken into captivity with the 'Glorious Glosters'. Where would they be? And the remains of the young American I had uncovered when filling sandbags. A thousand thoughts must have run through my head as I awaited that landfall in the morning – Liverpool and then home.

Although I was pleased to be back, my brain told me there was still a big world out there. How much of it would I see in the forthcoming years? Time alone would tell. I had the travel bug in my feet as well as my brain. I could already say 'been there, done that, seen it' about a fair slice of the globe, but I already knew I was unlikely to stay in one place for long. In July 1952, as *Empire Pride* lay off Liverpool waiting for the pilot to guide her into the

Mersey, that period of my life when I would be travelling once again was some way ahead.

Six long weeks and a day out of Kure, I came home. So many others had not been so lucky; they were never to see the medals they earned with their blood. As we pulled into the dock there were no military bands, no streamers, no press men or newsreel cameramen hovering to get a good story, and no joyful happy families singing *Land of Hope and Glory* for the fifth time, as there would be for returning 'heroes' from a later conflict. It would have been nice, but in 1952 these things were not done that way. It was just another damp, dismal day in the life of Liverpool, and of Britain. Although it was July, a chill wind swept Prince's Landing Stage as the gangways were positioned to allow the port authorities, important military visitors and customs raiding party to board. Later, leaving my home of the past six weeks with a happy heart, kitbag slung over my shoulder, I filed across a dreary, uninviting dock into a large grey shed.

'I do hope you haven't brought in more than 200 cigarettes,' from a miserable customs officer, was my 'Welcome Home, lad'. Her Majesty's Customs and Excise officials were about to make damn sure that every last penny due to government coffers was extracted from us. 'No, only 200,' I replied, when I had 400 Craven A stashed away for my father. Across the shed I could see an overzealous rummage squad taking great pleasure, or so it seemed, from ordering men to upend the contents of their kitbags onto the concrete floor. They might have got sadistic pleasure from watching them try to repack everything neatly – an impossibility – while telling them to hurry up, as they did not have all morning.

It all seemed very petty to me. Give a man a blue serge suit and a bit of gold braid and he thinks he is God Almighty, I thought. I must have had an honest face as I was not delayed, but was told to move on after indecipherable chalk marks had been scrawled on my kit. There was still no 'Welcome home', just 'Off you go then, I haven't got all day.' I guessed that my official welcome was being saved until I reached Woolwich Barracks.

I had heard that, shortly after my arrival at Liverpool, the locally recruited infantry regiment, King's (Liverpool) Regiment, with a large contingent of National Servicemen in the ranks, was sending its first battalion to Korea. I knew the people of the city would wish them well.

I had been waved through to the far end of the shed and told by a military policeman to 'stack your kit over there, stay with that lot until your train arrives, and don't wander off under any circumstances' – a long sentence of joined-up words for a Red Cap. But I had noticed that 'that lot' seemed to be getting smaller. Men were easing themselves out of the shed. I stacked my kit and then looked out to see why men were disappearing. The clink of glasses gave it away. Right there at the dock gate was a pub. Checking that I was not under the scrutiny of the MPs, along with a mate who also enjoyed living dangerously, I slipped away to find that the pub was absolutely filled to the gills with squaddies and dockers. It was only 1000 hrs, pub opening time in 1952, and I guessed the dockers were enjoying an early lunch. A very early lunch.

Those dockers were pleased to see us, telling us proudly that 'their regiment' would be heading for Korea shortly. They placed pint glasses in our hands and welcomed us home, not letting us put our hands into our own pockets to return the favour. As we were finishing our pints, the MPs came looking for us, threatening all sorts of punishment if we did not get ourselves into the shed, pick up our kit, and climb onto the waiting train. Those dockers had really made us feel welcome. I have never forgotten that crowd of happy, smiling faces. As our troop train pulled out of the docks, a few ribald remarks were made to petty officials everywhere, but particularly those in that customs shed, regardless of the colour cap they wore – navy blue or red.

Being British Rail, the train was absolutely crowded, all seats having long been filled while we were enjoying ourselves with the dockers. So it was standing room only as we passed once again those familiar villages and larger towns, where some troops disembarked close to their depots. Before long, Euston Station signboards appeared. From Euston, for all gunners it was an Underground ride to Waterloo, and a change of trains for Woolwich. Unbelievably, on arrival at home base there was no transport for us. I may be wrong, but I believe the wartime system of having a rail transport office (RTO) at stations where a good number of troops were garrisoned still existed. A bombardier went looking for the RTO to find out about transport. Whomever he spoke to said there was none. We were home again. There were no cheerful faces here to say 'Jump up guys'. We shouldered our kit and staggered up the long gradient to the barracks.

We walked in at the main gate where, just in case we had forgotten our manners, the sergeant of the guard demanded to know who our most senior man was. Sarge had been notified that, instead of the bombardier falling us in and marching us into barracks, we had just strolled along the pavement. Sarge seemed to be another sad individual, and he didn't welcome us home either. We were told to turn to the right under the arch that led to Field Wing, where another 'Woolwich commando' with three stripes but no medal ribbons, shouted, 'Get fell in, in three ranks facing me, come on, come on, hurry it up,' or words to that effect. Oh yes, we were back home again! He called us to attention, to right turn, and quick marched us over to an office block.

There, my demob procedure started immediately. Disinterested, clean-shaven, pink-faced young National Service clerks checked my credentials, asked questions, filled in forms, shuffled them into some semblance of order, banged rubber stamps, and made arrangements for my release medical, which would ensure that no body parts had fallen off along the way. Someone nudged me: 'That's Bombardier so-and-so.' The name did not register. Apparently, he was a formidable athlete and his home posting had guaranteed that he was available for the 1952 Olympics. He may have served his country well in athletics, but I considered I had better served my country.

We were back in the 'real' Army again. March here, march there, march back again. Only for a few more days would I suffer these indignities. We had been placed under the wing of another Woolwich commando. He seemed to take an instant dislike to me at our de-kitting to remove all kit that would not be needed at our TA units. And we had to pay for anything we had lost … or sold to the villagers through the wire at JRBD. He picked up the composite pack I had brought home. It went something like this:

'What the bloody hell have we got here, then, Gunner?'

'It is from a C7 ration pack, Sarge.'

'And what the hell is a C7?'

'US Army combat rations we ate in the front line, Sarge.'

'Don't tell me there were any Yanks in the front line?'

'Thousands of them, Sarge, but no Woolwich commandoes.'

Well, that did it. He threatened me with insubordination, the one they always used when they could not think of a genuine reason to have a man confined to barracks for, say, seven days. But instead he was lenient with me. He entered my name for main gate guard on my final night in the Army. And he confiscated my Composite pack, as it was likely to be 'stolen US military property'. In reality, he probably wanted to show it off to his mates or his family.

I passed A1 on my release medical, stood guard two hours on, four hours off, as my mates had a laugh at my expense. There would be no pint down in the town for me, no couple of hours at the Woolwich Empire laughing at what used to make us laugh in 1952, and no fish and chip supper in Greasy Annie's, as we called it, right across the road from the guardroom. On the morning of my discharge, following guard dismounting, our draft was marched to the pay office. Our expectations rose in anticipation. But money was held back from us until the very end. First I signed for a seven-day food ration card so that I didn't starve until I could get a full ration book at the Ministry of

Food office in Fareham. Finally came the reckoning. I received a proportion of what I had coming to me; the balance would be in the post. Trousering the money I had been paid (I believe it was about £30, the largest amount of cash I had picked up in my life) I had already calculated that my entire twenty-six months of conscription had cost a benevolent government a little over £300 ... but not much over. I ought to have signed on for regular service, as regular soldiers were paid more than a National Serviceman. Can you imagine the government trying that on today? Calling men up to cover a shortfall in, say Afghanistan, and paying them less than the guys they will be fighting – and perhaps dying – alongside? No, neither can I.

Surprisingly, a truck was laid on to take us down to Woolwich Station, possibly because they wanted to see the back of us as soon as possible, and they could not trust us to march there. We each had a large sealed buff envelope that had to be taken to our allotted TA unit before we dared to go home. My rail warrant was made out to Fareham, via Portsmouth, where, right across from the station, in Stanhope Street, was my TA unit HQ. I found the entrance into RHQ 383 Light Regiment (Duke of Connaught's Own) Royal Artillery Territorial Army. It was quite a title, but not as long as that of the Royal Artillery TA unit on the Isle of Wight that had something strange about 'Princess Beatrice's Isle of Wight Rifles' in the middle of it.

I had been told in letters from home that we had a new neighbour, a staff sergeant in the Royal Artillery who had got himself a cushy posting as Chief Clerk of the aforementioned TA unit. I entered, followed the signs, and came upon the Chief Clerk. For a neighbour, he did not have much to say, but then he was a staff sergeant, I was a gunner. I handed him my envelope. He looked up ... and told me my rights. About once a fortnight I was to report to the Gosport Drill Hall, and two weeks of my life each year was demanded for firing camp on Salisbury Plain. The regiment had three batteries, P, Q and R, one each in Fareham, Gosport and, I believe, Havant. I wondered why I was wanted at Gosport Battery when we had a perfectly good one in Fareham, but that was the Army ... He had dismissed me in kind, if not in a direct order, so I caught the Fareham train. As I was rather flush with money, after I had enjoyed the pleasure of dragging all my kit over the footbridge I decided enough was enough and squandered a couple of shillings on a taxi.

My mother had no idea which day I would be home. Like most people, we had no telephone. But she had seen the taxi arrive and came to the door to greet me. 'Welcome home,' she said. I had been welcomed home at last, although, in fairness, those Liverpool dockers had done a great job. She was pleased to see me, she said. I was very brown, slimmer, my hair was shorter, but apart from that, there was only the kettle to put on. Over a cup of tea I was asked if I had met our new neighbour. I said I had, but I told her he didn't say a lot. She told me he had hardly spoken to anyone.

I was asked questions about everything. I briefed her on most of the major events, leaving out the squalid bits. She had kept all the newspaper cuttings of anything to do with Korea, so she knew the sort of mischief I had been up to, she said, but most of the news items were about the American battles; there had been very little about British units. There was one cutting she might have produced at that time, or I could have seen it later, that had a photograph of the *Ted Ray Show*, which I had never even heard of. Under the photo was the caption: 'Ted Ray Entertains the Troops in the Front Line. The hills in the background are held by the Chinese'. Codswallop, as they say. I discovered later that the show was put on at HQ 1 Comwel Div. Well, if that was classed as 'the front line', I should have put in for danger money considering where I had spent most of my time.

In the middle of it my father arrived home from work, hung his jacket on the peg behind the kitchen door, came in and said 'Welcome home'. We had another cup of tea. Dad was pleased with the cigarettes, and my mother loved the music box I had brought home for her, which played *China Night*. I was back in the old familiar routine. But that would not suit me for long. I continued to plough through the news cuttings, and I did begin to wonder on which war the reporter had been reporting. I was reminded of Dennis Bedwell and his reporter.

I was asked if all the lads who had travelled out with me had also come home. I told them not all of them had, nor would they all. Forty years later, I discovered that eleven of the lads in my intake did not return from Korea. My father would have known about that, having had two ships torpedoed under him in the Second World War and seen good mates blown apart around him. It had been very dry of late, and the vegetables in the garden would not come to much, but there was a decent crop of pears on the tree. What had the weather been like when I left Korea? I said it would be very wet at present. Here they were crying out for rain, but my mates would be praying for it to stop. As always in polite English circles, the conversation had turned to the weather. What had Korea been like as a country? I could have told them it was a bloody-awful-stinking-shithole-of-a-place, but we did not swear in our family. I would have to watch my language now that I was home.

On my first full day in Fareham I changed into civvies, a strange feeling after so long. I took a walk into the town centre, stopping at the Maytree Café, the local meeting place for the growing motorcycle mob, to see if any old mates were there, but they were all at work. Seated on a stool at the counter was a man I remembered from my Sea Cadet days. He was in uniform, with

Royal Artillery shoulder titles. We passed the time of day and I asked him where he was stationed. He said he was in Germany, and home on leave. That surprised me. I had no idea leave was allowed from Germany. I told him I had just been demobbed at Woolwich. He enquired where I had been stationed. I told him I had just returned from Korea. He said, 'Oh! Been out there, have you?' finished his cup of tea, walked out, and to this day I have never seen him again. Oh yes, people were really interested in Korea.

On my first evening TA parade night at Gosport, I was introduced to about thirty men of Q Battery who were told I had just returned from Korea, where I had been in a mortar battery. I was unsure if they were impressed or not. After a roll call they were dismissed to their duties, some to polish the battery vehicles that were already gleaming from the last polishing, others to do the same thing on the guns. Meanwhile, the BC, a major, took me to his office to explain everything I needed to know about the battery. I could not see myself doing this for long. After a couple of days at home Korea was hardly mentioned, unless there was a report on the BBC *Six O'clock News*. I expect my parents thought the sooner I forgot, the better it would be for me to quickly assimilate back into the Fareham scene.

Of one thing I was quite certain: having been to war there would be no return for me to a boring civilian job; there would be no retreat to naivety, to innocence. Two action-packed years away from home had disoriented me, changing my outlook on life forever. Just a few days out of uniform and already I had itchy feet. My few precious photographs might have been only black and white, but my mind was filled with the colours I had seen. Already I was feeling like a forgotten soldier from a forgotten war.

Leaving aside the churlish treatment and pettiness that had been meted out at Woolwich, there was no deep interview to find out what a man had on his mind. No assessment was made of my mental capacity to cope with all I had seen. No legions of advisers were on hand to assist in my easy transition back into civilian life. There was a complete lack of concern at all levels for how I might have been affected by what I had experienced, or what effect it might have on me in the years ahead. I knew now how men returning from such places as Burma after the return to peace in 1945 would have felt. I personally didn't have any problems, but for those who would have welcomed help and guidance, there was nobody to turn to. Stiff upper lips were the norm. If any lad had felt the need for a sympathetic ear, he would almost certainly have been advised to get a serious grip on himself. Officialdom would have considered that he lacked 'moral fibre'. In the jargon of today, he would be looked on as a wimp. In 1952, wimps were not tolerated, as they displayed unmanly weakness.

Apparently, only those who had suffered most in the war in Korea, our POWs, were briefly assessed to ascertain their mental state before they were released to their families. Obviously it had been believed that a nice ocean cruise would be beneficial in helping them forget the treatment suffered as guests of the People's Republic. Many years later, I heard from some former POWs, and others from around the world, that mental illnesses were rather more common than had been publicised. Most men recovered well enough; some never did.

A very good Aussie mate spent time in psychiatric wards, even in a straight jacket in a padded cell. I know that if he was alive today, Ron would not mind me writing of his experience. In one particular clash at patrol strength called 'Cloncurry', as platoon leader he had to leave wounded men to their fate when he was ordered to get back before losing any more men. He could not wipe from his mind, or from his dreams, hearing the final shouts from his mates as the Chinese closed in after Ron believed his platoon could have saved them. He never forgot that he had to abandon them to certain death.

He would recall hearing his mates' Owen guns (like our Sten, only much better) firing until their ammunition was exhausted. For many years Ron had a recurring dream that he was standing on a Korean hilltop looking down into the morning mist, knowing that the Chinese were creeping up on him unseen. He had been diagnosed with 'full-blown combat neurosis' at the Veterans' Hospital, Concord, west of Sydney, who made an appointment for Ron to see a hypnotist who was a doctor. Over a period of three months Ron saw the hypnotist several times. When it was considered the right time, Ron was told to imagine he had taken his kitbag up on that hill, to look down into the mist again and imagine he could see the Chinese coming to get him. At the right moment he was told to throw his kitbag as far out and down as he could into the mist. Ron was not 'out of it' during this session; he recalled every bit of it vividly. He followed the instructions. Instantly, Ron was free of his demons, and he and his wife Betty could sleep easily for the first time in years. Ron told me, 'Forty years later, my life changed completely, and I started to live a normal life.' Such are the casualties of war. In 1953, during a second tour in Korea, Ron was decorated with the Military Medal for bravery in saving members of his platoon in another action. Sadly, Ron died in May 2006, just five weeks after Sheila and I had enjoyed his company in Sydney while on holiday. He was a good man and a good friend. Today, Ron would have been diagnosed as suffering from post-traumatic stress disorder (PTSD), but this condition was not recognized in the 1950s.

When I arrived home I had only one communication from the Army: postal orders for the balance of my pay. Like hundreds of thousands of National

Servicemen, we were never thanked for giving our time for that 'police action' in Korea. The reservists all received a letter of appreciation from the Chief of the Imperial General Staff (CIGS), Field Marshal Sir William Slim, a copy of which is included in an appendix to this book. The letter tells the reservists to be proud of their achievement. The Land Army girls who had kept the farms going in the Second World War were belatedly given a rather nice Certificate of Appreciation and a lapel badge. We had nothing, and we do not now expect a belated letter thanking us for our achievement. If a Korean War veteran wants to outwardly display demonstration of his service in fighting communism, he has to buy a lapel badge, as do the veterans from the Malaya Campaign, in which large numbers of National Servicemen fought between 1948 and 1960.

Not that any of us would have expected people to come up to us in the street and say, 'Thanks, mate, for doing a good job over there.' It was quite different at the end of the Second World War, when neighbours were aware that Tom had been fighting in the desert war against the Afrika Korps, Dick had landed in France on D-Day plus one, and Harry had returned physically wrecked from a Japanese prison camp in Thailand. After six years of crippling war, they were only too pleased to say a few welcoming words to Tom, Dick and Harry, friendly faces they knew, and they were aware of where they had been. There was one big difference – they had won their war.

Those good folk of Fareham who knew anything at all about our war in Korea in 1952 were very thin on the ground, and if they did know, they were unclear as to who, if anyone, was winning. Even after the eventual July 1953 ceasefire, they were in all probability just as baffled, not really able to identify which was which of the two Koreas. Unlike other wars, there is no grand monument to commemorate those who fought and died in that far land. We do, however, have a plaque that is decorated with the cap badges of all units that served in our Armed Forces in Korea. It is in the crypt of St Paul's Cathedral in London, where the public has to pay to see it. Opened by Her Majesty the Queen in 1987, thirty-four years after the ceasefire in Korea, its construction was only possible then due to the magnificent generosity of the London Embassy of the Republic of Korea and subscriptions from members of the British Korean Veterans Association. We did it our way, to demonstrate to the politicians that we care. It is a shame that it is not in a place where the public can view it, and hopefully gain a little knowledge and understanding about our war. But other governments have also stuck their heads in the sand.

Even in the United States, where there were pressures from much larger organizations to build some kind of memorial to commemorate the Korean

War, they had nothing until a magnificent display of nineteen stainless steel military figures, each more than 6 feet high, were officially unveiled in Washington DC on 27 July 1995 – the forty-second anniversary of the end of the Korean War. The figures represent an infantry patrol: fourteen representing the United States Army, three for the US Marine Corps, one for a US Navy corpsman (Navy medic attached to the Marines) and one for the US Air Force. The figures stand among shrubs that represent Korea's difficult terrain. Behind the statues is a 246-foot granite wall that has photographic images sandblasted into it depicting various service personnel who were involved in the war. It is quite magnificent.

Canada has a memorial wall in Brampton, Ontario, commemorating all who served in the Korean War, not only their war dead. The 200-foot long wall bears 516 bronze plaques, one for each Canadian soldier who died in Korea. The Australian memorial stands on Anzac Parade, Canberra. It was consecrated on Anzac Day, 25 April 2000. Boulders taken to Australia from the battlefield, and an obelisk with representative figures of the 17,000 Australian troops, air force and naval personnel who went to Korea to fight on land, at sea or in the air, stand among gravel and rocks to emulate the harsh Korean terrain. On the march past at the opening ceremony were 339 children, each carrying an Australian flag, one representing each of the Australians killed in Korea.

Through a serving Army officer in Canberra I made arrangements for one of the flags to be brought to the United Kingdom to be handed to living relatives of a Northamptonshire lad who had emigrated to Australia, joined the Army and went to Korea, where he was killed in action with 3 RAR. The family gratefully accepted the flag from my fellow veteran Michael White, who served in 42 Battery, and a small group of local Korean War veterans. They were also given a correctly badged Australian Army slouch hat that I donated.

For anyone interested in the statistics, the following figures will indicate that we did not fight in some tinpot police action: total United Nations dead, 114,932, and 204,584 wounded. Although China will not release the figures for her war dead, it has been estimated at anything up to 1 million, possibly more, and the figure for wounded must be horrendous.

So when the bugles stir the chill air on cold November streets in cities, towns and villages throughout the land on Remembrance Day, will the young and the not so young alike observe the two-minute silence with head bowed in respect for many more years in this twenty-first century? Or will too many continue to walk past our memorials, calling the veterans whose medal ribbons brighten a dull day 'silly old buggers, still glorifying war'?

Of one thing we can be sure: the people of South Korea remain forever thankful for our effort, their gratitude having flowed down the generations, and they remain indebted to the United Nations for their support, and for the preservation of their freedom. They understand that freedom is not free; it comes at a high cost. Their country has made a remarkable recovery since 1953, the current generation appreciating a standard of living that would have been beyond the comprehension of their grandparents.

But there is still one major necessity that remains to be sorted for the populace who were forcibly removed from ancestral villages and homes in the years 1950 to 1953. They must have the facility to travel the length and breadth of all Korea, north and south of the demarcation line, to visit ancient places from where their families were uprooted. Perhaps, given time, not too many years will slip away before there is an easing of the tension that is still very much in evidence. Dictator after dictator in North Korea has passed total control from grandfather to father to son: Kim Il-sung to King Jong-il to Kim Jong-un. A one-party state, where those causing a disruption, if anyone dared to cause one, would be taken away. In some reported instances gained from those few who have managed to escape from the north, whole families, including grandparents, are sent for 'correction of thought' to places we are not supposed to know about.

They exist in a country where a person is not allowed to live in the capital, Pyongyang, without an official permit, where the residents are told not to make eye contact with foreign visitors, and certainly not to speak to them without permission. A country where anyone managing to evade, or bribe, the border guards along the Yalu River, escaping initially into North China, can live with the hope that one day they might reach South Korea. There, they are automatically entitled to residence; they will receive a resettlement allowance and assistance in finding employment. They speak the same language, although the northern dialect is said to be harsher than the southern, but in reality probably no different than a comparison between Yorkshire and Hampshire.

Closer contact, better understanding between nations and less bickering among statesmen might one day totally eliminate the necessity for our young men and women to go to war. At present, there seems to be little hope of that, not helped in any way by the proliferation of nuclear programmes in too many countries where no consideration is given to whether the poor of the country have a decent standard of living. As long as one country has more territory, more oil, more water or more food growing capacity, tribal intolerances will persist, nation will war with nation, and dictators will continue to spread their evil. Only when national differences between the two Koreas are settled around the conference table at Panmunjom by the Military Armistice Commission Korea, will there be peace at last for all Koreans, on both sides of the 38th parallel, and the world's most heavily guarded border will become a relic of the past.

On veteran occasions I still wear a badge of crossed flags, but today it is not the trade badge of a regimental signaller worn on the sleeve. Now I wear on my lapel with pride the crossed flags of the United Kingdom and the Republic of Korea, the Union flag and the Taekuk-gi, a symbol of friendship and understanding between our two nations.

On peacekeeping duty in 1956 to 1957, the last British infantry battalion to serve in Korea, the Royal Sussex Regiment, with assistance from the Royal Engineers, erected a memorial close to the village of Solma-ri in commemoration of the last stand by units of 29 British Independent Brigade on the Imjin River in April 1951. Five simple stone tablets engraved in Korean and English have been built into the natural granite of the hillside, overlooking those same ridges that had been defended at great cost by the 1st Battalion the Gloucestershire Regiment and C Troop 170 Independent Mortar Battery Royal Artillery.

Every April, a moving ceremony is held at the site, with an honour guard and a bugler. The last post, followed by reveille, reverberates through the green valley as those strident notes are sounded amid the pines and blossoming shrubs that have been planted to heal the scars of battle. Other bugle calls of long ago, which filled the valley for three days and nights to direct movements of the enemy soldiers, sound no more. Neither do the bugle calls defiantly sounded in retaliation by Drum Major Buss of the Glosters, who had been ordered by his adjutant to retaliate against the Chinese by sounding every bugle call known to the British Army, except Retreat – although his notes will be remembered forever by all who heard them. Recent photographs show 'Gloster Valley', as it is known, to be a place of beauty, a fit place of commemoration for those who gave their lives in defence of the freedom of the Republic of Korea.

I was lucky; I came home. We left too many behind, good mates among them, but they are not forgotten. They will never be just a name on a grave marker. For them there will always be a small plot of Korean soil over which our Union flag will fly.

But now, let me take you back to 1952 ...

Although I departed from 120 Battery in June 1952, I feel it is relevant to include some of the main events that occurred in the battery from that time until March 1953, the reason becoming evident later. I have no idea if the following events were ever re-typed onto official Army Form C2118 (War Diary). They are taken from the personal handwritten notes that I received many years ago from Major D.A. Johnson MC, Commander of 120 Battery in June 1952, when he knew that I intended to write these memoirs.

By the end of July there was an acute shortage of 4.2-inch mortar ammunition in Korea. Each mortar battery, astonishingly, was rationed to ninety-six rounds per day; this was later reduced to forty-eight rounds. How they would have managed in the face of a major attack, I have no idea. Not to be thwarted, Major Johnson had noticed three 17-pounder anti-tank guns at a rear echelon of the Norfolks doing very little except gathering dust. He enquired if he could borrow one, along with a small supply of HE ammunition, and arranged for the gun to be towed to the battery position.

From 19 July to 6 August, the gun, manned by men with previous 17-pounder experience, including my late mate Peter Gore, was used on HF tasks each night from forward locations. Peter told me the first time the gun – correctly called the Ordnance QF 17-pound gun – was placed onto its circular platform a great deal of muscle was needed. The 4.2-inch mortar weighed in at a mere 806lbs, whereas the 17-pounder weighed 6,720lbs. Shooting continued until the weather changed to heavy rain, causing thick mud. Thankfully, during August, more 4.2 ammunition became available, so the 17-pounder was returned to its owners.

The 17-pounder had in fact become an infantry weapon in 1949. Most of the Royal Artillery Anti-Tank batteries were then disbanded, while by mid-1950 two had been converted to the 4.2-inch mortar, namely 27 (Stranges) Mortar Battery and 170 Independent Mortar Battery. The use of the borrowed gun was recorded as the very last use of the 17-pounder by a unit of the Royal Artillery in action against an armed enemy. The gun had been brought to Korea by the Ulster Rifles Support Company but never used, as by the time of their arrival there were no more sightings of enemy tanks. I have photographs of the gun with Peter Gore in the layer's seat. Nothing appears to have been recorded regarding the success, or otherwise, of the gun in action against known or suspected enemy OPs, but many years later, Major Johnson wrote in *Gunner* magazine: 'We must have at least caused a few Chinamen to suck their teeth in surprise.'

In July a further operation was planned for the infantry to take and hold Hill 227 for thirty-six hours, with Captain Harrison as FOO, although eventually the operation was cancelled. On returning to the gun position the BC's jeep was mortared, wounding him. Early in August, 42 and 120 Batteries changed positions, with D Troop moving to the north-east of Hill 187N and E Troop to the south-east of Hill 210. By mid-August, E Troop occupied a position in support of an operation of 28 Britcom Brigade, with tanks of 5th Royal Inniskilling Dragoon Guards (5 RIDG) deploying to the tops of ridges in close proximity to E Troop mortars. This was much too close as far as E Troop were concerned, as immediately a tank poked its gun and turret above the skyline the Chinese would start to shell it.

One tank sitting on the top of Hill 210 was particularly singled out, but most of the shells were ranging just over the tank, landing among E Troop gun pits, killing Gunner Banbury, which did not go down at all well with his mates, who made a few choice comments about tanks being so close at hand. Also wounded were Gunners Allen and McCricket, and Pak Jai-sok, one of E Troop's loyal porters. Such are the hazards of war.

Due to this unexpected and unwanted shelling on its position E Troop was relocated to a new position near Sanjom-ni. The road to this new position was under direct enemy observation, and it could only be approached by day on foot. Supplies were moved to the troop position at night, having been assembled on D Troop position during the day. Pak Jai-sok, who had been wounded in the shoulder, returned voluntarily after discharge from hospital, despite the partial loss of movement in one arm. This impressed Major Johnson, who said it was a good effort on his part, and it displayed something that was 'typical of the loyal spirit of our Korean porters'.

From the Sanjom-ni position E Troop could range on at least fifty known enemy mortar locations, firing 3,000 rounds against them despite continuing ammunition limitations. Live firing continued on observed targets throughout August and September, with 100 shells falling on D Troop position on 17 September, wounding Gunner 'Skin' Campbell, a man of many tattoos, including a fully-rigged sailing ship across his chest. I was later told that his main concern was not so much the lumps of metal that had to be removed from his body, but their precise locations, in the hope that his prized chest tattoo had not been wrecked.

Overnight on 14 to 15 September, there was the only instance of a 'premature' in a 4.2-inch mortar in Korea. A premature is the detonation of a bomb while still in, or just beyond, the barrel, the consequences of which in a mortar pit are devastating, as there is no gun shield to provide partial protection to the detachment as with a premature in a field gun.

G Troop 248 Battery was engaged in an intensive counter-mortar programme, when there was a premature in No. 2 gun. Lieutenant Mawson happened to be passing the gun pit when WO2 Woosnam, Sergeant Broadbent and Lance Bombardier Brettel were killed by the explosion, and a fourth man was badly wounded, as was Lieutenant Mawson. Almost immediately a serious fire broke out in the gun pit, where there were nearly 100 live bombs that would have caused much greater loss of life. Despite his own wounds, Lieutenant Mawson took charge, directing operations, offering what comfort he could for the dying and aiding the wounded. Although weak from loss of blood, he eventually had the fire extinguished and when he was certain that control was in the hands of a young officer, he had his wounds dressed. For his display of self-sacrifice and devotion to duty in a difficult situation Lieutenant Mawson was decorated with the George Medal.

Most of the shooting at this time was counter-mortar HF in support of 25 and 28 brigades. On 5 October, 29 Brigade relieved 28 Brigade in the left brigade sector, changing positions with 248 Light Battery, with D Troop locating near Naechon, and E Troop close to Hill 187S. The battery OP was manned in 1st King's Regiment area. On 12 October, Captain Graham assumed command of E Troop, relieving Captain 'Duggie' Hurndall, with whom I had performed in many OP parties. In the Second World War he had been a glider pilot, crashing his glider on the crossing of the Rhine, wearing wings above his medal ribbons. He was well liked by the signallers, and said when on OP duty, 'Call me Duggie and I'll call you by your name or nickname.' He reckoned that in a position where we never knew if any day would be our last on this earth, there was no need for much formality in the OP, where he would take his turn at making a brew, but when we were back at the guns, it had to be 'Sir' for Duggie.

The battery continued with night-time HF, using a single mortar from various roving positions to confuse the enemy. This had to be curtailed as cold weather had unexpectedly set in, and the positions were much too far forward to allow the gun detachments to light fires to warm themselves as they would have attracted the interest of the enemy. At this time Captain Peyton-Jones relieved Captain Jordan as battery captain, when Captain Jordan was posted to 14 Field.

On 29 November, 29 Brigade took over an area from US 7th Marine Regiment to the west of the Samichon River, in support of the newly arrived 1st Battalion of the Black Watch (1 BW) and the Duke of Wellington's Regiment (1 DWR). The Dukes had relieved the Welch Regiment in the centre of 29 Brigade positions. The 1 King's were located on the right of the brigade. The area taken over included a feature named by the Marines as The Hook – due to the shape of the feature, formed by a range of low hills – which had been the scene of recent bitter fighting during the ten days prior to handover. In the Black Watch area, 120 Battery moved close to Hill 121, and E Troop to Hill 146. An OP was manned on Hill 121.

At that time the enemy, who seemed to have good intelligence on United Nations deployments, broadcast surrender calls through loudspeakers to the

Scotsmen, telling them they would die on those hills, which would be followed by Scottish dance music. Shelling and mortaring onto The Hook became very heavy overnight of 18 to 19 November. A Company 1 BW was attacked by a large enemy force at 2100 hrs, 0100 hrs and 0400 hrs, penetrating two forward localities. The Jocks' position was not restored until first light. During this battle, 120 Battery fired 3,600 HE on DF tasks, FUPs and likely approach routes.

The first two days of December saw the relief of 29 Brigade by 25 Canadian Brigade in the two left-hand infantry battalion areas, 29 Brigade then relieving 28 Brigade of their left battalion area. All three brigades in 1 Comwel Div were in forward locations, each brigade leaving one infantry battalion in reserve. Then 120 Battery changed positions with 42 Battery, a move made in the first snow of winter. D Troop was now positioned east of Hill 187N, with E Troop to the north-east of the same hill. At this time Brigadier D.A. Kendrew assumed command of 29 Brigade.

A series of roving positions were occupied, named Valhalla, Arcady, Nirvana, Paradise and Utopia, which could only be approached at night. Whoever chose those names obviously had a sense of humour. One section – two mortars – was kept permanently in one of those positions, from where it carried out day-to-day shooting. There was an interchange of officers. Lieutenant D. Long rejoined 120 Battery as E Troop GPO, Lieutenant D. Lloyd moved to 42 Battery, and Lieutenant M. Robb transferred to RHQ 61 Light Regiment. On 18 December the roving section was mortared at Valhalla, with one vehicle destroyed. No casualty report seems to have been made, so presumably the driver escaped unscathed.

At the end of December, 14 Field had completed twelve months in Korea and were relieved by 20 Field from Hong Kong, to where 14 Field now departed. On Christmas Day, 20 Field fired their first 'M' (Mike) target, which was also recorded as the last one for 14 Field. (A Mike target involves all twenty-four guns in a regiment engaging the same target.) That having been accomplished, a Christmas dinner of roast turkey and pork, stuffing and all the traditional accompaniments was enjoyed, and an issue was made of one frozen bottle of Asahi per man. It beat C rations hands down.

Early in 1953 Brigadier Kendrew visited 120 Battery. As no further comment was recorded, it must be assumed that he was pleased with what he saw. On 14 January a combined troop made up from D and E troops deployed, putting down heavy fire in support of a patrol from the recently arrived 1st Battalion the Royal Australian Regiment (1 RAR), who were attempting to recover casualties from an overnight action. At this time 25 Canadian Brigade held The Hook, when an attack was expected. Recce parties were moved across the Samichon, but no attack materialized.

On 24 January a snatch patrol from the Dukes raided the feature Anthony at 0800 hrs in an attempt to take a prisoner, but returned with one dead enemy soldier. It might be assumed that he had been taken alive, although wounded, and that he had succumbed to his wounds as he was carried back. That would have annoyed the snatch patrol as a reward of five days' R&R in Tokyo awaited the first man to bring in a live prisoner for questioning. D Troop had moved forward to Valhalla, firing 700 rounds in support of the snatch operation. On 27 January the CRA, Brigadier Gregson DSO MC inspected the battery. On 28 January, 1 Comwel Div infantry were relieved in the line by the US 2nd Infantry Division, who were supported by Commonwealth artillery who had remained in the line.

Chapter Ten

Once More a Volunteer

Readers will have noted that after my stint as a National Serviceman I was disillusioned with civilian life, which seemed very tame. I suppose it would be true to say that I missed the thrills and the excitement, if I might respectfully refer to it as that. But mostly I missed the closeness of good comrades, the knowing that they were as dependent on me as I was on them, in the knowledge that I was doing a worthwhile job. So, what did I do? Mad fool that I was, I re-enlisted on a regular engagement. Obviously I had not shaken the military out of my system.

The recruiting sergeant in Portsmouth asked if I had a place in mind to where I preferred my body to be despatched. I had assumed that as 170 Battery had been replaced after one year by 120 Battery, the latter was due for relief and they had moved on to warmer climes. I enquired of the sergeant if he had details available regarding the current whereabouts of 120 Battery, but he said it was confidential information that he was not party to, but he would recommend a posting to the battery. 'Where was the battery when you left them?' he asked. I told him they had been in Korea. He looked quizzically at me, no doubt wondering if I was of sound mind. But his only question was, 'Are you mad?' which he delivered with a smile. I told him I had been passed grade A1(FE) at my release medical at Woolwich. He swore me in. I signed the Official Secrets Act, something that I had no recollection of doing when I had been called up for National Service, and he bid me good day, saying I would receive notification in the post regarding when and where to report. It took a few weeks before my papers arrived, during which time I thought maybe the Royal Artillery did not want me after all.

Of course I *was* wanted. And I had been wrong about 120 Battery being on the move. I ought to have realized that as they were an integral battery of 61 Light Regiment and it was the only mortar regiment in the Royal Artillery, and as their worth had been amply proved in that hilly terrain, they were going nowhere. Stuck at Woolwich for a few weeks, I pondered over whether I would regret this step. I began to wonder how committed I was about returning to Korea. Was there time for a change of heart? Could I picture myself In Dortmund, Dusseldorf or Paderborn? Could they send me to

Egypt, where I would hate spending my time on a gun site similar to the one I had volunteered to get away from at Lincoln? No, I would stick with Korea, the sole reason for my re-enlistment, and I would get to see more of Japan, Hong Kong and Singapore. I knew the right choice had been made. I took a disinterested view of the fatigue parties I was placed on, but they were made more pleasant as I was remembered by the WRAC Officers' Mess waitresses I had previously worked with. When I told them I was on my way back to Korea, they wanted to know if it was a punishment posting for having been a bad boy. I said I had volunteered. They too thought I was mad, as did some of the Korea draft lads I had been placed with.

The MO who had probed my inner depths on my previous release said he had seen me before, asking where I was going to this time. I told him Korea. He also enquired if I was mad. I thought he ought to be able to diagnose any displayed signs of madness as he was the doctor. The sergeant who had responsibility to ensure no Korea-bound men escaped his clutches was another who told me I must be mad. Maybe I was mad, but I believed I was doing the right thing, for me. While I awaited my troop train for Liverpool or Southampton I sat with the WRAC girls in the NAAFI as we related our recent experiences. I wondered what Korea had in store for me this time.

Sailing from Southampton on 12 February 1953, all the usual ports of call were left astern, and I arrived at Pusan on 13 March. Following the journey north on the EUSAK Express, I arrived at RHQ 61 Light Regiment the following day, together with another mad fool who was returning to 42 Light Battery for a second tour. I discovered that 1 Comwel Div infantry had been relieved in the forward defended locations by the US 2nd Infantry Division (2 Div), the Indianhead Division.

The composition of 2 Div was the 9th and 38th Infantry regiments, each of three battalions. Their third regiment, 23rd, was out of the line temporarily, during which time the famed Battalion Francais de l'ONU, the French contribution to the UN cause, and the Thai Infantry Battalion were attached. I have it in the back of my mind that the Netherlands Battalion was also attached, but I could be wrong. As there were no surplus artillery units, 1 Comwel Div field regiments and mortar batteries remained in the line. I had heard that the Thai Battalion had seen only limited action during the previous winter, however, unused as they were to the harsh winter climate. Now that spring was on the way they had been placed in forward locations.

The 61 Light Regiment still had the three mortar batteries – 42, 120 and 248 – plus the Bofors and sound-ranging troops in 15 Battery. The 14 Field had been relieved by 20 Field from Hong Kong, 16 New Zealand Field was still in the ORBAT, and I think either 1st or 81st Regiment Royal Canadian Artillery had replaced 1 RCHA. In addition there was a very welcome newcomer to the heavier support of the US Army artillery battalions in 74 (Battleaxe) Medium Battery, separated from its parent regiment in Hong Kong, armed with 5.5-inch guns, which fired an 82-pound shell over a maximum of 18,000 yards. While all this British artillery was engaging targets for 2 Div, *Gunner* magazine recorded that although British and Commonwealth artillery had supported United States infantry divisions on numerous occasions, this was the first time they had been an integral component of a US Army division. I recall that American officers were impressed with the speed with which we could bring the guns on target, requiring many fewer responses in the chain of command.

On arrival back at 120 Battery I found that all but one of the officers I had known had departed for pastures new, as had a majority of NCOs and Other Ranks – except, that is, for the draft I had taken out to keep them amused the day before I had left for home. I could not help myself reminding them of how they ducked for cover when a Kiwi 25-pounder had sent an outgoing shell over their heads. They would have learned a thing or two by now. One approached me, a ginger-headed lad who had been a gunner six months previously, but was now a fully-fledged bombardier. I congratulated him on his rapid promotion. He told me it was due to Bombardier Taff Jones being seriously wounded in November 1952 when, out with a D Troop line party, he had inadvertently walked into an unmarked minefield, causing him very serious injuries. One of the signallers had hurried to fetch our medic, Corporal Colin Lowes, RAMC, with some urgency. On arrival, fully appreciating that he could set off further mines, Colin had sent the other signallers to fetch a stretcher party, carried Taff out to what was presumed to be the edge of the minefield, passing again through 20 feet of live mines. In signing Colin Lowes' citation, Lieutenant General Bridgeford, Commander in Chief British Forces in Korea, said Colin 'had showed cold, calculating courage of the highest order, and that he reflected the greatest credit on himself and the Corps', recommending him for an immediate George Medal, one of only three awarded during the Korean War.

A visiting Pathé News camera team were in the vicinity when the ribbon of the George Medal was pinned on Colin Lowes in one of E Troop's gun pits in January 1953. I have no idea if the film clip was ever shown on British cinema screens. When the camera crew heard that D Troop was engaging enemy positions from a forward location, they asked if they could move forward to film the action. And that could be the only filmed record in existence of the 4.2-inch mortars in action in Korea. Thanks to my colleague David Drinkwater, a sergeant number one in D Troop, who in recent times contacted Pathé News, I have a copy of that brief film strip in my DVD collection.

Still comprised of D and E troops, I was returned to D Troop, which was now commanded by Captain G.S. 'Gary' Birtles, who immediately asked me for a war story. He was very interested to hear how life had been during the mobile phase of the war. He seemed a decent sort and I would be happy to perform OP duty with him.

The weather was still cold, with several hailstorms, but the worst of the winter was behind us. The combat clothing that was now issued to us was miles better than what had been available or was scrounged from US Army Quartermaster Corps depots in the 1950 to 1952 period. There was now no need to 'borrow' clothing from our American comrades in arms, although as we were with 2 Div, they would have been only too pleased to hand over anything we desired. They were very casual about signing for equipment, which would probably have had to have been done in triplicate in our army. I recall being sent back to a US Army depot for sandbags when our establishment had run out. There was a queue of vehicles all collecting thousands of sandbags. As each driver reached the front of the queue, the message was being passed back down the line that the Koreans, who were handing out the issues, did not care one jot how the paperwork was signed, just so long as they got a signature. I heard the driver ahead of me laughingly declaring that he had signed 'Walt Disney'. After loading many thousands of brand new, green rot-resistant sandbags, I signed 'Mickey Mouse'. Nothing was ever heard, so it was obvious no unit vehicle markings were recorded by the Koreans, and the US Quartermaster Corps who ran the place were very informal.

Within days of my arrival the battery fire plan was used in support of 9th Infantry, who had managed to encounter problems. Chinese artillery was heavy, with E Troop receiving roughly 300 shells on their location in two hours. Some damage was caused, including one vehicle destroyed, several more damaged but repairable, the troop commander's bunker destroyed, the ammunition pit set on fire, and all telephone lines and wireless aerials wrecked. All signallers from both troops were put to work to repair the damage, while fire-singed mortar bombs were carried a safe distance away for detonating by the Royal Engineers. Welcome back to the war, Jim.

Around the end of March, Major General Fry, Commander of 2 Div, presented the battery with what I understood was an 'Indianhead Citation' to all members of 120 Light Battery as a 'thank you' for our support. In 2011 I contacted 2 Div, surprisingly still based at Tokchon, Korea, asking for details of the citation. A senior NCO in the PR office delved into records for me, coming up with the information that the 'citation' was apparently the informal, hastily produced in the field 'Order of the Indianhead' – a certificate signed by Major General Fry awarded to any members of the division in recognition of an achievement that was not quite deserving of a medal.

The 23 Infantry Regiment returned to the 2 Div fold, relieving the French and Thai battalions, and 120 Battery now became principal heavy mortar support for 23 Regiment, commanded by Colonel Stilwell, son of General 'Vinegar Joe' Stilwell of Second World War fame. Our OP was established in 23 Regiment sector. In early April the officers of the battery were presented with a badged and engraved cigarette lighter by Colonel Stilwell on the occasion of the relief of 2 Div by 1 Comwel Div infantry on their return to the line. The lighter, retained for many years by Major J.A. 'Jerry' Harrison, was passed on to my colleague, David Drinkwater. David subsequently handed it to me for safekeeping. I still have the lighter in its rather worse for wear original box. Inside the lid is recorded:

> Presented to Major P.A. Johnson, Comd 120 Lt Bty RA by Col Stilwell Comd 23 Inf Regt on 6 Apl 53 in recognition of the support of 23 Regt by 120 Bty.

One side of the lighter has the colourful badge of 23 Regiment, and on the other is engraved '23rd Regiment, Korea 1952-53'. It is a nice souvenir of a unique occasion. We fired in support of 23 Regt patrols on several occasions.

At this time, when many targets were fired on, there was an exchange of positions, and 42 Battery, which normally supported 25 Canadian Brigade, took over our location while we moved to the old Samichon River area, the place that the recent inhabitants, 1st US Marine Division, had known as The Hook. Due to the rotation of infantry battalions in 29 Brigade, our mortars now supported the 1st Battalion of the Black Watch, the Duke of Wellington's Regiment and the King's Regiment, the one mainly recruited in and around Liverpool.

In D Troop our OP was sited on the forward slope of Hill 121, directly overlooking The Hook, where to minimize our movements in the open to enable us to enter the OP unseen from the rear slope, the Royal Engineers, aided by the splendid Korean Service Corps, were digging a tunnel right through the top of the hill, 80 feet long and 20 feet underground at the peak. The tunnel was completed in May, for which we were thankful, as we could now enter the OP without drawing fire, and there had been plenty of that when exposing ourselves on the skyline.

The Hook was a very hotly contested feature due to its position, and the fact that the occupier could look right down the valley to our supply lines. The first Hook Battle had taken place while I had been out of country, as had the second. The first was an assault against 7th US Marine Regiment in October 1952, the second fought by the Black Watch, 18 to 19 November 1952, which had been costly for the Jocks with twelve killed, twenty missing (later found to have been taken captive) and seventy-three wounded. Now, during May 1953, both D and E troops were subjected to heavy shelling and mortaring, heavier than anything I had experienced in the Guy Fawkes Battle in November 1951. Captain Birtles was wounded, and as I had established a good working relationship with him I hoped he would soon be plastered up by the medics and not be away from the troop for long.

It was noticeable that the Chinese had brought up much more firepower, and now they seemed to be particularly good at using it. Massed infantry assaults driven on by bugles, whistles and shouts I hoped were now history. But there was no chance of that. I would soon find out they still attacked by the same old method. One thing I had discovered was that our OP officers would turn a blind eye to my use of the Bren from the OP. If I saw men in the open that were not friendly, that were altogether too close, I would send them to ground with a quick burst. But I had to use ammunition sparingly, as I had only two magazines each of thirty rounds. When they were empty I had to scrounge more .303 rounds from the infantry, who did not appreciate handing too many over. I have to say that I preferred the old .30 calibre air-cooled Browning we had in the OP in 170 Battery, as that was belt-fed, whereas the Bren needed the thirty-round magazines replaced and to be refilled too often.

Shelling and mortaring by the Chinese became the normal day and night routine by mid-May, by which time Captain Birtles had returned to D Troop from hospital, having made a full recovery from his wounds. On 19 May, an enemy attack was believed to be imminent, due to heavy enemy sightings close at hand, which gave me targets for the Bren. But it was not until about 2230 hrs that we commenced counter-battery fire, as in excess of 1,000 enemy shells had been counted landing on The Hook. By first light on 20 May, the Chinese appeared to have gone to ground. After a fairly normal morning of occasional shelling and mortaring, during the afternoon in excess of 4,000 enemy shells and mortar bombs fell on The Hook. Many seemed to be of a heavier calibre than any encountered to date, and a large number were passing over Hill 121 to explode in our rear areas, making our supply lines vulnerable. On 20 May, a large enemy build-up was taking place in front of The Hook, with many enemy seeming not to bother about taking cover. Where had I seen that before? At times like that it was almost as though they were inviting us to bring fire down on them, possibly as it might disclose any weak points in our defended line. Men were walking about in the open, seemingly to test our strength, I would suggest, and to watch for our firing points.

It was known that information on the large increase in enemy manpower had come from a Chinese deserter who had been brought in a Duke's patrol at 0500 hrs on 18 May. As with earlier captives, they were not in the least concerned at how much useful information they imparted to an interrogator; they just talked and talked. And that could be the reason why I heard many years later that all Chinese who had been held in United Nations POW camps were not trusted by the authorities when they were eventually returned to China; it was considered they had been contaminated by contact with westerners. They probably found that the food was better in our POW camps than they had been accustomed to.

Around 2300 hrs on 20 May, both D and E troops commenced firing on registered targets and suspected FUPs until around 0230 hrs on 21 May. The Duke of Wellingtons had now been placed in occupation on The Hook ridge, and it was beginning to look as though a third Hook battle was imminent. During 21 May, 120 Battery fired 1,600 HE rounds on observed FUPs, and on counter-mortar tasks. The following day we counted more than 800 incoming rounds on and about our OP on Hill 121. In retaliation we returned nearly 2,100, some on defensive fire when enemy troops were seen to be much too close to our base plate positions. We continued to respond against observed targets, and on three more occasions I brought the Bren into action to halt enemy intrusion before they came any closer. With the infantry machine guns and small arms all picking targets, it was bedlam.

Meanwhile, a raid against enemy locations was planned by 1 King's, who were on the right bank of the Samichon, on the Yong Dong feature known to the Scousers as The Dong. A river crossing was called for at the start of the raid, during which some kingsmen (a regimental title for a private) were killed and others wounded when straying into an unmarked minefield. Recovery of the casualties was of paramount importance, so the raid was prematurely curtailed. Enemy soldiers were still coming close enough for me to pick off several single targets again.

By then it was noticeable that every time we sent grid references back to the mortars, which fired a large number of rounds at the targets, there would be immediate retaliation from the enemy, and men were being killed and wounded. On 23 May approximately 3,000 shells and mortar bombs fell on The Hook area, causing considerable damage to our defensive earthworks, and virtually destroying our barbed wire defences. At that time 1 Comwel Div decided to move A Troop of 42 Battery from the Canadian sector, to be placed under command of 120 Battery and increase available fire power where it was needed. A Troop was deployed to our rear, from where they could provide covering fire to both D and E troops in the event that a rapid extraction was necessary.

By late on 23 May we had been advised to pay particular attention to enemy movement to our immediate front, as our own infantry and men from the Royal Engineers were being sent forward to effect repairs on our demolished wire defences, a perilous task for infantry and sappers. Having immediately identified what was happening, the enemy fired a great many star shells to illuminate the scene, and my mate and I took turns with the Bren in an additional effort to keep enemy heads down.

At that point it was obvious to all that The Hook was the feature of most interest to the enemy. The taller hills of the feature dominated the lower hills, making it imperative that it was not surrendered. The sappers and the men of the Korean Service Corps (KSC), conscripted for road building, tunnelling, etc, in lieu of military service, performed wonders in providing protective cover for us. Apart from the 80-foot tunnel to the OP from the 'safe' side of Hill 121, deep communication trenches had been excavated, roofed over with heavy timbers, as had the infantry and gunner accommodation bunkers.

On 22 May our mortars, including those of A Troop under command, fired close to 2,100 HE, and now G Troop of 248 Battery, which normally supported 28 Britcom Brigade, was deployed east of the Samichon in support of and on call to 120 Battery as and when we needed them. G Troop mortars would be able to cover the whole of the potential battle-area-to-be. On 23 May the heavy incoming continued. 1st Royal Fusiliers from 28 Brigade had been placed under command of 29 Brigade, and moved into a blocking position to our rear. We had noticed that the Chinese had spent much time and effort to our immediate front improving existing earthworks and bunkers as fast as we destroyed them, and excavating new communication trenches that were ominously close. Several times I brought the trusty Bren into action against the enemy diggers, who were particularly busy overnight.

On 24 May the heavy incoming fire continued unabated, but slackened off somewhat on the 25th. The Black Watch had now been relieved by 1 King's in the area of Hill 146, where our E Troop was dug in. By 26 May incoming fire had become lighter. Were the enemy saving ammunition for a full-scale regimental assault? Whether or not something big was being planned, it had been decided by the 29 Brigade commander that G Troop could be safely moved back to their former position in support of 28 Brigade in the area around Hill 355, more than 4 miles away to our north-east. A mate, Gunner Roy de Moulpied, a Channel Islander, suffered several wounds from mortar fragmentation when driving our battery commander to the OP. The BC escaped uninjured, but the jeep was a bit dented. Walking wounded, Roy cheerfully returned within a few days.

Brigadier Kendrew, 29 Brigade Commander, visited all forward locations on 26 May, after which there was an interchange of infantry battalions. Overnight on 26 to 27 May, all 1 Comwel Div artillery was called upon several times to fire DF tasks as the enemy had encroached too close. A major bombardment commenced at 2300 hrs, causing many casualties. Someone, probably a cavalryman with nothing better to do back at Divisional HQ, decided to fit some tanks of 1st Royal Tank Regiment (1 RTR) with searchlights to illuminate the enemy lines, at the time causing a huge increase in enemy fire against us in an attempt to shoot the lights out. It was fine for the guys in the tanks; they could just sit out any bombardment by closing the hatch, and the decision-maker on the searchlights was safe at least 4 miles behind the line at HQ. We who did not have several inches of armour to protect us invoked curses on the tankeys, hoping they would go and play in someone else's backyard.

The 27 May passed in similar fashion. We fired on many observed targets, and others called for by the infantry, but first light on 28 May saw dramatically increased enemy artillery. Around that date I heard that several men from Gunner units had been reported killed in action, including Sergeant Colverson, Bombardier Hudson, Lance Bombardier Archer and Gunners Archibald and Caws, some of whom would have been in the field regiment, as I only recognized Sergeant Colverson.

At about 2000 hrs the long anticipated Third Hook Battle commenced with a ferocity not seen since Operation *Commando* in 1951. The main thrust was against the Dukes, who quickly had two platoons overrun, but a counter-attack reported at 0200 hrs on 29 May that they had re-established the position within 300 yards of D Troop mortars. In total, our mortars, including A Troop, fired 7,600 rounds of HE in less than eight hours on DFs, FUPs and on approach routes onto The Hook. One visible target was a considerable number of enemy soldiers approaching much too close for my continuing good health. Engaged by E Troop, they were ordered to fire the unofficial 'charge reduced' at minimum range. Charge reduced was achieved by stripping four of the six secondary propellant charges from the fins of the bombs. As a signaller I am not certain if it was an official order straight from the Royal Artillery gunnery manuals, or if it had become a necessity at times in Korea to combat the hordes, due to their close proximity. They would infiltrate to well inside the minimum capability of the 4.2-inch mortar, so something had probably been invented on the spot. Of course, where the bombs might land was anyone's guess … 200 yards … 500? It could not be assessed with accuracy, but as long as our bombs did not fall among our own infantry, that was all that mattered.

The Chinese had started to shell us with large-bore artillery that had been brought up to within our range quite unexpectedly. Several infantry weapons pits and our OP were severely damaged by non-stop shelling and mortaring, which continued unabated. Two Centurions of 1 RTR were dug in with us, one taking a direct hit on the turret, which probably gave the battened down crew headaches. There was slight damage. I believe the tank was withdrawn for repairs and replaced by another. By that time too many bunkers had collapsed under the intensity of the incoming barrage, burying some of the infantry lads in the forward platoons. It took a while to dig them out, but luckily they all survived. The Chinese had actually got right into our trenches where hand-to-hand fights ensued.

Our defences, which had been carefully constructed, were now a shambles. All the carefully laid aprons of barbed wire that had been intended to slow enemy infantry advances had been practically destroyed, and many of the mines that had been positioned with care to our front had been detonated by the incoming barrage. Communication trenches that had been deep enough for all but the tallest men to walk through with heads below ground level were almost non-existent. When moving around in the open, where hot metal was flying, we were now completely exposed, and our OP was reduced to little more than a shell scrape. Re-supply of charged batteries was becoming a problem.

We all waited for another attack, which we knew would be particularly unpleasant. In 120 Battery, as in all units in 1 Comwel Div, we had become aware that a major enemy attack could be expected without warning. The nearest enemy entrenchments were virtually within shouting distance of our OP and forward locations. Our mortars kept up a continuous harassing fire (HF), heavy in volume, over the following three days. Consequently, supplies of HE were running dangerously low in D and E troops, as well as in A Troop still under command. In fact, it had become a major challenge, which could only be alleviated if supplies could be brought to the gun positions with some urgency.

To start the ball rolling, our battery captain, the second-in-command, had organized a line link between the battery commander's Tac HQ with RHQ 61 Light Regiment and the RAOC Forward Ammunition Platoon. By that means, approved by 1 Comwel Div HQ, he had been able to borrow all available transport, and 25 Canadian Brigade came up with the goods. This supply line, a round trip of close to 30 miles over poor dirt roads, was maintained by the drivers of RCASC with twelve 2½-ton GMCs in a continuous flow, bringing supplies to each troop gun site, so that by first light on 29 May, an average of 2,600 rounds of HE162 were available to each troop. That would be insufficient to counter another full-scale assault, but we could at least keep the mortars in action over the following three days as the Canadians continued with the supply operation. Those RCASC drivers, at times under shellfire from the Chinese long-range guns, maintained the supply operation throughout the preliminary enemy bombardment, which would not cease for the next three days.

Hill 146 was now being targeted, and we were calling down fire virtually on top of our own OP and the forward infantry. Many enemy shells were again falling on our rear area in an attempt to disrupt our supply lines, and most of our telephone lines had been blown out. Wireless was now our sole means of communication provided spare batteries could be brought up from BHQ and the rear echelons. Sergeant Simpson was awarded the Military Medal for bravery in keeping all three gun troops and our OP supplied with fresh batteries, continually making a dash for it while under direct observation by the enemy, who directed fire on his vehicle, but it did not deter him in his mission. By keeping our communications live, we were able to stop many of the enemy from leaving their FUPs, but too many were still managing to gain a foothold on our hills.

During the battle a great many shells fell on both D and E troops' gun positions, causing casualties in both. D Troop suffered five: Troop Sergeant Major Shaw, Sergeant George Howard (died of wounds twenty-one days later in NORMASH) and Gunners Clements, Jones and Ginger Stevenson, whose back was literally peppered with metal fragments. Casualties in E Troop were Lieutenant Jeffcoate, Gunner Perry and Sergeant Simpson, who was wounded while on his battery delivery run, although he continued with his task before seeking aid for his wounds. Thankfully, he recovered rapidly and returned to the battery

Much of The Hook defences had been destroyed by enemy shelling and mortaring, and some enemy soldiers had crept up under cover of the heavy barrage to infiltrate our communication trenches, to use grenades and pole charges against the defenders. We were afforded the opportunity of bringing our Stens into action for a few moments, something gunners do not have to do under normal circumstances, firing directly at the enemy who had approached into our trenches, hoping we would not run out of .38 ammunition. They had encroached much too close for comfort, in anything but normal circumstances.

At that time the US 25th Infantry Division, with the attached Turkish Brigade, relieved the 1st Marine Division on our left flank. The grapevine reported that before the Marines departed, their commanding general had been heard to say, 'I sleep well at night as I have the Commonwealth Division on my right and the sea to my left, and I know both will still be there in the morning.' He was, of course, making reference to some other United Nations forces who had a tendency to 'bug out' at the first sign of an enemy attack without first warning neighbouring units, leaving the flanks of those units badly exposed. We had slept well with the Marines on our flank; now we had 25 Div to test.

This move brought a huge increase in available artillery, the Americans bringing with them four batteries of 155mm self-propelled howitzers, two batteries of towed 155s, one battery of 8-inch howitzers, a rocket battery and a battery of enormous 240mm split trail howitzers. Royal Artillery pilots of the light aircraft from 1903 Air Observation Post Flight reported very large concentrations of enemy some distance beyond the front line who had aimed small arms fire at them. In addition to the aforementioned increase in available artillery, 1 RTR had put the 20-pounders of their main armament to good use on observed targets. Although Korea was not good tank country, the Centurions could climb steeper gradients than any American tanks, getting right to the crests of the ridges. Our only complaint against them was those infernal searchlights.

It had been reported that in the final hour of 28 May, the first day of the final Hook Battle, 1,000 shells fell on one company of the Dukes, although I believe an accurate count of incoming on all Commonwealth units would have been an impossible task. While the Chinese were maintaining this continuous barrage against the four low hills that comprised our defensive line, all available artillery had been brought into action in our defence. Later, it was reckoned that between 29 and 31 May 38,000 shells and mortar bombs of all calibres had been expended against the enemy, 32,000 by 1 Comwel Div and 6,000 by the supporting US I Corps artillery. It is not certain if that figure included those fired by 1 RTR tanks, who were in hull-down positions in forward locations.

The huge increase from US Army units was appreciated. The units involved were 4th, 11th and 936th Field Artillery battalions with towed gun/howitzers, 204th Armored (*sic*) FAB with self-propelled 105s and, old friends from my very first days in Korea, 17 FAB, 'The Persuaders', with their superb 8-inch howitzers. Additionally there was a welcome contribution from the massive split trail 240mm howitzers of 159 FAB, which had only arrived in Korea on 1 May after removal from the mothballed state they had been in since the end of the Second World War. Apparently, they could fire shells fitted with nuclear warheads, although it was unclear if any had been brought to Korea.

I heard that the first shell fired by one of these monsters was a demonstration shoot for an admiring general who had been brought up to an OP to observe the fall of shot. Apparently, on impact the shell buried deep into the hilltop, not only pulverising several cubic feet of soil and rock, but also detonating an ammunition store. The general must have been impressed.

I have no idea how the mammoth guns were manipulated on Korea's narrow dirt tracks, having never seen one on the move, although I saw one later in its huge gun pit, and it was quite impressive. Each gun was well over 30 feet in length and at least 8 feet wide in mobile mode. Two heavy-duty tractors, rather like our Scammells, only larger, were used to move them, one at each end. Each gun had a detachment of fourteen men.

Once again, our gun positions had taken a heavy pounding from enemy artillery, and our OP was almost non-existent, as was the communication trench leading to it. But thankfully by 31 May it seemed that this latest offensive by the Chinese was over. We were glad of the respite that allowed us to start rebuilding our defences.

At that time A Troop was returned to 42 Battery and The Hook forward positions were now occupied by 1 King's, relieving the Dukes, who had taken 149 casualties, of which twenty-one were killed and sixteen missing. Chinese dead were estimated at 1,000, judged from the number of bodies visible in front of our forward positions. We counted almost 170 in close proximity to our position on Hill 121, and some bodies were right up to within 20 feet of the most forward Australian position on Hill 111, as evidenced by a photograph I have seen in the Australian War Memorial in Canberra. The Aussies had allowed a brief 'white flag truce' to permit the Chinese to collect the remains. The photo shows a group of four Chinese, two with white face masks, the others lifting bodies onto stretchers, with an interested Australian soldier watching from about 15 feet.

For a while after 31 May, life on The Hook became ominously quiet, the major event on our side of the ruined defences being the coronation of Queen Elizabeth II on 2 June. At 1000 hrs we stood for a minute in contemplation to enable those who wanted a quiet moment in prayer, although the ceremony in London would not take place for another six or seven hours due to the time difference. Our silent moment was broken by a rather weak 'Three cheers for Her Majesty' from one of the infantry officers, which was followed by red, white and blue smoke shells fired by the British, Canadian and New Zealand field regiments, which might have made a few enemy soldiers wonder if it was Chinese New Year already. I heard later that someone at 1 Comwel Div HQ blew a fuse when he heard that 61 Light Regiment did not contribute to the colourful display, without realizing we had only white smoke bombs, and they could not be wasted due to the supply problem. There had been a coronation parade somewhere to the rear, but I have no idea who represented 120 Battery.

Around that time we were given to understand that the peace talks were progressing nicely at Panmunjom, but we would shortly find that the war was far from over. Rumour had it that the Chinese might be about to make a last-ditch attempt to grab as much real estate as possible before an armistice could be settled. With that in mind we were put on high alert for twenty-four hours in each twenty-four hours.

I am given to understand that in addition to the huge expenditure on artillery ammunition during the third and final Hook Battle, more than 500,000 small arms rounds had been fired at the enemy. I wondered if my use of the Bren had been included. And to illuminate the scene one American gun had been tasked to fire a star shell every two minutes over the entire period of darkness at a little amount extra for Uncle Sam's military accounts.

There has never been a battle of anything like the same intensity in the years that have followed – not in Vietnam or any of the Middle East conflicts. Never again will there be such massive reliance on artillery and mortars by both combatants, at least not with conventional warheads.

Following the June coronation and some replacement of infantry on The Hook, the final action of the Korean War for British combat arms started to build up again on 15 July, when sporadic incoming mail recommenced, and we continued to fire on targets as they presented. On 19 July, the feature that the US Marines had named East Berlin in the sector to our left, which was then held by US 25 Div and the Turkish Brigade, was lost to the Chinese. A small piece of much fought-over ground had been relinquished in one of the war's final battles, but I understand there was a lot more activity far away to the east in the Pork Chop Hill and Punchbowl regions. Although we were quite unaware of it at the time, the truce was only one week away. Not that there was any relaxing on the front line. Continuous shell and mortar rounds continued to fall on our positions, and we sent over like for like.

By 20 July we had a new enemy to combat, a serious fly infestation that became a major hazard in our OP. Food could not be put down, and trying to eat it while continually batting away attacking flies, as well as those that settled around the rim of a mug of tea, was no easy task. They covered everything. July in Korea is either hot dry or hot wet, and we were receiving both. Hill 111 on our left flank was heavily bombarded on 22 July, and what was estimated as a divisional attack, about 7,000 in number, was mounted against the more recently arrived 2nd Battalion Royal Australian Regiment, who had relieved their 1st Battalion in the line. The Aussies were kept very busy in their first experience of warfare Korean style.

Some elements of the enemy thrust reached to within 300 yards of E Troop base plate position. Our mortars fired 7,800 HE overnight. It was ominously quiet on 25 and 26 July. Were the Chinese drawing breath before making yet another full-scale assault against us? We would soon find out. The expected, or likely, the unexpected, was about to happen. After being stood down on the morning of 27 July 1953, we were called together to be told the news that a truce had finally been agreed at 1000 hrs between the United Nations Command and the communist forces, to be effective at 2200 hrs that day. The war was over. But we still held our breath until 2200 hrs had passed, having been on 100 per cent stand-to since last light, just in case, hardly daring to believe our original enemy, the North Korean Army, who had started the war on 25 June 1950, had really accepted the truce terms when the bulk of the negotiations would have been done by the Chinese People's Volunteers. Two years had passed since the first peace talks had commenced at Kaesong in the summer of 1951.

Many cynics thought it was too good to be true. Three years, one month and two days of war was over. We had managed to contain the communist forces from overrunning the south, but what a disaster zone we had made of their country in the process.

We were informed that hostilities had actually ceased, through the *Crown News*:

Monday 27 July 1953

TRUCE TODAY

It was announced today from General Mark Clark's Tokio [*sic*] HQ that the truce agreement would be signed at 10 o'clock today at Panmunjom. It is three years and a month since the Korean War began. After meetings yesterday morning, liaison officers finally reached agreement on the signing a few minutes after 2 pm. It was stated that to speed the signing and to prevent casualties, and because of the unacceptable conditions required by the communist forces for the appearance of their senior commanders, the truce will be signed by the senior truce negotiators, General Harrison for the UN and General Nam Il for the communists. Both sides have agreed upon a procedure by which after the negotiators have signed, the agreement will be sent to the overall commanders for their endorsement. General Clark will sign at Munsan, the allied truce camp a few miles from Panmunjom. The communist commanders, North Korean Marshal Kim Il-sung and the Chinese General Peng Te-huai, will sign later at a place thought to be their HQ at the North Korean capital, Pyongyang. The major provisions of the truce are that all hostilities will cease 12 hours after the armistice has been signed. This refers to land, sea and air actions.

Secondly, all troops with their equipment will withdraw from the demarcation line drawn across Korea, along the battle front. The distance of withdrawal is 2 kilometres, about 1¼ miles.

Thirdly, allied troops and arms will withdraw within 5 days from islands off the North Korean coast.

Fourthly, blockade of the coast of Korea is not allowed.

Fifthly, there will be an immediate freeze on the reinforcement of troops and arms, in both North and South Korea. Each side will rotate no more than 35,000 men in a month on a man for man basis. Neither side may raise the level of either men or arms above that which they have in Korea at the time of signing the armistice.

A Military Armistice Commission will take control of supervising the truce and settling any violations. The Commission will consist of 5 UN and 5 Communist members, 3 of each side being of the rank of general or admiral.

Lastly, to supervise the buffer zone and the Han River estuary ten observer teams of joint UN-Communist members are established, to work under the Commission.

President Rhee yesterday called a Cabinet meeting to discuss the truce. No statement was issued on the deliberations.

On the battle line severe fighting continued on a number of sectors. In the region around Kumsang, a 3,000-man attack was launched by the communists with little success. A smaller one on the positions east of Panmunjom held by the US Marines was beaten off.

It was learned later in the day that the Korean Minister for Defence stated that South Korean troops will withdraw in accordance with the terms of the armistice. He stated that they intended to observe the truce for 180 days. The exchange of prisoners is expected to commence before the end of the week.

At first light on 28 July, with no stand-to having been ordered, I looked carefully out from our OP to see a surprising sight: groups of Chinese soldiers sitting in the open, smoking and talking, no more than 30 yards from us, which indicated just how close they had actually extended their trench system in the last few days. Beyond them I watched as stretcher bearers moved around seeking the remains of their late comrades, right up to our infantry's slit trenches, almost in front of our OP. The condition of most of the remains being removed suggested that many had been there since the battle of 19 July, which would account for the dreadful fly infestation we had been hard-pressed to control with small cylinders of a chemical that was usually very effective against the flies and mosquitoes, but probably did nothing for our respiratory systems.

Officers had ordered no fraternization with the Chinese, who just sat there, probably as pleased as we were that the fighting was over. But some of the bolder lads walked down the slope to exchange cigarettes with them. The Chinese soldiers were definitely on the best end of the deal, receiving British Players or American Lucky Strike in exchange for their poor quality 'Peace' brand, in small blue paper packets printed with a white dove within a wreath of leaves – propaganda smokes.

And on that day, the first day of peace, *Crown News* headlined the following:

Tuesday 28 July 1953
Temp max 89 min 69

SPECIAL ORDER OF THE DAY
BY
MAJOR GENERAL M.M.A.R. WEST CBE DSO
GENERAL OFFICER COMMANDING
1ST COMMONWEALTH DIVISION

Today our division celebrates its second birthday. It is young in age but old in experience and renowned valour. Throughout its short life the Commonwealth Division has upheld the tradition and glory of the Crown and Commonwealth and each of us can be proud of having played his part. With the coming of the armistice no one can see the future of either or [*sic*] the Commonwealth Division, but for the time being let us carry on without relaxation – there is much to be done.

The front page continued with a résumé of the events in the Panmunjom tent, where the chief communist negotiator arrived by jeep and the chief UN negotiator had arrived by helicopter (one-up-man-ship?). Each side signed nine copies of the truce agreement, three of each in English, Chinese and Korean. After the signing General Nam Il looked at his watch and walked out.

It was then that the hard work began. The terms of the armistice dictated that both sides agree to vacate their 27 July positions within forty-eight hours, after which only limited, approved access to the new Demilitarized Zone (DMZ) would be enforced. Each side had to withdraw 1¼ miles to new marked boundary lines, leaving a no-man's-land 2½ miles wide. Our most pressing task was to remove guns, ammunition and communication equipment to the rear, as well as any reusable timber we were able to recover for use at our truce position.

For 120 Light Battery, I was surprised to find that we would move back to develop a liveable camp on the site of the ruined village of Oridong, a place that I recognized instantly from April 1951, just to the west of Hill 195, where in B Troop 170 Battery we had made our escape with the Belgian battalion. Our task looked daunting. It had been ordained on high that an area would have to be flattened to form first a gun park, then wagon lines, and finally areas where four large tents could be erected each for D and E troops, three tents for BHQ, and another for a cookhouse. The battery office tent and those for senior NCOs would be on the other side of the valley, and the officers' mess and living accommodation right at the top of the valley. It looked like an awful lot of hard work with pick and shovel. But who would come to our rescue? The Royal Engineers, that's who, with a splendid bulldozer that soon pushed down both sides of our valley and graded it flat for us to continue from there. The last traces of the houses that had stood there for many years were bulldozed instantly, removing thatch and rats in one fell swoop.

The majority of Commonwealth troops moved back to new locations on the former Kansas Line, mostly south of the Imjin, whereas 61 Light Regiment, 3rd Royal Australian Regiment and 16 New Zealand Field Regiment remained on the Wyoming Line, about midway between the DMZ and the Imjin. It appeared that our three units were the stopgap force that would be expected to hold back the red hordes in the event that they decided not to abide by the truce agreement and tried to force a return back to the 38th parallel. I hardly felt confident that with my Aussie and Kiwi mates we could delay a thrust from a determined enemy long enough for the lads south of the river to pick up their rifles. In addition to our occupation on Wyoming Line we also had to dig reserve positions on Kansas Line, south of the river.

We arrived at the Oridong position on 31 July, following two days of back-breaking toil demolishing bunkers and moving everything that was moveable back to the south. Our battery sergeant major became most annoyed at the number of sightseeing tourists from BHQ and the rear echelons that seemed to have arrived to view the front line for the first time before it was no more. BSM Charlie Cole 'invited' a number of them to join in. It started to rain, which meant they would soil their polished boots in the mud and, like us, get soaked to the skin.

Some time in August we were called together for a parade on the nicely flattened ground to be informed that the General Officer Commanding 1 Comwel Div had sent congratulations to 120 Light Battery for putting in a good account of themselves and notifying the following decorations, which had been published in the *London Gazette*, three of which we already knew about: Corporal Colin Lowes RAMC, the George Medal; Captain Childs RA, the Military Cross; Sergeant Simpson and Gunner Tom 'Groucho' Bond, the Military Medal; and WO2 Charlie Cole the MBE. Major L.G. Wilkes, Captain G.S. 'Gary' Birtles, WO2 Sam Davies and WO2 'Curly' MacDonald were Mentioned in Despatches. We were also informed that a small number of Coronation Medals had arrived at RHQ 61 Light Regiment, but I never heard who the lucky recipients were.

In no time at all we had a smart gun park where all mortars were located in a single line facing north. From that date we lived a fairly peaceful existence, punctuated with training exercises. Digging and occupying our Kansas Line fallback position was practised, ours being right at the spot where C Troop 170 Battery and the Glosters had been taken into captivity in April 1951. On occasion the job was made most unpleasant when unearthing human remains that had been there since the Imjin River Battle. Several searches, each named Operation *Skunk Hunt*, consisted of forming a long cordon and moving forward in line across the hills in an attempt to locate suspected spies whose messages on units, locations, troop deployments, etc., had been intercepted by the intelligence people.

We no longer had to duck each time we heard a loud noise and I had little to keep me occupied until much later, when I was put in charge of a generator that would light up the tents with two 40-watt bulbs in each. It was powered by a Coventry Eagle horizontally opposed two–cylinder engine, which might have been fine on a motorcycle, but was not man enough for this job from the start as it struggled to illuminate 120 Battery. A lad who had served an electrical engineer apprenticeship in the John Samuel White shipyard at Cowes on the Isle of Wight, 'Ding-dong' Bell, handled all the technical side of it. As usual, we had to scrounge the required cabling from the US Army Signal Corps. I just had to run the generator for the few months I had left, before I had finished my allotted year in Korea.

But before I went anywhere the motorbike engine gave up, and for 120 Battery it was back to candles for illumination. What was I to do? I saw Ding-dong in a huddle with 'Q', our BQMS, who gave him a case of Asahi, then told us both to head down the MSR to a huge US quartermaster depot. We were to trade the beer for a jeep engine. On arrival at the depot, which was stacked with huge packing cases, seeing that we were Limeys, a soldier wandered across to ask the usual 'Have you guys got any beer?' We told him we had, although it was not for sale, but to exchange. He told us, 'Go see the major,' indicating a man with a large pearl-handled .45 Colt revolver strapped to his thigh. We told the major what we wanted for the beer. He said that was fine, no problem, but first he asked to look at my rifle. We still had to carry loaded weapons everywhere, just in case.

Giving the rifle the once-over, he reckoned it was just what he wanted for shooting elk 'back stateside', saying that if I left him the rifle and the beer we could take 'a whole goddammed jeep', pointing to a huge stack of wooden crates, each stencilled with the cost to the US taxpayer of the contents – one Willys-Overland jeep. Needless to say, he could not believe that in our army it was a court martial offence to 'lose' a personal small arm, so we returned to Q without the engine. After commenting that he ought not to have sent boys out to do a man's job, within days he had acquired an engine by his own nefarious means. He had got together with a REME technician from RHQ, who made a coupling between engine and genny, and it was not long before we were lit up once more.

Where would I go next, I wondered? But it was not long before my name came up again for R&R, which was very pleasant, and I'm glad to say that there were no engine failures on either of the flights. Then I waited to hear of my next posting, which I hoped would not be Egypt, where I had originally planned to serve, but somewhere pleasant, and warm – anywhere away from freezing winters.

Well, I discovered that my name was on a list to join a training team in Malaya, where initially I would be at a pleasant sounding place called Kota Tinggi, then later at Batu Pahat and then Yong Peng, training others to kill communist terrorists who intended to turn Malaya into a communist state, while not actually killing any myself – although I was pleased about my proficiency on the Bren, in case of need.

I arrived in Singapore on 22 March 1954 and was taken to a transit camp at Nee Soon. Someone asked where I was heading, and when I told him I was on my way to Kota Tinggi, he told me I would be sorry. I was not bothered, as that was a typical comment about any posting by the initiated to the uninitiated. Perhaps it was not going to be like a holiday resort after all.

He was right. Kota Tinggi was the base for the Far East Jungle Warfare School. It sounded like fun. I had to complete three exhausting weeks there to become 'jungle aware', and learn how to avoid being poisoned, clawed, bitten or eaten by anything that swam, flew, slithered, climbed or crawled, of which there was a vast menagerie in the Johore Jungle, before moving on to Batu Pahat, where the 1st Battalion the Fiji Infantry Regiment was housed. After one or two further moves it was back to Singapore for me, then a four-day voyage to Hong Kong, where I spent the best part of my army life in yet another mortar battery, 27 (Stranges) Light Battery, stationed in Far East Farm Camp, at the 21st milestone, Castle Peak Road in the New Territories.

The camp was where HQRA and the Commander Royal Artillery, Brigadier Jago, were housed.

The first gunners of 27 Battery had been sent to Korea in September 1950, two months before 29 Brigade had arrived in the country. At first they did not know what to do with me. I was surplus to requirements as a signaller, but the interviewing officer advised me that as we were not killing anyone in Hong Kong, apart from in road traffic accidents, he had a vacancy for a storeman in the Q Stores, or another in the Technical Stores. I decided that Technical Stores sounded more interesting than one where I would spend my day issuing out new socks and pieces of 4x2 for pulling through a rifle bore. I was told not to get too comfortable, as Tech Stores courses were taught at 3 Base Ordnance Depot (3BOD) in Singapore.

Packing my kit again, I was back in Singapore before you could say Jack Robinson, slogging away in a classroom at 3BOD, passing out with flying colours, and then it was another four days by trooper back to Hong Kong. I had finally made it. I was told to get all my shirts to the camp tailor to have my lance bombardier stripes sewn on. But it did not stop there. My intelligence must have been noted. Or was it just that the technical storeman in a light battery was a bombardier post? So, it was a truck ride of 21 miles for me to 6 Command Ordnance Depot (6COD) in Waterloo Road, Kowloon. Again, passing all the requirements for military stores accounting, I had hardly unpacked back at Far East Farm when I was told to get my shirts across to the tailor again to have my bombardier stripes sewn on. This was great: gunner to lance bombardier to bombardier in less than nine weeks. Why, I would be a brigadier by Christmas!

Hong Kong was the very best place for peacetime soldiering. I made myself at home in my own 'bunk', where I was master of all I surveyed. As my duties were needed 24/7, in the modern idiom, I was excused guard commander duty ... and just about everything else, apart from when on exercises with the Gurkhas or with some of the battalions I had served in OPs with in Korea. The Royal Norfolks were in the New Territories when I arrived, as, I believe, were also the Welch Regiment. One interesting duty I had to perform was in the OP on Crest Hill, which overlooked the crossing into China of the Kowloon-Canton Railway at Lo Wu. It was somewhat incongruous watching Chinese people going about their daily business walking each way over the border when I had been recently involved in killing their brothers in Korea, 1,400 miles to the north.

Before my time was up at the end of my three-year Far East posting I was asked if I would consider signing on for a further six months in Hong Kong, for which there was a substantial bounty. As it was the best peacetime posting in the Army, and the overseas allowance paid in Hong Kong brought my pay up to the level of a basic UK-based sergeant, I signed on the dotted line.

After three years and five months actually in the Far East, plus two months of travel in troopships, I left for home on 31 July 1956 on HMT *Empire Fowey*. The scheduled date of arrival at Southampton was 26 August. Shore leave was taken in Singapore. Would I see that fascinating city again? Of course I would, many times as a civilian later in life. There was no shore leave in Colombo as the locals were rioting about an increase in the price of red onions in the markets, and smoke was rising ominously from several parts of the city. Aden had not changed, but as we were about to board our ship, the local shopkeepers told us they would see us again next week, which seemed a bit odd. But they were right. The Egyptian government had nationalized the Suez Canal, and no Royal Navy ship or trooper was permitted passage. Several Royal Navy ships were anchored in the bay at Port Suez, the southern end of the canal. A motor launch came across to us, and a high-ranking naval officer climbed aboard. Shortly afterwards, we were ordered to the troop decks. What was going on? We were told we could take down several addresses and write a quick air letter home, telling family they could write to us at any one of the addresses we were being given – the ship's agents in Mombasa, Durban and Freetown, Sierra Leone. I posted a letter to my parents, giving them the agents' addresses for mail. Then it was back to Aden, just as the shopkeepers had predicted.

Well, I looked forward to a letter in Mombasa, but we bypassed the place completely, entering the harbour of Zanzibar instead. It was an interesting place, very tropical, but where was our mail? Durban next; it will catch up with us there, we thought. But no, we went to Cape Town instead. No mail there either, although we had a great time ashore. As we were the first British troopship the locals had seen since the end of the Second World War, they came to the docks in droves to take us out and wine and dine us. We knew that our mail would catch up there. Wrong again; it was probably still waiting for us in Durban. Next we went to Dakar, Senegal instead of Freetown, where a French Foreign Legion band and Corps of Drums entertained us on the dockside. We had given up all hope of picking up any mail by then, which was just as well, because there was none. Dakar was probably typical of the French African colonies, but had little to offer apart from street cafés where the beer was cool and where hawkers were trying to sell us stuffed giant lizards as we tasted the local brew.

Finally, I arrived home, better late than never, docking at Southampton and wondering why two aircraft carriers were loading onto their flight decks vehicles that were being hastily painted in desert sand camouflage. I was due to leave the Army as a regular, after my three years and six months. I had decided that the Army had enjoyed me for long enough and I had worked it out of my system. I was sent on my accumulated leave of seven weeks, four days, straight from the ship, and was told I would be notified by telegram of my next posting. Not me, I told them. I was due out. Not yet, matey, I was informed. The Suez Emergency was in force, and there would be no discharges while it lasted. That explained the vehicles being sprayed on the aircraft carriers. Britain and France were at war with Egypt. With the Suez debacle, and revolution in Hungary, what had I returned to?

By the time I finally left the Army on 14 March 1957, I did not know what to do with myself. I decided to emigrate to Canada. I reached the stage of booking passage on the *Empress of Canada* from Liverpool, but with about two weeks to go before departure, I received a letter from the Ontario Government Office telling me there was a recession there at present. Go if you must, was the message, but don't come crying to us if it doesn't work out. But I had not yet kicked off the wanderlust. Next I gave the Merchant Navy the benefit of my undoubted qualities for one year, completing six round voyages to South Africa, two on RMS *Capetown Castle* and four on *Winchester Castle*, Southampton to Durban and back, via Madeira outbound and Las Palmas on the homeward stretch. Life at sea soon palled; it reminded me too much of troopships, of which I had had enough. In 1960, Sheila and I were married. Did we settle down? No. Sheila had become committed to my desire to see more of the world and, more importantly, to better ourselves. We emigrated to Australia, leaving Southampton just before Christmas 1960.

To return to more important matters, there is no doubt that North Korea started the war that cost millions of lives, but to read the official Chinese government publications, they laid the blame entirely on the heads of Syngman Rhee and his government. I have a book published by the Chinese Military Museum in Beijing that makes it quite plain to readers:

> The Chinese People's Volunteers was [*sic*] organized soon and went to Korea in October 1950 to fight shoulder to shoulder with the Korean people against the US aggressors … the poorly equipped Chinese People's Volunteers defeated the UN forces headed by the US, which had modern technical equipment and forced the opponent to sign the Korean Armistice Agreement on 27 July 1953.

I think the People's Volunteers would have expected better treatment when they returned to China, particularly those who had been captured by UN forces. Of those, many opted to settle in Formosa (Taiwan) but the (approximately) 6,000 who decided to return to their homeland apparently made the wrong decision. According to a *Washington Times* news cutting in my archives, they were publicly humiliated, refused work and even deprived of Communist Party membership. Personnel files were marked '*Wei gui, nei kong*', which, I am told, can be translated as 'returned from abroad, control in use'. They were not, as they had anticipated, welcomed as heroes.

And what of 61 Light Regiment, the only Royal Artillery regiment ever put into the field with three batteries of the 4.2-inch mortar as main armament? They returned to Larkhill, Wiltshire in early 1955, after three years in Korea. They were re-titled 61 Field Regiment, and were equipped with the 25-pounder. Then 120 Light Battery eventually disappeared into 'suspended animation', gone forever.

Over the years I have been told by my fellow veterans that I must be one of very few men who fought in both the Imjin River Battle, 22 to 25 April 1951, and the Third Hook Battle, 28 to 31 May 1953, although I maintain that the latter was, in reality for 61 Light Regiment, continuous from 21 May. Sometimes I have been asked which was worse, and that is difficult to answer. On the Imjin River, where it was impossible for one brigade to hold such a broad river frontage, we were attacked by 27,000 infantry soldiers with limited artillery support. The left-flanking units were so quickly engulfed that they could not withdraw. A difficult fighting withdrawal was put into effect on the right flank, after yielding territory to the enemy. In the final Hook Battle, the Chinese attacked with large-scale infantry assaults against a much smaller defended area, benefitting from a huge increase in firepower, with orders to drive us from our hills. They were unsuccessful.

Whether attacked by thousands of massed infantrymen or bombarded by incredibly concentrated artillery barrages, my experiences of both battles were equally daunting. A man in the most forward locations who can say in honesty that he was not scared stiff on occasion in either battle, would be a liar, or a very brave man.

Chapter Eleven

Freedom is not Free

Hostilities in Korea came to a close on 27 July 1953. Two days later, the War Office held a debate on defence policy, and the future of National Service was on the agenda. By that time the number of young men who had been called to serve under the National Service Act 1947 and had returned to civilian life topped the half-million mark. Another 320,000 conscripts from the total army strength of 440,000 were in varying stages of their two years' service, possibly as many as 7,000 in Korea. Call-up was said to be running smoothly at the rate of 169,000 a year. In 1953, the intake of conscripts was divided – 118,000 for the Army, 47,000 for the Royal Air Force, while the Royal Navy, which would rather have managed without them, accepted just 2,700, who were most likely to be kicking their heels on a concrete battleship ashore in Portsmouth, Devonport or Chatham.

The day prior to the debate in Parliament, the first day of peace in Korea, an independent source published the finding of their investigation into the 'Effects of National Service on the Lives of a Nation's Youth'. The impact of enforced conscription when Britain was not actually at war with any other country had, so it seems, not been smooth, and as youths were returning in droves every fortnight to civilian life, their complaints were escalating.

Sufficient numbers were turning out to be misfits in a military context as to merit concern in the corridors of power. It was reported that between 15 and 20 per cent of those receiving call-up notices each year were unreceptive to any form of military training, and all three services would have preferred not to suffer them. Approximately a quarter of a million reluctant youths were compelled to register each year on reaching eighteen, a number that was whittled down by medical examination, deferments, exemptions and outright rejections. During the first few hard weeks of basic training, the unsuitable, the unsavoury, the unfit and the bed-wetters were sent on their way with a rail warrant and a corned beef sandwich back to their home town, leaving their bored and dispirited comrades to continue polishing coal scuttles in Newcastle, or demolishing much of the picturesque German landscape with their war games.

In 1953 the greatest numbers of our troops were based in West Germany, to combat those red hordes that never materialized. There were many people at that time who considered the vast number of conscripts who were still under training or who were serving in the United Kingdom were not being used to the best advantage, forgetting that in the recent past the nation had applauded them when the Army had kept much needed food imports moving in London docks when a strike was crippling the nation. 'Too much free time on their hands' was a common complaint. Officially, after completing his basic training, a home-based conscript was entitled to one forty-eight-hour leave pass – a long weekend – each month. I found out later in life that, in practice, 'after-duty passes' were also freely obtained that permitted leave of absence every weekend from after duty on Saturday until reveille on Monday morning, which worked out fine for anyone stationed reasonably close to his home.

One consequence of so many uniformed personnel being on the move at weekends was that every London terminus and most mainline stations were crowded with hundreds of polished, pressed and Blancoed conscripts all heading in one direction on a Friday night and in the reverse direction on a Sunday night. With almost no conscript owning a car, all long-distance coaches, particularly those heading to Victoria Coach Station, London, did a roaring trade with squaddies, sailors and airmen on the move. Military police (they were always in pairs) at rail stations close to military garrisons and at all major city stations would call over anyone in uniform, first to check they had permission to be on the move, and then to closely scrutinize the miserable, cringing wretch cowering in front of them for anything they decided did not look sufficiently military. But everyone to their own job, and some of the Red Caps were also conscripts.

The more penurious hiked the highways, holding out a thumb to the sound of any vehicle approaching from the rear. Favourites for a lift were the long-distance truck drivers, who were often glad of the company, but also many car drivers would pull over to give a lift to a man in uniform. It was all part of the growing up process in those days.

Managers in industry were often unimpressed when the quiet, reserved, pimply-faced youth they remembered came back bigger, wiser, fitter and loud-mouthed, seeking his old job back, with a chip on his shoulder and considering that the company, the country, someone, somewhere owed him something to compensate for his two lost years. Service chiefs agreed that not all youths had been put to useful tasks during their period of conscription although many thousands had benefited considerably and, according to one general, had attained the stature of courageous manhood 'as has been amply proved in places like Korea and Malaya'.

So, it would appear that the thousands of conscripts who served in Korea were not necessarily a waste of space. And without wishing to repeat myself overmuch, it is a fact that the citizens of South Korea, rather than our own governments over the years who have forgotten, appreciate our significant contribution towards ensuring their future, as is made abundantly clear to veterans who manage to make the trip back to their country. A genuinely warm and hospitable welcome awaits all who are capable of making the journey.

For many years I had listened to tales related by veterans who had been back. I was told that the old dirt road out of Seoul through Uijongbu was now an excellent four-lane highway. I could easily picture Route 11 as having changed considerably, but as it is close to the DMZ, I doubted that it would be plastered with billboards advertising Budweiser and McDonalds or have service stations complete with fast food outlets. The narrow, twisting track through Gloster Valley going north through Solma-ri and Choksong to the bridge over the Imjin River will have been widened and hard surfaced, although maps still show it twisting between the rocky outcrops much as it did in 1951.

The new bridges over the Imjin are of steel and concrete, but veterans told me it was no longer possible to visit the Hill 195 area, where the Imjin River Battle started for me. Where the old bath unit stood I could picture boats for hire in summer, ice skates in the winter. In those places where once death was an expectation for the refugees crossing the river with all their possessions on their backs, today the population enjoy their leisure time. Today, nobody starves, nobody freezes. Everyone is well dressed, suitable to the season. There will be no more of the barefoot orphans that had our pity, but whom we were sadly unable to help.

Over the years I gave much thought to going back to Korea, but if I did it would not be on the tourist trail. They have every right to be there, but crushed into a group of camera-wielding tourists would, I thought, not be for me. If I ever took my nostalgia trip, I would want to climb again those lonely ridges, walk the silent valleys and search the hills for the places I had known while I was still capable, although I doubted that I would achieve all of it. One year, in spring, after winters freeze but before the wet humidity of summer, I would want to attend the annual ceremony in Gloster Valley, and stand there in the company of my fellow veterans to remember the lads of C Troop who went down fighting, who had no alternative but to surrender and spend two years and five months in North Korean prison camps.

I would stand there and hear again the voices of Jock and Geordie ... of Liverpool, the West Country, Ulster and Yorkshire ... and I would remember. But it would be so different. In those far-off days the Royal Regiment of Artillery could field sixty-nine regiments and an assortment of independent batteries. Eighty-five infantry battalions could be despatched to the trouble spots of the world provided the problem had not been resolved before their troopship arrived. Today, there are no postings to the peacetime pleasures of the 1950s. No more to Jamaica, Hong Kong or Singapore, or to the burning sands of Egypt, the rocks of Aden or the Malayan jungle.

It must be difficult now to scrape together an infantry battalion of not many more than 550 personnel, including some borrowed from other battalions to make up numbers, compared with the 1,000-strong battalions of the past. We do supply men to the United Nations peacekeeping duty in Cyprus – a strange duty considering that in 1952, when Australians, Greeks and Turks could all have celebrated Anzac Day together behind the Aussies line, now the UN have the task of keeping Greek and Turk apart.

A military life now that there is no compulsion to join on reaching eighteen is not for most, while many would-be recruits would fail basic fitness tests. And famous regiments have gone forever. They will never be re-formed under their illustrious titles, many of which go way back in history. Traces of the famous Scottish regiments can be found in the splendidly named Royal Regiment of Scotland. The Royal Regiment of Artillery had been reduced to fifteen regiments at the last count, the gunners all fully trained in infantry skills, whereas I was taught only the basics, and I made the rest up as required. Throughout the 1970s and continuing until well into the 1980s, Gunner regiments took their place patrolling the streets of Northern Ireland and the dangerous countryside of South Armagh, rotating with their infantry comrades.

Today's politicians are once more surrounding the conference table in Whitehall to decide on which military units can be demobbed early, so that the Ministry of Defence can balance its budget by reducing headcount even further. We have no requirement, they say, for so many in uniform. They said precisely the same about the number of National Servicemen in July 1953.

How quickly the lessons of the past are forgotten. The government could not have been without us in Malaya, Kenya, Aden, Cyprus, Korea, and all those trouble spots now only remembered by those who were there. In more recent times ... in the Falklands, Kuwait, Iraq, Bosnia, Kosovo and Afghanistan. Where next, I wonder, will the cream of Britain's youth be needed? And when they return home, after hailing them as heroes and pinning on medals, will the discharges continue as they are considered surplus to requirement?

To those who would reduce our fighting capability even further, I say take heed of the words of the Chinese militarist and philosopher Sun Tzu, written around 500 BC:

You may not need soldiers for one hundred years,
but you cannot be without them for one day.

It had been my intention to close these reminiscences with the wise words of Sun Tzu. However, there is much more to tell.

There are many who say it is inadvisable to return to the places that lie deep in our memories, but deciding to disregard such advice, I took advantage of the Korean government-sponsored veteran visit scheme, submitting my application in 1995. I was accepted and made my pilgrimage back to Korea in April 1996 – in my sixty-fourth year.

I had no idea of how I would feel when stepping back onto Korean soil. Would I just be chasing ghosts? It was not the same. The country to which I returned was so vastly improved from the devastation I had known in war, although I had, of course, kept abreast of the massive modernization, industrialization and commercial development of the Republic of Korea since hostilities had ended.

My Korean Air flight departed London Heathrow at 2200 hrs on 17 April, overflying much of northern Europe, right across Russia, then landing at Kimpo Airport, Seoul, at 1700 hrs the following evening. The brand new Boeing 747-300 made the trip in less than twelve hours. The last time I had been at Kimpo, I reflected, was on my return from my third R&R in Tokyo, when it had been known as US Airbase K14. Now it had been transformed into a fine international airport, as modern as anywhere.

Travelling to my five-star hotel, the Sofitel Ambassador, I witnessed first-hand the progress that had been made. Dusty dirt roads where non-stop military traffic had forced ox carts into ditches had been completely transformed into multi-lane highways, jam-packed in the evening rush hour. The high-rise apartment blocks, row after row of them, stunned me. Where there had been a couple of repaired bridges over the broad Han River, now there were more than I could count, many double-decked, combining road and rail traffic.

The Sofitel Ambassador was a fine example of modern hotel construction, from the lobby with a stream trickling through, containing multi-coloured koi carp. Check-in had been organized in advance, and within minutes I was whisked to my room. I had been advised by our group leader, Frank Fallows, not to use the drinks from the mini bar as the prices were exorbitant, as is usual in luxury hotels, so out on the street I walked a few yards to a side alley where a little old lady sold everything I could possibly need. I bought bottled water, juice, soft drinks and a few nibbles for the quiet hours. The only conversation that passed between us was our '*kamsa hamnida*' as we bid each other 'thank you'.

The first evening was taken up by an official welcome in the residence of our Ambassador to the Republic of Korea, where we were welcomed with speeches by military and civil dignitaries. Every last detail of our visit had been planned by our defence attaché, Brigadier Colin Parr OBE and retired Major General Chang Tae-wan, President of the Korean War Veterans in Seoul, to ensure that our once-in-a-lifetime return to Korea would be truly memorable.

Next morning, provided with a fleet of air-conditioned coaches, each with a Korean lady guide, our group, which had now been swelled by Australian, New Zealand and Canadian veterans, was taken along a major highway to the area around Suwon, where our first visit was to a replica Korean folk village, which is a major tourist attraction. Here, house styles from all over the country had been re-erected. The buildings took me right back to that smoky smell I mentioned earlier. The only incongruous modern device on one of the houses was an air-con unit purring softly. On the day of our visit swarms of polite schoolchildren had arrived in brightly coloured clothing and were laughing and joking. What a difference. Some asked us to sign our names in their books. I wrote mine in English and Hangul, the Korean language, which made them laugh. The children, so well behaved, were a delight. At lunchtime, the meal was taken in a typical Korean restaurant, where we cooked our own tender slices of beef and vegetables on a charcoal grill in the centre of the table. Those of us who had thought we had mastered chopsticks ended up asking for a spoon and fork. The meal was delicious, although few were game to taste the *Kimchi* – Korea's national dish of fermented vegetables and spices.

Our next excursion was to the DMZ and Panmunjom, where our hosts were a US Army unit whose motto was 'In front of them all'. After a handover from our civilian guides to military NCOs, we were given the full tourist treatment, being told not to make rapid hand movements at the North Korean border guards, who were watching us watching them. We were allowed into the building where armistice talks continue today, making one circuit of the actual table, which meant a few steps were made into the north. Some of the veterans who had arrived in Korea during the peacekeeping period said they could now say they had set foot in North Korea. Most of us had been there before.

After a meal in the soldiers' mess, with those compartmented aluminium trays, our next stop was a visit to Outpost Dora, where a fabulous panoramic view for miles into North Korea was the highlight. The view looked so familiar; I could swear we were close to Hill 199. But for me the next day would be the icing on the cake.

There are war memorials the world over – in deserts, on mountain passes and jungle trails, in green fields where poppies grow, and in quiet remote places of scenic beauty. They are wherever battles have been fought, where the fallen are remembered. Solma-ri is a small village close to Hill 235, the position onto which the Glosters and C Troop of my battery were ordered to withdraw on the morning of 25 April 1951. For them there was no escape. The memorial ground at Solma-ri is supremely simple. It would be possible to pass by without realizing it is there. There is no razzamatazz, no monstrous, elaborately carved obelisk, no massive wall covered in hundreds of names. Just five simple granite tablets engraved in Korean and English, proclaiming that, for four days and nights, men fought valiantly in the cause of freedom. It is a beautiful setting, very rural, very green, a quiet place where a man can stand alone with his memories. In April 1996 I stood there, and I remembered.

A Gurkha pipe major and bugler had been brought from our Hong Kong garrison, in a party headed by Major General Bryan Dutton, the last General Officer Commanding (GOC) Hong Kong Garrison before the colony was handed back to China. After a short service conducted by a chaplain from Hong Kong, and a speech by Brigadier Parr, the bugler sounded the last post and reveille. The pipe major played laments as wreaths were laid on the memorial tablets at the top of steep steps cut into the rock face. It was a time of nostalgia for me, standing on that ground. A picnic lunch was taken in park-like surroundings close to Hill 235. Balancing a plate of food in one hand and a drink in the other, I tried to free a hand to shake the outstretched one of a US Army officer of obvious senior rank. He introduced himself with 'Hi. I'm General Norwood. It is my pleasure to meet you, Sir.' Sir – to me!

The general enquired exactly where I had been in the battle. I told him I had been with the Belgians on Hill 195. Next he enquired if I was an enlisted man or a draftee. I told him I came into the latter category, and that I had volunteered, twice, for service in Korea, which seemed to go down well. I did feel like asking him if he could arrange a visit to Hill 195 for me and some of the former Ulster Rifles and Fusiliers in our group, but I knew the Korean Veterans Association (KVA) had a very tightly planned programme for us.

On the next day we paid our respects in the Kapyong area, first at the Canadian memorial under the shadow of Hill 677, at Naechon, and then it was on to the joint Australian/New Zealand memorial at Mokdong-ri, where a ceremony had been arranged by the embassies of both countries in conjunction with the UN Korean War Allies Association (UNKWAA). This was on the eighty-first anniversary of the action by ANZAC troops at Gallipoli of 25 April 1915, and the forty-fifth anniversary of another by troops from both countries at the Battle of Kapyong, 24 to 25 April 1951. Wreaths were laid by two Aussie mates, Ron Cashman and Eddy Wright, both ex-3RAR, as the pipe major played another lament.

The busy day was completed by a march through the main street of Kapyong, a typical small Korean country town, where it was pleasing to see that we were joined by local veterans of the war. Another short service was held in the small but beautifully maintained memorial to all Commonwealth troops. Several times I was approached by ordinary people in the street who offered a hand of friendship, which I was pleased to accept. They had noticed the banner on the side of our coach proclaiming that we were United Kingdom veterans of the 'June 25 War', as they know it.

Back on the coach I looked around at the various cap badges worn by my fellow veterans. Today, not one of the infantry regiments is in the order of battle. In 1996, some had been placed into vague geographical amalgamations, others had gone forever. No more would we see cap badges of the Middlesex Regiment, or the Argyll and Sutherland Highlanders. Nor those of the Royal Ulster Rifles, Royal Northumberland Fusiliers or the Gloucestershire Regiment of 29 Brigade. Or the King's Own Scottish Borderers, the King's Shropshire Light Infantry, Royal Leicestershires, Royal Norfolks, the Welch Regiment, the Duke of Wellingtons, Black Watch or Durham Light Infantry, the Royal Fusiliers or King's Regiment, all proud titles, gone forever. Let's not forget also the regiments that sent battalions in the peacekeeping period: the Royal Scots, the Essex Regiment, the Royal Warwickshires, the King's Own Royal Regiment, the North Staffordshires, the Northamptonshires, the Royal Irish Fusiliers, the Dorsets, the Queen's Own Cameron Highlanders and the Royal Sussex Regiment – all once proud regiments of the line, each with its own traditions and ceremonials that commemorated daring deeds performed on battlefields the world over.

Towards the end of our week in Korea we paraded at the magnificent National War Memorial, where we paid our respects to the fallen of our host nation. It was a tranquil place of rest for the service dead of the Republic of Korea in a truly splendid setting. We were awed by the sheer beauty of the place as our wreath was laid and the trumpets sounded. The United States has a similar final resting place at Arlington, Australia has theirs in Canberra, where the names of all who lost their lives in battle are recorded, from the Boer

War to Afghanistan. At long last, in Britain, we have the National Arboretum in Staffordshire, commemorating our war dead from 1945 onwards.

On our penultimate day in Korea a banquet was held in our honour in the lavish Lotte Hotel. Tables were arranged so that at each sat a retired senior Korean service officer. The meal was first-class, as was the entertainment, first by the Canadians, then the Aussies, who gave us *Waltzing Matilda* as only they can sing it, before a rendition of *Kiss Me Goodnight Sergeant Major* was sung with gusto. I am unable to remember the British contribution, but it might have been a rather weak, spur of the moment *Land of Hope and Glory*. Then we stepped onto the stage to be presented with the Ambassador for Peace Medal and Certificate.

For our British group the final day started with a journey from Seoul on a superb non-stop express train to Pusan, which was beyond comparison with anything operated by any of the rail companies in the United Kingdom. The journey was so smooth it was difficult to comprehend the speed we made through the countryside, barely able to read the station signboards of the towns and cities we had known in a past life. Arriving at Pusan almost to the second of our schedule, we were taken by the local KVA members to the United Nations Military Cemetery on the outskirts of the city. Once again, the setting was magnificent. A short service by the Hong Kong chaplain was followed by the last post and reveille sounded by the Gurkha bugler. Then we were dismissed to wander around and seek out the graves of old comrades who had not returned home. I headed straight away to locate plot 24, row 12, grave 1,835. On it I read 22275407 Gunner R.E. Dowkes Royal Artillery, Bob's final resting place. Next I sought out the marker for 22287077 Gunner H. Breakwell, and 22157787 Gunner J.F. Kilburn in graves 1,549 and 1,705 respectively. I planted small crosses bearing a red poppy on each grave and stood in silence for a few moments. I noticed that my colleagues had also fallen silent at the graves of their remembered comrades, who were resting forever in that splendid place, which is maintained by local people and schoolchildren. It is a fine thing that they do.

I am not ashamed to say I shed a tear or two when I stood at the graves of those 170 Battery lads, as I did when I stood at the monument for all who have no known grave, and those who did not survive the POW camps in the far north – men who did not grow old. It all came back in a flood of nostalgia on that sad occasion for us all, tempered by the lawns and flowers of the beautiful setting, each British grave with a rose bush. Someone once said 'Freedom is not free'. No, it is not; it comes at a heavy cost.

Then it was back to Pusan Station to board the Seoul Express, which left on the dot, wafting us almost silently back to our hotel rooms for a final night.

During the flight home it was announced that there was party of Korean War veterans on board, and this received a genuine handclap from the Korean passengers. A large cake decorated with the Korean flag, our Union flag and the BKVA insignia was brought through by the cabin crew, a slice for each of us. It was a nice final touch from our hosts who had cared for us so well.

When I had arrived at Kimpo the previous week I entered next to 'reason for visit' on my immigration card: 'Korean War Veteran revisit'. On leaving, the immigration officer checking my departure card leaned across the desk and asked me, 'When were you last in Korea?' I told him I had first arrived in 1951. He leaned further, shook my hand and said, 'Thank you for coming in 1951, and thank you for coming back.' What the typical Korean thinks about our assistance in stopping the spread of communism in their country had been summed up for me in those few kind words. In turn, I thanked him, and passed through to airside with a spring in my step.

Marching with my comrades from the Commonwealth at Solma-ri, Naechon, Mokdong-ri and Kapyong, it struck me that this is what it is all about, being a veteran of war: to be among men who had suffered far more than I had when called to do so by our government, men who had risked their lives so that another man's country should be free, to be unconditionally accepted by them as a mate. I believe we can all look back and say that the individual part we played in the overall strategy of containing communism might well have been infinitesimal, but collectively we did manage to change for the better the lives of the people of the Republic of Korea. I certainly do not regret for one minute having volunteered – twice.

A unique occasion took place in London in July 1999. The National Committee of the British Korean Veterans Association issued invitations to the veteran associations in all twenty-one nations whose military or medical personnel had participated in the conflict, requesting their presence at an international reunion. Never before had they all been invited to meet together in the United Kingdom. A week-long programme was planned, and our committee had sent out in advance notice of the events to all the major media channels. However, every event was disgracefully boycotted by them, as no British reporters, photographers or television crews attended any of them. And that just about sums up the feeling that we all carry with us that we truly fought the Forgotten War.

At one major event I had been handed the role of official photographer of the British Korean Veterans Association (BKVA). On arrival I was ushered to the media compound, where a few people were gathered. I felt encouraged when I noted that a camera team, complete with satellite dish, was busy recording the event. After a while one of the crew came up to me and asked,

'Where is the BBC?' The team was from one of the largest TV channels in South Korea, and everything was being sent back as a live feed to Seoul for the evening news broadcast. I regret that I could not think up anything polite to say to him regarding why there was no BBC or independent TV channels represented, or any news reporters in attendance at any of the events during the week of the international reunion.

The major activities included a superb service in St Paul's Cathedral, London, followed by a fine lunch in the Great Hall of the Guildhall. There was also a garden party at Buckingham Palace, a Beating the Retreat Ceremony by the band of the Welsh Guards, tours to Windsor Castle and the grand old lady that rests on the Thames, HMS *Belfast*, a veteran of our conflict, and a gala dinner at the Paragon Hotel. All were splendid affairs, very well attended by the overseas groups. I saw one of the Canadians I had met at Naechon three years previously. He told me that the highlight of his visit was to march behind the Welsh Guards band along streets he had known of since childhood but had never expected to see. Now he would take treasured memories back to his homeland.

Perhaps the event that was most meaningful to many of the men who were attending was the parade and inspection on Horse Guards. After gathering informally in Wellington Barracks, meeting comrades old and new, I caught up with several of the Australian veterans group. I spoke to some Belgians, a Turkish officer and his formidable bodyguard and flag bearer, two Ethiopians, the United States contingent, three Kiwis from 16 RNZA, a number of NORMASH doctors and nurses, the Canadians, the French and Greek standard bearers, and, of course, the party from the Republic of Korea, who were handing out decorative fans. It was a marvellous occasion. A Guards regimental sergeant major called the various national groups to order, national flags and veteran association colours to the front. We then marched along Birdcage Walk to Horse Guards, once again headed by the band of the Welsh Guards. Old heads were held high as their tired legs tried to keep up with more sprightly comrades.

Standing at attention on that hallowed ground, the scene of so much military ceremony over the years, while HRH the Duke of Kent, deputising for the Queen, inspected the hundreds of assembled veterans. The Duke was interested to speak with many of the men from among the various nationalities on parade. Most were only too pleased when the order was given to 'Stand at ease, stand easy', as the parade marshal, a very tall Guards RSM, either forgot to stand us at ease or thought that as royalty was on parade we ought to remain at attention. Following inspection, the Duke addressed us with these words:

It is good to see such a fine gathering on the Horse Guards square in London this afternoon, representing the armed forces of the many nations who fought together under the United Nations flag almost fifty years ago.

During those years, 1950 to 1953, you were engaged in a war fought to preserve the newly fledged Republic of Korea. Your efforts were successful. The campaign took place at a great distance from the homes of all those sent to assist the people of South Korea, yet you gave the best of yourselves to it and suffered grievously in doing so.

It is right that this hard-fought struggle should be duly commemorated and the opening of your programme, the assembly at St Paul's, was a reminder that many of those who went to Korea lost their lives at sea, on the battlefield, and in the air. I am sure you were reminded, too, of your own experiences, not the least during the bitter winter weather in the peninsula, and the comradeship that you enjoyed in surviving such hardships.

I know that some of you feel that the war in Korea was forgotten almost as soon as it ended in 1953, but I believe that it will never pass into oblivion for at least three reasons.

Immediately, your association of international veterans is a living reminder of the event. In the longer term, the national memorial, now well established in the countries that you represent, will provide a permanent record of the men involved in the operations. Above all, perhaps, the people of the Republic of Korea, preserved from conquest to develop as a democracy with their unique culture intact, remind us continually of their appreciation of all that the United Nations contributed to the outcome. Her Majesty the Queen has asked me to send you her best wishes for the success of your programme here in the United Kingdom, and a safe journey back to your homelands.

It is good to know that the Queen remembers the war that had run barely half of its course when she succeeded her father King George VI to the throne on his death in February 1952. The British Korea Medal, awarded to all Commonwealth participants, was the first new campaign medal to which she gave her approval after her succession, the one we proudly wear 'first in line' before the United Nations Service Medal. In the past some of us have argued that the medal, bearing the uncrowned head of the Queen, ought to have the King's head on the obverse for all who served in Korea or in Korean waters during his reign. After all, the reservists, the original members of 27 and 29 brigades, and many ships' companies, had already left Korea and left the service before the King died, without ever having served in the armed forces during the Queen's reign. Two medals were required, as in the case of the General Service Medal 1918-1962 (struck with King George V's, King

George VI's and Queen Elizabeth II's head successively until 1962), awarded, for example, for service in Malaya with the King's head until 1952, then the head of Elizabeth II from February 1952. Money, no doubt, came into the equation.

The Queen's first investiture was to award the Victoria Cross to Private William Speakman, Black Watch attached to King's Own Scottish Borderers, for heroism and leadership in the Guy Fawkes Battle, November 1951. But regardless of the argument over which head should appear on our medal, we are all proud to wear it.

Much has happened to the Royal Artillery units that fought in the Korean War, not the least being the transformation of 170 Mortar Battery, which underwent many changes. Shortly after arriving back at Stanley Barracks, Hong Kong, the battery paraded for inspection by the GOC Hong Kong Garrison, Major General Lewis. He immediately wanted to know why all men were wearing the emblem of the United States Presidential Unit Citation, a medal ribbon-sized piece of bright blue silk within an anodized gilt surround (the same as the blue on the ribbon of the United States Distinguished Service Cross). The battery commander responded by saying he believed that was the intention when approval for wear was given. The general said he would investigate and give the answer to the battery commander when it was decided, but for the interim period all members could continue to wear the emblem. In February 1952, the response was received that only C Troop men were permitted to wear it, and not in its correct form, as there was no precedent for the wearing of such a device on the right breast as in all other armies to whom the citation had been awarded, but as a cloth badge at the shoulder, beneath the Royal Artillery shoulder title.

In 1954 the Queen approved the award of the Honour Title 'Imjin' to the battery, and henceforth it would be titled 170 (Imjin) Battery Royal Artillery, and Imjin Day would be commemorated on 23 April each year, St George's Day. On 1 February 1956 the battery returned to the United Kingdom, amalgamating as an integral battery with old friends from 29 Brigade, 45 Field Regiment, who then lost 116 Battery, with whom I had been attached temporarily in March 1951. The 116 Battery was placed in 'suspended animation' and would only be reactivated in the event of an emergency, such as Korea had been. The newly titled battery was henceforth known as 170 (Imjin) Field Battery, stationed in Dortmund, West Germany. On 7 February 1961, 45 Field Regiment was ordered to convert one battery from field guns to medium, from 25-pounders to the 5.5-inch gun, and 170 Battery was selected, becoming 170 (Imjin) Medium Battery. At that time the last National Servicemen left the battery. May 1963 saw the remaining

25-pounders in 45 Field Regiment convert to the new 105mm pack howitzer, when it was renamed 45 Light Regiment, although 170 Battery retained the 5.5-inch guns. The regiment had now been notified that it was to relieve 26 Field Regiment in Malaya, based at Terendak.

However, 170 Battery would once again become virtually independent, based in Seremban. In November 1963 the battery was ordered to join 99 Gurkha Brigade in Borneo during 'confrontation' with Indonesia to provide close support to 2nd/6th Gurkha Rifles, which proved a successful operation. They returned to Malaya on 15 March 1964, rejoining the parent regiment at Terendak prior to an eventual return to the United Kingdom. In October 1988 I was invited by Battery Commander Major Lane to attend the unveiling in the Officers' Mess, Woolwich, of a painting by Ralph Webber depicting C Troop in action on the Imjin River. The painting was unveiled by the guest of honour, General Sir Anthony Farrar-Hockley, who had been adjutant of the Glosters on Hill 235 in April 1951.

The unveiling was attended by one old regular soldier, one reservist and one National Serviceman. Reg Kitchener represented the regulars, George Philipson the reservists, and I was there as the embodiment of conscripts everywhere. We were delighted to see the former C Troop commander at the occasion, Captain (by then Major, retired) Frank Wisbey, who had gone into captivity with General Farrar-Hockley. Ralph Webber approached me to enquire if I thought he had got the colouring about right. I said that he had, asking how long he spent in Korea when painting it. He said he had not set foot in Korea, but he had based the colours and the general view of the Imjin Battle, with the mortars in action, purely on advice from veterans.

From that date until well into the 1990s the battery served in Germany, Colchester and Northern Ireland, where they operated in an infantry role. In April 1993 I attended a parade at Woolwich for the disbandment of 45 Light Regiment. It was a splendid weekend, when I met up again with Reg Kitchener and George Philipson. I met other old comrades from Korea, as well as some officers I had known there. On disbandment of the regiment, 170 Battery was transferred to 19 Regiment at Kirkee Barracks, Colchester, where they amalgamated with 25 Battery, with yet another title, 25/170 (Imjin) Battery. That amalgamation is historically interesting as 25 Battery is the only other Royal Artillery unit to have also received a United States Presidential Unit Citation, a fact that has been rather forgotten. It was awarded for their support of US Army forces near Asten, Holland, in the Second World War. The two 'citation batteries' had become one. On 9 June 1999, the battery marched out of Kirkee Barracks on moving to amalgamate with 47 Regiment at Thorney Island, Hampshire, the former Royal Air Force airfield now known as Baker Barracks. I attended at Colchester in the company of my old colleague Peter Gore, our wounded man from Operation *Commando*.

In April 2001 I was invited by Battery Commander Major Eddy Grace to provide a talk to a group of young gunners who had raised their own funds to enable them to travel to Korea for commemoration of the fiftieth anniversary of the Imjin River Battle. Prior to battery transport collecting me, I provided a fifteen-minute interview with the morning show host, Richard Cartridge, at BBC Radio Solent, also arranged by Major Grace. Later, in the Battery History Room at Baker Barracks I displayed a framed map showing the position of all 29 Brigade units when we first came under attack at 2200 hrs on 22 April 1951, the first night of battle, and demonstrated with markings the Chinese assault by the 63rd Army and our withdrawal along Route 11. After I had my photograph taken with the map and the Imjin Gun by a photographer from Portsmouth's *The News*, the map was presented to the battery.

My notoriety had spread. I had a call from the BBC Overseas Service, London, to say they had listened to my interview and asked if I would do a live transmission for them. I accepted. On the day, I was collected by a BBC car and taken to the Southampton studio. I was ushered into a small soundproofed room where I was told to put on headphones and wait for a voice to wake me up. Connected to the London studio, I provided an extended interview on the April 1951 battle. After a few days I received a letter from the BBC thanking me. Enclosed was an audio tape of their recording. I discovered it had been transmitted to their Far East listeners. I hoped that had not included North Korea, or I might now be on the 'most wanted' list of their secret police.

By that time the battery had converted to the High Velocity Missile (HVM) in an air defence role. I was given the once-over of a Stormer-mounted HVM unit. Major Grace asked if I had seen inside one, and when I told him I had not, he told me to jump inside, whereupon a lance bombardier showed me the ropes in each of the positions of the three-man crew. I thought the Stormer Armoured Fighting Vehicle (AFV) was a neat piece of kit, with the eight missile pods mounted on the roof of the 13-ton tracked vehicle, which is capable of 50mph. The Starstreak missiles, once fired, reach a maximum speed of mach 3.5. The AFV is produced by Alvis, the manufacturer of quality cars in the past.

On Imjin Day 2002, Peter Gore and I were invited by the BC to partake in the pinning on of red roses to the assembled battery on the main square outside the gun shed. As the battery marched onto the square Peter and I had to agree that they looked equally as smart as we had been so many years ago. With the battery at 'open order' we were marched onto the square with our escort of two warrant officers. Peter pinned on the roses to the front rank, I took the second rank, and the BC covered the rear rank. A number of young gunners were then called to the front to receive lance bombardier stripes, which I thought displayed how different our modern Army was compared to that of sixty years earlier. After the parade was dismissed we repaired to the Battery History Room for a fine buffet and drinks. Then Peter and I were each presented with a blue silk-lined box that contained a half-bottle of scotch and a cut-glass goblet engraved with 'Imjin Day 23 April 2002'. I still have mine, the scotch remaining un-drunk. I will probably put it on the BBC's *Antiques Roadshow* one day.

Later we were taken to the WOs' and Sergeants' Mess, where we would be sleeping that night. But first, drinks were consumed, followed by dinner and a continuing of the occasion by an all-ranks get-together in the Junior NCOs' Mess. As guests Peter and I were not permitted to buy a round of drinks. I understood the party broke up at 0100 hrs the following morning, but I am unable to remember much about that. After breakfast we went our separate ways, having enjoyed a good weekend with today's young officers and soldiers of the battery.

In more recent years the annual commemoration of Imjin Day has been combined with St George's Day, held outside of Baker Barracks, in the main square of Emsworth, in the Borough of Havant, the closest village to Thorney Island. The entire village takes a major part in the proceedings, including many events for the local schoolchildren, who involve themselves enthusiastically. My fellow veteran and colleague Norman Davies, a former Royal Signals warrant officer, is heavily involved with the Mayor of Havant and local organizers. They do a splendid job. All veterans are invited, not only those of the Korean War. The parade of veterans with soldiers from 47 Regiment, and/or 12 Regiment, which is also based at Thorney Island, is finished with a fine curry lunch back at Baker Barracks. All agree it is a good day, one of the best, and it is good to meet old comrades again. And so it was … until I was hit by a bombshell.

On 26 January 2011 I received a handwritten letter from Major Mike Sargent, the new battery commander. It included an invitation, but it was not to ask me to pin on red roses. I was shocked to find that veterans were invited to Baker Barracks to attend the 'Suspended Animation Parade' of 25/170 (Imjin) Battery on Thursday, 10 March 2011. The letter stated that the Band of the Royal Artillery and the Pipes and Drums of 19 Regiment, known as the Scottish Gunners as that is their area of recruitment, would be in attendance (25 Battery had, of course, been inherited from 19 Regiment). Major Sargent hoped I would encourage as many Korean War veterans as possible to attend. Following the disbandment parade, a buffet lunch would be served in the Junior NCOs' Mess.

My old battery was being dumped from the order of battle. My colleagues and I knew only too well that the Ministry of Defence was having a hard time balancing the budget and shedding personnel in line with government directives. As my old unit was the only Gunner battery to have been awarded an honour title by the Queen, I thought, and hoped, that it would be retained. Sadly, it was not to be.

The battery had been formed in India in 1857 as part of the Bombay Artillery, and remained there until 1875, when it moved to England, and then Ireland in 1877. In 1889 the battery returned to India, when the title was changed to 70 Field Battery. In 1899, the battery was again stationed in Ireland. The battery went to France in 1914 as part of the British Expeditionary Force, where it was involved in the retreat from Mons and most of the major battles on the Western Front. Between the two World Wars the battery served with the British Indian Army in Afghanistan, where they have served again as infantry since 2002. After more moves between England and India they were again sent to France in 1939, as part of the new Expeditionary Force fighting its way to Dunkirk, from where it was extracted off the beaches. Re-armed, the battery next fought in the North African Campaign and in Italy. Then, from Norton Barracks, Worcester, it was moved to Korea in November 1950 as an independent mortar battery. Now it would exist no more.

On 10 March 2011, a handful of veterans defied a biting wind to watch a very smart 25/170 Battery march onto the square to the Royal Artillery's quick march, *The British Grenadier*. The battery commander (BK), Captain A.J. Carter, and WO2 (BSM) Jones headed the seventy-one officers and men of the battery. I could not help making a comparison with 170 Mortar Battery, where in Korea we had a strength of 175 officers and soldiers, plus eight attached Royal Signals, Army Catering Corps and REME, and eight BCRs in the replacement depot in Japan, arriving in theatre with a total complement of 191. Nowadays, many fewer personnel are required to operate the much more sophisticated equipment needed to kill the enemy.

The battery was inspected by the Regimental Honorary Colonel, Major General C.C. Wilson CBE, who also inspected us veterans. When the BC introduced me as a former member of 170 Mortar Battery, the general enquired if I had been taken prisoner, to which I responded by telling him I had not been in C Troop, and that in B Troop we had managed to withdraw with the Belgian battalion. Following inspection, the battery flag was lowered for the last time, folded ceremonially and presented to Major General Wilson for safekeeping. Sunset was played by the band and the last post was sounded, this time not followed by reveille, as the battery would not rise again. The battery then slow-marched off parade for the last time to the Pipes and Drums playing *Flowers of the Forest*. They marched away to obscurity, almost certainly gone forever. The personnel would be posted throughout the existing regiments of the Royal Artillery.

My old battery had joined the ranks of all those famous infantry regiments that are no more. So now only 14 Regiment Royal Artillery based at Larkhill, Wiltshire, and 74 (Battleaxe) Battery in 32 Regiment are the only remaining Royal Artillery units with a direct connection to the Korean War, although 19 Regiment, who provided the Pipes and Drums, served in Korea during the peacekeeping period.

In 2012 there were fifteen regular and seven Territorial Army regiments of Royal Artillery, which with eleven armoured regiments support our reduced corps of infantry, consisting of thirty-seven battalions. Although given the speed with which the government removes them from the ORBAT, that figure could be even lower by the time this book is published.

So, what are we left with? In 1950 an infantry battalion at war strength had at least 900 men, whereas today they are lucky to go to war with something closer to 500, sometimes only achieving that figure by men borrowed from other battalions in the same brigade. We have today, apart from the five battalions of the Royal Regiment of Scotland, five regiments of Foot Guards, each with a single battalion. There are two battalions each of the Princess of Wales's Royal Regiment, and the Royal Regiment of Fusiliers (although I hear that their second battalion might be for the chop), the Duke of Lancaster's, the Royal Anglians, the Royal Welsh and the Royal Gurkha Rifles. I would mention here that the Indian Army, recognizing the soldierly bearing and fighting ability of these famed Nepalese warriors, in 2009, had forty-six battalions of Gurkhas, more than our entire Corps of Infantry.

The Yorkshire Regiment, the Mercian Regiment and the Parachute Regiment have three battalions each, and there are five battalions of The Rifles, currently the largest infantry regiment in the Army. Also operational are the 22nd Special Air Service (SAS) and the Special Forces Support Group. The Royal Gibraltar Regiment, consisting of one artillery troop and three infantry companies, one of which is a Territorial Army unit (although usually fulfilling ceremonial and normal garrison duties on The Rock), has been on the permanent establishment of the British Army since 1990. The Royal Irish Regiment also has a single battalion.

I am given to understand by my fellow Korean War veteran, Norman Davies, that 47 Regiment will continue to hold the annual ceremony in Emsworth square each April, although the word 'Imjin' will play no part in it. He will continue to hold discussions with the regiment, the office of the mayor and others, ending up with a fine finished product. It will continue to be enjoyed by all, whether schoolchildren, organizers, the civilians who line the streets to cheer the marching soldiers, or the veterans. St George's Day, call it what you will, to me, 23 April will always be Imjin Day, whether or not the battery still exists.

Those infantry battalions of 29 British Independent Infantry Group and all supporting arms fought valiantly against an army that in some respects was better armed. Apparently they had a mix of Russian, Japanese, American and British rifles, of varying calibres. Supply of the correct ammunition must have given them nightmares. We had the .303 SMLE (short magazine Lee Enfield), a single-shot bolt-action rifle, needing each round loaded by hand. It was accepted that the Russian designed burp gun was superior to our Sten, although neither had a particularly spectacular killing range. The burp gun was designed in 1941 and mass produced for the Soviet Army, as the Pistolet Pulemyot Shpagina (Shpagina machine gun), or PPSh-41, an inexpensive weapon for the infantry using 7.62mm ammunition either in the 35-round box magazine or 71-round drum, like the American Tommy gun.

In 1953, several ordnance companies were said to be working on a semi-automatic self-loading rifle to replace the Lee Enfield, which had hardly changed from 1914, but even that met with opposition in some regiments who were admired for their smart rifle drill. At the time the usual 'un-named officer' was heard to declare that the Lee Enfield rifle was perfectly suited for the current arms drill, and he saw no reason to change it. It might be assumed that he had never been surrounded my massed enemy infantry, as any soldier who had might have asked which he would prefer in such a situation, a rifle that was perfect for drill on the barrack square, or one that might save his life with its improved rate of fire.

Today our recruits are better trained, and for longer than my twenty-five weeks, producing a soldier who is far better equipped for the role of the modern infantryman. Could any of our soldiers in Afghanistan, for example, imagine what it was like to go into action with a single-shot bolt-action rifle, each round hand-loaded? Since 1985 to the present, our service personnel have been armed with the SA80 Assault Rifle in several variants, the L85A2 variant firing standard NATO 5.56mm rounds having been in use since 1987, although that could change.

So 47 Regiment Royal Artillery will continue to provide a contingent to march through Emsworth, and we veterans will attend as long as we are able, although fewer will march and more will be on parade in wheelchairs. Red roses will be pinned on, and a curry lunch will be enjoyed in barracks. Writing this at the age of eighty, I hope to attend for a few more years into the future, but who knows when I will also be placed in suspended animation?

We continue to live in troubled times, yet talk is of a reduction of up to another 20,000 in our army over the next few years. The government's National Security Strategy published in 2010 promised 'to use our national capabilities to build Britain's prosperity, extend our nation's influence in the world and strengthen our security'. I ask the question, 'with what?' A couple of under-strength brigades and the Territorial Army? Well, I sincerely hope that will be enough.

Nevertheless, somehow the world seems a better place when a man can feel proud of his involvement in the history of another man's country. For all of us who were there, who survived the hard times and came home, the comradeship that exists between us, the bond between mates seems to grow stronger as the days that are left to us grow shorter.

At the beginning of these pages, in Chapter One, I said that I have nothing gloriously heroic to boast about. And, of course, I have not. I have just told the story as I saw it. Have I killed men? Yes, I have – both indirectly by sending orders to the mortars to fire on observed targets, possibly directly with the Sten and definitely with the Bren. I have withheld many names, and the more gory parts, as they would have added nothing of interest to the text. Let me just say that a battlefield by its very nature is a compilation of a series of very unpleasant scenes, as it was in Korea, as my comrades who saw much more close-up action than I did will confirm. I was just a gunner with a story to tell … and that was some 'police action'.

I have been told that it is unusual for me to be able to lay claim to having been in the two major battles in which the British Army was involved in Korea. I maintain there was a third. Operation *Commando* is often brushed over as having just involved the capture of some important hills. It ought to be remembered that seventy-five were killed and 347 wounded in driving the enemy from those hills, many more losses than in the Third Hook Battle, while also taking seventy-four prisoners. Can readers imagine the public outcry in this day and age if we lost that many soldiers in five days? Why, wives and mothers, fathers and brothers would batter down the ornamental gates at the entrance to Downing Street, calling on the prime minister to 'Bring our boys home … Now!' So I will conclude on an optimistic note that it might not be necessary, or indeed possible, for much longer to send our dedicated, first-rate service personnel to countries where they are not welcomed, some of which might be ungrateful recipients of our taxpayer-funded international aid programme. Ah, well, an old soldier can daydream, can't he?

Many of the events I have recalled might not be quite the way some of my comrades in arms will remember them. Well, I also commented in Chapter One that if three veterans of the same battle are in a room together, you will hear three different stories. This is mine.

In Remembrance

The following officers and soldiers of the Royal Regiment of Artillery gave their lives in the Korean War, in defence of the principles of the Charter of the United Nations. Their names are inscribed on the Gunner Memorial in the Garrison Church of Saint Alban the Martyr, Larkhill, Wiltshire. The memorial was opened by Her Majesty the Queen on 8 August 1990. They have individual grave markers in the UN Military Cemetery, Pusan, or those who have no known grave are commemorated on the memorial there.

L/Bdr K. Alder	L/Bdr R. Archer	Gnr K. Archibald
Gnr A.J. Baldock	Gnr M. Banbury	L/Bdr R.J. Barwick
Gnr V.F. Bayley	Gnr A. Bond	Gnr H. Breakwell
L/Bdr M.A. Brettel	Gnr D. Broadbent	Sgt R.H. Broadbent
Gnr J.W. Camp	Sgt J. Cawley	Gnr G. Cawood
Gnr C.M.L. Caws	Gnr J.A. Cloake	Gnr R.S. Coe
Sgt J.A. Colverson	Gnr R. Cruickshanks	Gnr T.L. Curtiss
Sgt H.W. Danes	Gnr R.E. Dowkes	Gnr W.A. Edwards
Gnr R. England	Capt R.D. Fleming	Gnr T. Fox
Gnr S. Foy	Gnr T.F. Gibson	Gnr G. Grayston
WO2 J. Harrion	Major W.G. Harris MC	Gnr R. Harrison
Gnr W. Hewitt	Capt L.P. Hicks	Gnr D.G. Hill
L/Bdr R.E. Hindle	Capt W.M. Holman MBE	Sgt G.W.A. Howard
Lieut A.B.S. Hudson	Bdr H.J. Hudson	Gnr C.A. Humphrey
Gnr K. Jaynes	Capt A.V. Jenkins	Gnr K. Jepson
Gnr P.J. Keating	Gnr J.F. Kilburn	Capt J.L. Lane
Gnr D. McCafferty	Lieut A.J Measor	Sgt F.T. Mersh
Gnr J. Micklethwaite	Capt W.M. Miller	Gnr R.J. Mitchell
Sgt P.J. Moir	Gnr R. Morrison	Gnr J. Murphy
Gnr G.W. Naylor	Gnr R.B. Newman	Gnr G. Nutman
Lieut J.R. O'Brien	Gnr A. Ogden	Gnr A.W. Russell
Gnr J.A. Snell	Gnr L.G. Taplin	Capt J.K. Thompson MC
Gnr J. Tracey	Gnr E. Waller	Capt J.B. Warren

Capt R.F. Washbrook   Gnr K. Williams   Bdr S.E. Williams
WO2 C.R. Woosnam   Gnr L. Wright   Gnr G. Yates

The following Royal Artillery personnel lost their lives in Korea during the peacekeeping period, 28 July 1953 to 27 July 1954:

BQMS A.E. Mapplebeck   WO2 J. Mills   Gnr D. Parker

They rest in peace in the Land of the Morning Calm.

Prisoners of War

Seventy-four officers and soldiers of the Royal Regiment of Artillery were taken into captivity in the Korean War. They suffered great hardship, deprivation and sometimes torture in the most inhumane manner. In August 1953, sixty-five were released. Nine died in the camps.

170 Independent Mortar Battery

WO2 G.E. Askew MM	Sgt S.E. Aselby	Sgt E. Boswell
Gnr D. Boulton	Gnr R.L. Broomer	Gnr A. Bruce
Gnr L. Burns	Gnr N.R. Campbell	L/Bdr T. Clough
Gnr J.A. Cooper	Bdr T. Daly	Gnr M.E. Dunnachie
Gnr E.E. Edson	Gnr J.C. Gabbs	Gnr F.G. Gardner
Gnr J. Harris	Gnr J. Hepple	Gnr B. Hesford
Gnr J.W. Hildrew	Gnr M.G.A. Lorimer	L/Bdr M.A. Mackay
Gnr D. Mackie	Bdr E.W. Maryan	Gnr J. Mason
Gnr H.R.G. McFarlane	Gnr M.S.H. Menaud	Bdr J.R. Muncaster
L/Bdr T.L. Nutting	Bdr G.F. Oliver	Gnr T. Ormesher
Gnr E.G. Pochin	L/Bdr D.N. Rayment	Gnr M.B. Rees
Gnr D.A. Roberts	Gnr R.W. Ross	Gnr N.E.A. Smith
Gnr J. Stocks	Gnr E. Stott	Gnr J. Tracey
Gnr N. Usher	Gnr S.J. Vickerson	Sgt J.G. Watson
Gnr S. Williamson	Capt F.R. Wisbey MC	

45 Field Regiment

Gnr J. Arnall	Bdr L. Bristow	Gnr E.G. Bushby
Gnr R.E. Button	Gnr J. Cameron	L/Bdr G.M. Clark
Gnr E. Clinton	Gnr A.H. Collins	Capt C.S.R. Dain
Bdr D.G. Fitzgerald	T/Capt A.H.G. Gibbon GM	Capt W.M. Holman MBE
Gnr L. Leak	L/Bdr R.A. Lintott	Gnr M. Mair
Gnr J. Martin	Gnr G.H. May	Gnr G.W. McDonald
Gnr J. Micklethwaite	Bdr F.W. Moore	Gnr S.D. Morgan
Capt A.M.L. Newcombe MC	Gnr M. O'Neill	L/Bdr E.S. Simms
Gnr J.A. Snell	Gnr R. Thompson	Gnr K.R. Tolley
Maj G.T. Ward TD	Capt R.F. Washbrook	Gnr W. Wood

Appendix C

**WAR OFFICE, WHITEHALL,
LONDON,S.W.
TELEPHONE,WHITEHALL 9400.**

**PERSONAL MESSAGE FROM
FIELD MARSHAL SIR WILLIAM SLIM, C.I.G.S.,
TO OFFICERS AND OTHER RANKS OF THE ARMY RESERVES WHO ARE RETURNING
TO CIVIL LIFE AFTER SERVING IN KOREA**

I wish to tell you how much your service in Korea has been appreciated.

At the time you were recalled, to the Service the Army was fully extended and it was only possible to complete the force which we were pledged to send to Korea by recalling certain reservists,

The British Army has rarely been required, to fight under more difficult conditions than those you met in Korea.It is to your credit that, under those conditions, you earned, the admiration, not only of your own country and of all Nations fighting in Korea but the hearty respect of the enemy.

As old soldiers in a force which contained a high proportion of young officers and other ranks your experience, efficiency and sense of duty were an example to them.

Most important of all you have helped to strike a blow in the defence of the free world, which has, I think, done much to lessen the likelihood of further wars.   You've done something to be proud of; be proud of it.

Thank you and good luck to you on your return to civilian life.

November, 1951
25S5C W

Appendix D

The Distinguished Unit Citation is awarded by the President of the United States to the Army

General Order 286 of the Eighth United States Army Korea dated 8th May 1951

Battle Honors – Citation of Units

By direction of the President, under the provisions of Executive Order 9396, the following units

are cited as public evidence of deserved honor and distinction.

The 1st Battalion Gloucestershire Regiment, British Army, and Troop C 170th Independent Mortar Battery Royal Artillery attached, are cited for exceptionally outstanding performance of duty and extraordinary heroism in action against the armed enemy near Solma-ri, Korea on the 23rd, 24th and 25th April 1951. The 1st Battalion and Troop C were defending a very critical sector of the battle front during a determined attack by the enemy. The defending units were overwhelmingly outnumbered. The 63rd Chinese Communist Army drove the full force of its savage assault at the positions held by the 1st Battalion Gloucestershire Regiment and attached unit. The route of supply ran south-east from the Battalion between two hills. The hills dominated the surrounding terrain north-west to the Imjin River. Enemy pressure built up on the Battalion front during the day 23rd April. On 24th April the weight of the attack had driven the right flank of the Battalion back. The pressure grew heavier and heavier and the Battalion and attached unit were forced into a perimeter defence on Hill 235. During the night heavy enemy forces had bypassed the staunch defenders and closed all avenues of escape. The courageous soldiers of the Battalion and attached unit were holding the critical route selected by the enemy for one column of the general offensive to encircle and destroy I Corps. These gallant soldiers would not retreat. As they were compressed tighter and tighter in their perimeter defence, they called for close in air strikes to assist in holding firm. Completely surrounded by tremendous numbers, these indomitable, resolute and tenacious soldiers fought back with unsurpassed fortitude and courage. As ammunition ran low and the advancing hordes moved closer and closer, these splendid soldiers fought back viciously to prevent the enemy from overrunning the position and moving rapidly to the south. Their heroic stand provided the critically needed time to regroup other I Corps units and block the southern advance to the enemy. Time and again efforts were made to reach the Battalion, but the enemy strength blocked each effort. Without thought of defeat or surrender, this heroic force demonstrated superb battlefield courage and discipline. Every yard of ground they surrendered was covered with enemy dead until the last gallant soldier of the fighting Battalion was overpowered by the final surge of the enemy masses. The 1st Battalion Gloucestershire Regiment and Troop C 170th Independent Mortar Battery displayed such gallantry, determination, and esprit de corps in accomplishing their mission under extremely difficult and hazardous conditions as to set them apart and above other units participating in the same battle. Their sustained brilliance in battle, their resoluteness, and extraordinary heroism are in keeping with the finest traditions of the renowned military forces of the British Commonwealth, and reflect unsurpassed credit on these courageous soldiers and their homeland.

By command of Lieutenant General Van Fleet

L W Stanley

Colonel, AGC

Adjutant General

Leven C Allen

Major General US Army

Chief of Staff

Honours, Decorations and Awards

The following honours, decorations and awards were received by officers, senior NCOs and soldiers of the Royal Regiment of Artillery, for gallant or meritorious service in the face of the enemy in Korea. This definitive record represents the culmination of months of painstaking research by my late colleague Ashley Cunningham-Boothe, Royal Northumberland Fusiliers, to whom I am indebted for permission to publish. Those marked * were awarded posthumously.

Distinguished Service Order

Lieut Col T.G. Brennan CBE Maj R.A. Pont

Officer of the Order of the British Empire

Maj A.J. Batten DCM	Maj D.J. Cable MC	Lieut Col H.S. Calvert MC
Lieut Col D.C. de Cent	Lieut Col J.H.	Maj P.M. Victory MC
Lieut Col M.T. Young DSO	Slade-Powell DSO	

Member of the Order of the British Empire

Maj W. Bull	Capt R.A. D Butler	WO2 C.J. Cole
Major J.A. Fletcher	Maj J.A. Gregg	Capt (Q) J.P. Hartland
WO1 J.F. Hartney	Capt B.H.P Heaton	WO2 A.L. Hunt
Maj J.H.P. Jones	WO1 R.G. Smith	Capt K.F. Stott
Capt M.H. Turner	WO1 G. Walkingshaw	Capt H. Woodley

Military Cross – 1st Bar

Capt J.A.C. Baxter MC   Maj W.M. Mackay DSO MC

Military Cross

Capt P.D.R Childs

Capt A.P.H.B. Fowle

Lieut R.H. Hanna

Lieut G.H. Lakes

Capt G.J. Strickland

Lieut G.A. Wood

Capt J.C. Danskin

Capt J.L.H. Gordon

Capt J.A. Harrison

Lieut R.A. Monilaws

Lieut E.P. Walsh

Capt Hon. J. de Grey

Capt N.C.O. Grant

Maj J.D. King-Martin

Maj F.S.G. Shore

Capt P.L.D. Weldon

George Medal

Capt A.H.G. Gibbon

Lieut B.A.F. Mawson

Military Medal

WO2 G.E. Askew

WO2 A.M. Ellis

Bdr A. Newbold

Gnr H.J. Spraggs

Gnr T. Bond

Bdr E. Lewis

Sgt C. Onyett

Gnr S.G. Young

Gnr W.G. Elcoat

L/Bdr G. Machin

Sgt J.B. Simpson

British Empire Medal

WO2 C.H. Anderson

WO2 L.A. Whitehead

Mention in Despatches

Gnr G. Berry

S/Sgt V.C. Cannon

Gnr A.E. Crisp

Maj C.S.R. Dain

L/Bdr P. Dixon

Maj T.V. Fisher-Hoch

Maj R.N.L. Gower

Major H.G. Huleatt

Lieut (Q) J.F.D. Jones

Gnr P.Y. Law

Capt F.C. Matthews

Capt D.W. McGhee

Capt A.M.L. Newcombe MC

Lieut Col G.R.G.
   Bickley

Gnr I. Croft

WO2 F.J. Davenport

Maj L.V.F. Fawkes
   DSO MC

Sgt J.D. Hales

Capt W.M. Holman
   MBE*

Gnr G. Lowry

L/Bdr A.N. McCormack

WO2 J.P. McDonald

L/Bdr C.K.G. Nash

Capt G.S. Birtles

Sgt P.H. Chapple

Maj K.R. Cronin

WO2 S.T. Davies

WO2 J.G. Fenner

S/Lieut H.W. Godfrey

Sgt M.A. Hayde

WO2 A.A. Horsell

Sgt M. Joyce

Maj D.J. Macrea-Brown

Capt D. McDonald

Capt J.G. Morgan MC

Maj J.E. Nicholls

Sgt D.J. Oldham
Lieut P.A. Powell
Capt D.F. Ryan
BQMS J.W. Siddle
WO1 G.K. Stewart
Gnr E.S. Stowe
WO R.C. Talbot
Sgt I.H.T. Thomas
WO2 W. Tighe
Capt R.F. Washbrook*
WO2 A.A. Wells
Capt J.G. Wilkes MC
Capt F.R. Wisbey MC

Gnr M. Partridge
WO2 W.F.J. Riddle
Sgt W.J. Salisbury
Maj L.E.E. Skuse
Capt A.G.E. Stewart-
Cox DFC
Capt B.J. Templeman
Maj C.P. Thompson
Sgt S.R. Titheridge
Capt A.G.C.M. Waters
TD
Sgt D.T. Willey
WO2 G.T.S. Wood

Maj R.A. Pont
Lieut E.J.U. Russell
L/Bdr L.J.T. Searle
Sgt R.A.J. Smith
Capt A.S. Stepto
Gnr G.W. Strong
Maj E.V. Thomas
Capt J.G. Thorneloe
L/Bdr E. Walsh
Capt P.L.D. Weldon
WO2 E.F. Wick
Maj R. Wilson DSO TD
L/Bdr J.H.K. Wood

Foreign Awards

The following awards were conferred by the President of the United States of America.

Silver Star

Maj T.V. Fisher-Hoch   Lieut Col M.T. Young DSO   Maj H.C. Withers MC

Bronze Star with 'V' Device (for valor)

Gnr P. Soanes

Bronze Star

Capt D.W.V.P. O'Flaherty   Maj E.V. Thomas   Capt P.M. Victory OBE MC
DSO

During the Korean War, a number of Royal Artillery officers served as pilots and observers in Air Observation Post Flights. The following decorations and awards were bestowed for individual acts of bravery while engaged on flying duties:

Distinguished Service Order

Maj J.M.H. Hailes

Distinguished Flying Cross

Capt L.R.B. Addington	Capt D.J. Browne	Capt F.A. Cox
Capt J.A. Crawshaw	Maj R.N.L. Gower	Capt D.A. Hall
Lieut J.E.T. Hoare	Capt D.B.W. Jarvis	Capt G.W.C. Joyce
Capt W.T.A. Nicholls	Capt K. Perkins	Capt A.G.E. Stewart-Cox

Air Medal (United States)

Capt R.M. Begbie	Capt D.B.W. Jarvis DFC	Lieut W.P.R. Tolputt

The following officers were decorated by the Government of France. The ranks shown are not in all cases the same as at the date of the award.

Croix de Guerre

Lieut Col T.G. Brennan MC	Capt H. Fairgrieve	Brig G.P. Gregson DSO
Capt J.G. Morgan MC	CBE DSO	Maj F.S.G. Shore MC

Sources & Bibliography

Alexander Turnbull Library, Wellington, New Zealand.

Australian War Memorial, Anzac Parade, Canberra, ACT, Australia.

Carmichael, J., Imperial War Museum, London, 1994.

Cunningham-Boothe, A. (Ed), *Marks of Courage*, Korvet, Leamington Spa, 1997.

Daily Mirror, London, May 1951.

Department of Defense, National Archives & Records Administration, Washington DC, USA.

Department of War Transport, London.

Gunner magazine, London, 1951.

Harrison, Captain J.A., MC, personal notes on 120 Light Battery, 1952-53.

Kitchener, Sergeant O.R. 'Reg', personal audio tapes, 1994.

Korean War Picture Album, Chinese Military Museum, Beijing, 2000.

Lane, Major C.F., 170 (Imjin) Battery historical records, Woolwich, London, 1988.

London Gazette, Nos. 360738 and 847297, 29 June 1951.

Mackley, Ian, personal archive material, New Zealand, 1996.

Maryan, E., personal memorabilia, New Zealand, 2004.

United States Marine Corps Archives, Flickr Photostream, Pusan, 1950.

Washington Times, 25 June 2000.

Wilson, Charles, Mirror Group PLC, London, 1988.

Wright, Lisa, P & O Steam Navigation Company, London, 1989.

Index